*THE **INFLUENCER** FACTORY*

THE **INFLUENCER** FACTORY

A Marxist Theory of
Corporate Personhood
on YouTube

GRANT BOLLMER

and

KATHERINE GUINNESS

STANFORD UNIVERSITY PRESS
Stanford, California

Stanford University Press
Stanford, California

Printed in the United States of America on acid-free, archival-quality paper

Library of Congress Cataloging-in-Publication Data
Names: Bollmer, Grant, author. | Guinness, Katherine, author.
Title: The influencer factory : a Marxist theory of corporate personhood on
    YouTube / Grant Bollmer and Katherine Guinness.
Description: Stanford, California : Stanford University Press, 2024. | Includes
    bibliographical references and index.
Identifiers: LCCN 2023029785 (print) | LCCN 2023029786 (ebook) |
    ISBN 9781503637924 (cloth) | ISBN 9781503638792 (paperback) |
    ISBN 9781503638808 (ebook)
Subjects: LCSH: YouTube (Electronic resource) | Internet personalities. | Social
    media—Economic aspects. | Capitalism—Social aspects. | Corporations—
    Social aspects. | Self—Economic aspects. | Self—Social aspects.
Classification: LCC HM851 .B67415 2024 (print) | LCC HM851 (ebook) |
    DDC 302.23/1—dc23/eng/20230724
LC record available at https://lccn.loc.gov/2023029785
LC ebook record available at https://lccn.loc.gov/2023029786

Cover design: Matt Avery.Monograph
Cover illustration: iStock

CONTENTS

ACKNOWLEDGMENTS

This book was conceptualized, researched, and written during the peak years of the COVID-19 pandemic, while we were living in Colorado Springs, Colorado, and Durham, North Carolina. We could not have written it without our friends, family, and colleagues, who helped us, in countless ways, throughout these years. We'd also like to acknowledge the many influencers and content creators we watched on YouTube over this time, as well. While this book may seem deeply critical of influencers and influencer culture throughout, it emerged from a genuine love of and enjoyment from the many things these influencers produce online.

We would like to highlight several people and events that contributed to the development of this book. Yiğit Soncul organized and invited us to present parts of this book in the online roundtable "Influencer Aesthetics," at the University of Winchester. We would like to thank him and the audience for this roundtable, as well as the other participants beyond Yiğit and ourselves, Mari Lehto and Rachel O'Neill. We also presented parts of this project at the Society for Cinema and Media Studies annual convention, which was held online in 2022, and at the NC State Communication, Rhetoric, and Digital Media Ph.D. Program Symposium in 2022. We would like to thank the audience members of both presentations, as well as the organizers of these events. This especially includes Fernanda Duarte, Nick Taylor, Malcolm Ogden, T. R. Merchant-Knudsen, Lindsey Scheper, and

Charlotte Wilkins, who organized and ran the NC State Symposium, and Chloe Higginbotham, who ran the panel we were on.

This book wouldn't exist without the support of Erica Wetter and Caroline McKusick, along with everyone else at Stanford University Press. We'd like to thank them for their support and labor in developing our manuscript into this book. We'd also like to thank the three anonymous reviewers of the manuscript for their enthusiastic support and helpful comments.

Portions of this book were used in two special topics courses Grant taught at NC State: "Media Economics" and "Influencer Culture." He would like to thank the undergraduates who participated in both courses, along with the colleagues and graduate students he's discussed this project with (beyond those mentioned above), especially Anne W. Njathi and Adriana de Souza e Silva. He'd also like to thank Katherine Guinness for everything she does. Katherine would like to thank those who tended to both her physical and academic well-being over the course of writing this book, including, but certainly not limited to, Grant Bollmer, Jos Marshall, and Michelle Parrinello-Cason. Also, thanks to Ayla for her invaluable influencer insights.

INTRODUCTION

"Existence in late capitalism is a permanent rite of initiation," argued Max
Horkheimer and Theodor Adorno in *Dialectic of Enlightenment*, their classic analysis of midcentury American capitalism. "Everyone must show that
they identify wholeheartedly with the power which beats them."[1] Today,
in the age of influencer culture, the power that beats us determines the
relative value of individual lives through the ability to gain and maintain
attention, intimacy, relatability.[2] Yet the infinite scroll of social media
appears as a constant stream of the same, in which one's "success" or
"failure," as an individual, as a person, as a worker, is reduced to the instrumental measurement of attention given through the metrics supplied
by platforms. This reduction of social life, personal life, and economic life
is tacitly accepted by many. One either gains attention and is valuable or
remains unseen and invisible, a failure, to disappear and remain beyond
value. Beaten. "Unless I am seen, then I am a failure," says the influencer—
and that is that.

An "influencer," in most popular understandings of "influencer culture," is one whose value derives from gathering interest for brands, maintaining social bonds between consumers and commodities, and cultivating

identities that attract attention on social media.[3] Although we are given glimpses of their lives on our phones and computer screens (reveling in what seems to be extreme wealth, unboxing large hauls of products, organizing elaborate games and events, remodeling their homes, driving their cars, cleaning out their closets), these influencers are not our friends, even though we may imagine or desire them to be. Behind the luxury, leisure, and indulgence we witness, being an influencer involves deep precarity concealed behind an opulent veneer.

For most, being an influencer requires continuous work, work that is often rewarded inadequately. Popular reportage on influencers dwells regularly on the countless narratives of quitting and getting burned out from influencing. According to Emma Chamberlain, one of the most successful and popular influencers of the past few years, "If you're not producing constantly, you won't grow [in popularity]. That's what drives the algorithm. There's pressure to be producing at a level that is unrealistic. Inevitably people burn out or they become too obsessed with being consistent, and they never take time off to evolve their creative side, so it becomes stale."[4]

If one accepts the constant drive to work, one may be "paid" in a few free products—obviously not the same as a wage. As journalist Taylor Lorenz explains, alongside "an ever-growing class of people who have leveraged their social media clout to travel the world, frequently in luxury," who are courted by businesses directly, there is also an overwhelming growth of "D-list" influencers who request the same treatment. Kate Jones, manager at a luxury retreat in the Maldives reports, "Everyone with a Facebook [account] these days is an influencer. . . . These people are expecting five to seven nights on average, all-inclusive. Maldives is not a cheap destination."[5] Many hotels now have a standard influencer request form and contract. Even for the influencers who make the cut and receive free goods—at Jones's luxury retreat, it's 10 percent of applicants—it's rarely clear when the next job may come or the next brand will call.[6] Influencers often see their work, and the comped amenities that their work provides them, as their primary labor and pay, although they may face controversy for demanding even this noncash compensation. Influencer Natalie Zfat responded to such criticisms: "Could you think of any other business industry where it would be frowned upon for someone to reach out to a potential client and offer them an opportunity? You'd never see Coca-Cola berate an ad sales-person at CNN for calling them up and sharing their rates."[7]

Some influencers may rent expensive cars and mansions, attempting to gain attention through extravagance and the perceived wealth of freebies.[8] Others live life as a scam, working to integrate themselves into various social circles to syphon attention and money from others, faking wealth to get attention. While this "scamming" is often downplayed or disguised as genuine, some social media stars revel in the moniker of "scammer." Caroline Calloway, for example, first gained attention for her popular Instagram posts discussing life as an American student at Cambridge. When it was revealed that her posts were ghostwritten, she leaned in to the scandal and attention by selling a variety of products flouting her inauthenticity, everything from a face and body oil named "Snake Oil" to writing workshops that were compared to the infamous Fyre Festival.[9] Calloway later failed to deliver on a lucrative book deal and advance for her memoir, then declared she would self-publish the book, funded through a series of grifty moneymaking schemes, including tarot card readings and selling signed books (not her own book, just books she owns and signs). Calloway's own book, which became available in 2023 for preorder with an unspecified release date, is, of course, titled *Scammer*.

Some of the most renowned influencers go to great lengths to hide their marketing. Kim Kardashian, whose existence is perpetually on the fringes of influencer culture, and who offers a popular image of fame and luxury emulated by many influencers, was fined $1 million by the US Securities and Exchange Commission for not disclosing her promotion of EMAX cryptocurrency.[10] Kardashian's veiled interest in finance and business points toward the obscured relations behind influencer culture that we take up in this book. When Emma Chamberlain contrasts herself with another exceptionally popular YouTube star—Jimmy Donaldson (better known as MrBeast)—she describes an emergent new kind of selfhood in late capitalism: "I look at YouTube more as a creative canvas, whereas MrBeast is a business. This is strategic. It's not intimate. Do we really know MrBeast? What does MrBeast's bedroom look like? What does MrBeast eat for breakfast? No one knows. He is this vehicle for entertaining content. . . . His personal presence is not to be ignored—people know him now—but he's business-minded, and I think I'm more emotional, creative-minded."[11] It is this intersection of authenticity, identity, and commerce that this book is interested in. And, as we will detail, Chamberlain diagnoses something important (which applies to her as well): when people move beyond a level of precarious hustle, then their existence online is one in which identity and commerce converge.

Influencers are more than people we see and interact with on Instagram, TikTok, or YouTube. Influencers are an integral category for the reproduction of the social relation that is capitalism. When an influencer labors to become interesting, relatable, or worthy of attention, the internet becomes a factory to produce the self as commodity. This book examines this articulation of capital and selfhood. It employs influencer culture as an entry point into a set of relations that far exceed social media. In attending to the videos and images of influencers, it draws out numerous obscured infrastructures of contemporary capital, infrastructures that relate to a deeply questionable reinvention of subjectivity and social existence. In these pages, we will sketch the emergence of an economic context in which "successful" individuals achieve wealth, fame, and luxury by imagining themselves and acting not as individuals *but as if their existence is equivalent to that of a vertically integrated corporation*, a context in which rights and abilities are denied human citizens and transferred to corporate entities—a historical moment we term the *Corpocene*.

Influencers, in many ways, are extensions of past understandings of influence, advertising, and spectacle. There are precedents for today's influencers throughout the entirety of modern capitalism.[12] We might point toward people called "opinion leaders," who, in the 1950s, served as intermediaries to carry propaganda from the mass media to the communities in which they lived, shaping political opinion and consumer choice.[13] In the 1990s, opinion leaders became "influentials," a holy grail of marketing research. If one could identify "influentials," then one could manipulate the tastes, consumer habits, and political beliefs of civil society.[14] Earlier, in the work of French sociologist Gabriel Tarde from the late 1800s and early 1900s, we see the source of new trends and new ideas branded as "geniuses" whom others would unconsciously and passively mimic.[15]

And in 1899, Thorstein Veblen first published his ideas about "conspicuous consumption," which emerged from his observations of a "pecuniary emulation" that confers status among the bourgeoisie.[16] Written at the end of the Gilded Age, Veblen's *Theory of the Leisure Class* observed that class stratification could be understood, in part, through different attitudes toward labor and consumption. While the working class may believe in the essential dignity of manual labor, the "leisure class," Veblen argued, invested instead in domination through useless "conquest," meaning competitive games, hunting, war, and sport—activities dedicated to waste rather than productivity. This wasteful excess confers status through competitive esteem judged by others.

Veblen describes "conspicuous consumption," in which expensive goods are flaunted, as typical of this class. For the leisure class, consumer goods should be purchased and ostentatiously displayed. The relative value of a specific good comes not from anything in the product itself—its quality, its utility—but from an excessive price value that makes that good exclusive. The value of an individual comes from the price of their belongings. Conspicuous consumption is highly competitive: "pecuniary emulation" refers to how members of the leisure class mimic and attempt to best each other by squandering money on increasingly excessive purchases. These tendencies, for Veblen, were never entirely the province of the *nouveau riche* of the Gilded Age, the apparent main target of his book. In fact, he saw the leisure class as essentially conservative, a class that perpetuates archaic social forms descending from the tribal and feudal stages of European society, embodied through bourgeois manners and etiquette.

Today's influencer culture carries with it a similar privileging of waste, leisure, conspicuous consumption, and pecuniary emulation. But today's influencers, however much they mirror Veblen's understanding of class differentiation, are distinct from the opinion leaders, influentials, and "geniuses" of the past. We argue that influencer culture distinguishes itself through new forms of class antagonism, an almost bizarre parody of proletariat and bourgeoisie. One group becomes raw material for brands, laboring endlessly, hammering themselves into visual commodities that are eventually used up and discarded. These are the people we typically think of as influencers. This precarious population, struggling to make deals with brands and foster audience interactions, can be contrasted with a far more exceptional kind of influencer who, at first glance, appears to descend directly from the members of Veblen's "leisure class."[17] These influencers do not seem to work for a living and instead mostly engage in activities of luxury and expenditure. Those that rise above a certain level of precarity seem to do so through sheer consumptive excess—as if they've discovered a particular trick or hack to work less and indulge. But, we suggest, this appearance is an illusion. This second category of influencer—those who appear as a wasteful "person" engaging in excessive spending—*is an embodiment of a vertically integrated conglomerate*, moving beyond the production of self as commodity to the ownership of the means of production of the self.

Examples of these conglomerated persons are rare, but they constitute the "elite" of influencer culture, embodied in figures such as Jeffree Star, Jimmy Donaldson (MrBeast), and Emma Chamberlain. The members of this second group merely seem to be particularly successful versions of the members of the first group, as if their existence is a difference in degree, not kind. This is not the case. Even though he may appear to be a successful beauty influencer like any other, Star owns supply chains and warehouses, manufacturing makeup and merch through his companies, Jeffree Star Cosmetics and Killer Merch, to name only the two most prominent companies associated with the influencer. Donaldson, whose excessive stunts are viewed by millions and emulated by many who see MrBeast as "relatable," owns parts of MrBeast Burger, a fast-food chain, and Feastables, a food company that mostly makes chocolate bars. He has invested in numerous tech start-ups and financial technologies, such as Backbone (an iPhone game controller) and Current (a mobile finance app). Emma Chamberlain, whose videos are often celebrated for her "real" persona (which, you'll recall, she contrasted with MrBeast's "business" persona), has transitioned from YouTube to interviewing celebrities for *Vogue* and acting as a brand ambassador for Lancôme, along with founding and maintaining ownership over a coffee company, Chamberlain Coffee.

Star, Donaldson, and Chamberlain's business ventures reveal that they are best understood not as creative laborers but as capitalists whose public image is inextricably linked with a range of partially obscured corporate ventures. Throughout this book, we are interested primarily in this second group of influencers, these conglomerates who appear as people and own warehouses, who control supply chains—traditional methods of capital accumulation derived from the manufacture, distribution, and sale of commodities. We chart the structures of capitalism that guide the "success" of these figures, and we examine how the model of a conglomerated, corporate person they embody has been disseminated throughout influencer culture, a model of aspiration that broadly shapes social media today.

In other words, when thinking about class differences obscured in influencer culture, we find that *one class is capital personified, and the other strives to achieve the status of capital personified.* The striving class has bought into the belief that contemporary capitalism depends on social relations, on personal connections, embracing precarious flexibility and constant hustle as a route to future success and security. The other class, while its members also appear to engage in these same practices, has instead invested in the manufacturing of consumer goods, the ownership of social media platforms and apps, and the trading and speculation of real estate. Theirs is a class in which the logic of selfhood becomes indistinguishable from the logic of the corporation. This, we will demonstrate, is the fundamental ruse of contemporary influencer culture. In the name of identification, intimacy, and authenticity, of being "real" and being "relatable," today's influencer culture is asking audiences to identify with a way of conceiving of themselves—a mode of subjectivity—that follows the logic of a vertically integrated conglomerate, desiring this model of the self as the image and model of "success."

Understanding this class distinction, we will demonstrate, requires significantly rethinking, and perhaps even rejecting, many theorizations of labor and capital that stress the "immaterial" dimensions of production in a digital age. The concept of "immaterial labor," as defined by Italian philosopher Maurizio Lazzarato, refers to activities such as creative thought and the maintenance of emotional relations, activities necessary for the reproduction of capital that have long been neglected because of their seeming lack of physical form.[18] Lazzarato's ideas have been widely taken up to describe technological transformations in capitalism after the 1970s, transformations that coincide with the rise of marketing, public relations, and the cultural industries. With digital, networked media, value regularly seemed to be less about the manufacturing of products than the crafting of brands, the interpretation of data, and the rise of "services" in a range of economic sectors, in which physical commodities were replaced with images, emotions, and information. "Immaterial" forms of labor regularly seem to be what's at stake with the work of influencing. Yet, as we will show, an emphasis on immaterial labor today serves to obscure new forms of vertically integrated production that return us to the manufacturing and circulation of consumer goods. Even though the "elite" discussed in this book appear to be mostly invested in branding and communication, what we show, instead, is the centrality of manufacturing and supply chains undergirding what may otherwise seem to be the most "immaterial" forms of labor online.

Of course, images, relations, information, and emotion are all central to labor online. But a singular emphasis on immaterial aspects of production obscures class antagonisms that persist today. The countless precarious influencers, invested in building brands and maintaining relationships, appear to be a mass of potential *surplus population*—that is, workers who are potentially redundant from the perspective of capitalism, who can be cast aside without any real impact to the larger system.[19] This does not mean that capital cannot extract value from this population; it does so in the form of rents and debt but only to a point—credit card bills pile up; houses and cars are leased; one "hustles" and fakes it until they make it . . . or until they are eventually used up, thrown away, and forgotten. The potential "redundancy" of most influencers is found in how any specific individual can effectively be discarded once the debt becomes excessive, once value can no longer be eked from the worker's body as it ages, as it breaks down in exhaustion, as it burns out. As one relatively popular Instagram influencer, Lee Tilghman, once known as @LeeFromAmerica, told the *New York Times* in 2023, after years of constant work creating branded content, she found herself exhausted, feeling empty and alone, desiring an office job, a boring job. "You don't get it," Tilghman recalled saying to a coworker in her boring office, who couldn't believe she'd trade in her life of glamorous influencing: "You think you're a slave, but you're not. . . . When you're an influencer, then you have chains on."[20] Her years of influencing left Tilghman depressed and stressed, worn out from constant striving to achieve luxury. And, like so many other influencers who have quit and been forgotten, Tilghman's exit from influencing doesn't particularly matter from the point of view of capital. For every @LeeFromAmerica there once was, countless others are willing to take her place and become the next personality to go viral.

Influencer culture is a factory, in which countless individuals on the internet labor daily, most often for pittance wages, manufacturing a commodity called "the self." This commodity must appear distinct, unique, different, a product that is exchangeable and valuable. And it must be produced, made, fabricated using tools given and controlled by monopolistic industries—fashion, cosmetics, social media, technology—often to sell these very things back to the audience watching on their phones and computers. Yet these workers do not have the ability to organize themselves as a class because the product they make is effectively worthless, because this product is the self. Rather than the sale of their labor power, the product is the very possibility that one is a unique individual with unique connections and unique abilities—labor power and personal identity fully converge. As the promise of individuality is a delusion—Adorno and Horkheimer might say that individuality under consumer capitalism is, at best, pseudo-individuality[21]—these precarious workers are precarious because they perpetually differentiate one from another, negating the possibility of class solidarity. And, at the same time, not one is meaningfully distinct from any other. As individuals, they are fungible and unnecessary. As Horkheimer and Adorno claimed, "The self, entirely encompassed by civilization, is dissolved in an element composed of the very inhumanity which civilization has sought from the first to escape. The oldest fear, that of losing one's name, is being fulfilled."[22] The demand to *be* an individual, to *be* a self, to *be* a unique and exchangeable commodity realizes what Adorno and Horkheimer were describing: the liquidation of selfhood in the name of capitalist rationality.

But this liquidation of selfhood is slightly different when it comes to people like MrBeast, Emma Chamberlain, or Jeffree Star. The second type of influencer, embodied by these figures, *is* capital. They are an embodiment of a vertically integrated conglomerate, moving beyond the production of self as commodity to the ownership of the means of production of the self—the machinery and materials that manufacture the product called the self. Person and means of production are conflated. Jeffree Star oversees the manufacture of the makeup he brands with his name, stored in warehouses he manages, shipped through logistics companies he operates, to mention just one example we'll draw on throughout this book. Star does not merely advertise a product to others, influencing through social relations fostered by social media. He owns and controls the entire supply chain that sources, makes, and ships the makeup he and many others, who essentially pay Star for the privilege of producing a marketable, glamourous identity, use to craft the glamourous people seen over social media.

There are precedents to these vertically integrated "people"—Oprah Winfrey or Martha Stewart, for instance, to name two of the earliest examples of branded individuals,[23] whose personal identities and names gave coherence to large conglomerations of consumer goods and products sold through the lure of the individual. Yet nobody truly believes Oprah's conglomerate, Harpo Inc., to be self-identical with her as a person. The same goes for Martha Stewart Living Omnimedia, which continued operations even with Stewart in prison. But, as we will return to later in this book, Star is often presumed to "be" his brand. When it comes to the conglomerated individuals of influencer culture, corporate diversification and integration are concealed, bound together with the personal identity of the individual we see onscreen. Fans are often more likely to believe that these individuals are faking their wealth than they are to believe those they watch are truly "different" from any other precarious, struggling influencer.[24]

HOW WHITENESS INFLUENCES INFLUENCER CULTURE

This book is guided by a refusal to believe that "successful" influencers are essentially the same as those living and struggling and burning themselves out. As we mentioned above, in this book we mostly examine "successful" influencers in the construction of their online personas. Throughout, we look for the moments in which the presence of production, the presence of capital, intrudes. Our guiding principle is that the videos of influencers, their "content," inevitably point toward the material foundations of contemporary capitalism, even if these foundations are rarely the focus.

Within the class relations of influencer culture, the bourgeoisie are made up largely of rich, white people, and there are specific reasons for this. While not everyone discussed in this book can truly be situated as "elite," we do believe that everyone discussed here is following a specific model of influencer, a model that intrinsically follows, to some degree, a normative acceptance of whiteness, linking wealth and success with a tacitly racialized understanding of human worth.

Numerous media scholars have examined those struggling in the contemporary influencer industries, often foregrounding dimensions of gender, race, and class.[25] Cultural production, like culture in general, is inherently structured by these categories. American culture, rooted in white supremacy, privileges whiteness, and internet culture in the United States is no exception.[26] If we want to understand the oppressive qualities of contemporary digital culture, then we must examine whiteness, wealth, and other qualities privileged as natural, as normal, as desirable today.

It is widely known that Black influencers are, as Shani Orgad and Rosalind Gill put it, "likely to be underpaid by brands relative to their white counterparts undertaking identical promotional labor."[27] Race impacts the visibility and income opportunities afforded almost all influencers. Marketers assume, to use the words of one, that "Black influencers are not able to deliver the results (i.e. sales, followers etc.) that white influencers are able to," even if follower counts are the same, leading to racialized interpretations of metrics and unequal pay for otherwise equivalent labor.[28] At the same time, signifiers of race are often appropriated by white influencers for attention and exoticism, a practice termed *Blackfishing* by the journalist Wanna Thompson.[29] "Blackfishing" is a concept that echoes bell hooks's classic argument about "eating the other," where appropriating racial otherness becomes a way to add "spice" to the blandness of white culture.[30]

Black influencers face difficulties negotiating visibility on social media through the automated, algorithmic manipulation of feeds and moderation of content. Systems of algorithmic recommendation, which are essential for negotiating visibility over social media, reproduce—and often intensify—forms of discrimination that exist beyond the internet. Safiya Umoja Noble uses the phrase "technological redlining" to describe how technologies of automation "reinforce oppressive social relationships and enact new modes of racial profiling."[31] Ruha Benjamin terms this technological discrimination "the New Jim Code," which she defines as *"the employment of new technologies that reflect and reproduce existing inequities but that are promoted and perceived as more objective or progressive than the discriminatory systems of a previous era."*[32] This is part of a long-standing pattern. Charlton McIlwain, in *Black Software*, a historical study of race and computers, has argued that while Black people have often existed at the vanguard of technological innovation as hobbyists, entrepreneurs, "organizers, evangelists, activists, and knowledge brokers" who positioned Black culture in the foreground of the internet's "popular social development," the history of technology in America is also a story of how digital technology has been used to negate Black agency and limit the "hopes and dreams, aspirations, human potential, and political interests" of Black people.[33]

Algorithmic data analytics, according to Wendy Chun, descend from eugenics and presume a fundamental "homophily" to ground all sociality—enforcing a "love of the same" that tends to exclude all that deviates from this sameness. As Chun argues, even though data analytics initially were framed as leading to a kind of postrace, postidentity "utopia," "social networks perpetuate angry microidentities through 'default' variables and axioms. By using data analytics, individual differences and similarities are actively sought, shaped, and instrumentalized in order to capture and shape social clusters."[34]

Thus, the algorithmic manipulation of attention by the platform tacitly reiterates the norm of whiteness, linking this norm with wealth and "success." Even though one labors to be interesting and distinct online, this distinction must remain "relatable," within a narrow space that cannot deviate excessively from the norm of whiteness.[35] Benjamin describes "the power of this plainness as the invisible 'center' against which everything else is compared and as the 'norm' against which everyone else is measured. Upon further reflection, what appears to be an absence in terms of being 'cultureless' works more like a superpower. . . . To be unmarked by race allows you to reap the benefits but escape responsibility for your role in an unjust system."[36]

This privilege given to whiteness has obvious consequences, directly shaping how pay, visibility, and attention are distributed online. Even popular Black influencers are often treated as secondary to white influencers, placing them in a position where they must work harder for a similar amount of attention and less pay. Take, for instance, a series of well-publicized events thrown by Tarte Cosmetics, in which the company invited many TikTok-based beauty influencers to events, first in Dubai and then in Miami. For the Dubai trip, fifty influencers were invited, yet only one invitee, Monet McMichael, was not white.[37] The subsequent Tarte trip, to the former estate of the singer Prince, outside Miami, was also called out for racial disparities, this time by one of its invitees, Cynthia Victor, a beauty influencer of Sri Lankan descent known on TikTok as Shawtysin, for the privileges she witnessed given to the white attendees. While Victor was invited for one week, the white influencers on the trip were invited for two and were often given better rooms and more promotional goods and opportunities than she was.[38]

Outside of the United States, the emphasis on the visibility and necessity of whiteness is often even more explicit. In her study of Instagram influencers in Nairobi, Kenya, Anne W. Njathi describes the case of Empresal Sally, who died on December 12, 2021, from complications related to a skin-lightening procedure. Sally, a thirty-nine-year-old mother of four at the time of her death, whose Instagram account was filled with images of luxurious, international travel, "believed her appearance was her best commodity, and invested in having the most appealing physical presence as possible."[39] As Njathi argues, skin-lightening is widespread among many of the most popular Kenyan influencers, such as Vera Sidika, often described as Nairobi's Kim Kardashian, who also popularized the hashtag #BleachedBeauty to describe the lightness of her skin and, therefore, her economic value as one who can attract attention.[40] As Benjamin explains, "race itself is a kind of technology—one designed to separate, stratify, and sanctify the many forms of injustice experienced by members of racialized groups, but one that people routinely reimagine and redeploy to their own ends."[41] When race does appear in influencer culture, it often does so through its appropriation by white influencers[42] acting as a way to "extend" white bodies and the reach of whiteness[43] or, as evidenced by Tarte trips and skin bleaching, appears as a liability for the "effective" circulation of capital.

In other words, platforms algorithmically privilege whiteness through the enforcement of homophily, through forms of automation that reproduce structures of racist social organization, and some influencers respond by manipulating their bodies through risky practices that likewise hold up whiteness as an ideal. This does not mean that platforms exclude people who are not white, but it does mean that it is radically more difficult for influencers who are not white to get attention and to get paid—and thus to move into the position we have described in which one becomes capitalist rather than a worker.

Even the whitewashed veneers of luxury and opulence that we see in influencer content cannot conceal the material reality of capitalism today and, in fact, as we show over the course of this book, can serve as a route directly into the hidden abode of production. The global infrastructures of capital—warehouses, supply chains, shipping industries—are profoundly racialized.[44] The chapters of this book emphasize the *ownership* of varied, large-scale forms of capital, including homes, cars, and warehouses. We show that property ownership is a significant, obscured part of "success" in influencer culture. Given long-standing governmental policies that discriminate by race to prohibit or discourage property ownership by non-white people,[45] this is another way that influencer culture reproduces a norm of whiteness.

It is easy to assume that "influencers" are a general mass, a group of people whose differences are about scale and significance rather than differences in kind. Race is one way of articulating forms of discrimination perpetuated by platforms and marketers, one way of identifying varied forms of stratification that emerge from platforms and attention that leads some to greater precarity than others. But the solution to this discrimination should not be to help capital further integrate disparate individuals and groups into economic exploitation. Or, the "problem" of influencer culture should not be reduced only to how platforms distribute attention in a biased way that reproduces, among other things, racial disparities. We can see the limits of approaching platform discrimination in this way through the failure of labor organization online, which returns us to our general problem of class within influencer culture.

The general precarity of most influencers is widely acknowledged. One solution often proposed for the precarity is unionization, an argument that frames influencers as equivalent to any other cultural worker.[46] Influencers "are facing a kind of existential crisis," reports the *Atlantic*. "They have never been more valuable to their home platforms, yet they're still struggling to turn that value into meaningful leverage."[47] Among other factors, the algorithmic mediation of attention, the demands of platforms and advertisers, and the constantly shifting attention from audiences all contribute to the precarity of struggling influencers.

There have been multiple attempts to unionize influencers and content creators, though many, like the "IG Meme Union Local 69-420," a union for Instagram meme account owners, seem more like a joke than an actual attempt at unionization. The author and YouTuber Hank Green founded the Internet Creators Guild in 2016, which shut down after three years for lack of interest. (It's also notable that Green isn't primarily known as an influencer today; he and his brother, John Green, who vlogged together in the early 2000s, are both exceptionally popular novelists and entrepreneurs, themselves vertically integrated individuals who have transcended the precarity of influencer culture.) The Screen Actors Guild has an "influencer agreement" that positions brand relationships under the purview of the union's bargaining guidelines, though it's unclear how many people have taken advantage of this agreement or if influencers who are not primarily actors could even secure SAG membership. A lawyer who represents online creators was quoted by the *Atlantic*, noting how "not one client" he has worked with has ever been interested in unionization or collective bargaining. Influencers, he says, "are small businesses on their own and they don't need help from others. . . . It's only if you're starting out or you're a micro-influencer that you want to band together for strength in numbers."[48]

The most significant and successful form of organized influencer protest has been a "strike" in which Black creators withdrew their labor from TikTok to resist the common appropriation of dances choreographed and created by Black influencers. When white influencers would repeat these dances, they often would gain far more attention and visibility (and therefore money) than the Black influencers who initially created the dances,[49] a fact that illustrates yet again some of the arguments about the privilege given to whiteness by social media platforms. But because visibility on TikTok, like other social media platforms, is determined by constant posting of new content, this "strike" hurt neither TikTok nor anyone other than the creators who withdrew their labor.[50]

Our suggestion is that these attempts at unionization and worker organization are limited because they fail to grasp the specificity of class differentiation in influencer culture. Labor grievances are focused on the relative integration, or lack thereof, of individuals into the larger capitalist system. The framing of the labor politics of influencer culture in this way ignores how many of the most prominent and successful influencers are not creative workers but are themselves capitalists who conflate their own identities with corporations they found, own, and manage. And because capital, in the United States, descends from a range of racialized structures that implicitly and explicitly privilege whiteness, combined with algorithmic structures and racialized understandings of the value of attention that also privilege whiteness, this means that the class structure of influencer culture, with its capital-owning "elites," also privileges whiteness. Our goal throughout this book is to study this privilege, which too often, like whiteness itself, passes as "neutral" and aspirational.

THE CORPORATE PERSONS OF YOUTUBE

Believing that the model of success online is at least somewhat "neutral" is easy, unfortunately. In the idealized life cycle of an influencer, "success" appears to come from working hard or understanding the logic of platformed attention. Begin by generating popular content—a start that might involve a high level of fraudulence, investing in fake followers, bots who comment on posts, gaming the system of algorithmic visibility. If an influencer gets popular enough, with enough videos going viral, with enough followers (real or not), they might get paid by a platform, receiving a tiny, partial share of the profits from advertising shown in conjunction with their videos. If their popularity expands further, the influencer may get offers from brands, generating sponsored content, doing product reviews, presenting personalized ads—opportunities that may be paid but more often are compensated with free promotional goods. Then, if one is exceptionally popular, brands may desire collaborations, putting the influencer's face and name on their products. The influencer may become the face of a specific brand.

There is precarity, disposability, and discrimination implicit in this life cycle: even highly prominent and popular influencers can disappear if they're revealed to be "toxic," if their fans turn against them or grow bored. That precarity is only mitigated if one can transition out of the influencer life cycle, a stage achieved by a miniscule few, revealing the limits of this meritocratic narrative of popularity. Here, one ceases to be an influencer, properly speaking, and becomes a corporation that appears as an individual human. In this stage, one owns the brands that they advertise, brands like Jeffree Star Cosmetics, MrBeast Burger, or Chamberlain Coffee. These brands may not even be attached in a direct way to the individual's image, and the influencer may disappear from the branding for the products associated with their name. Emma Chamberlain often does not appear in the ads for her coffee, for instance, and Jeffree Star's extensive business activities are regularly obscured. Some make the transition to full-fledged corporation by investing in companies that manufacture goods for other influencers and own warehouses that distribute products for others; Jeffree Star, through Killer Merch and his fulfillment centers, does precisely this. In this final stage, the influencer is a very traditional capitalist and cannot be understood as one of many workers struggling in the creative economy.

This move from branded collaborations to owning and manufacturing is a central part of our analysis. Our focus on influencers and influencer culture is directed toward understanding the everyday, lived reality of capitalism today, in which individuals are steered toward identifying directly with corporations, in which today's *community*, if we can even use this term, is a community of brands and corporations passing as human beings.

The broad internalization of the logic of capital as the foundations for subjectivity and sociality has led to what the Marxist theorist Jacques Camatte terms "the domestication of humanity," the process that "comes about when capital constitutes itself as a human community." It "starts out with the fragmentation and destruction of human beings, and the final outcome is that capital is anthropomorphized."[51] Capital today, Camatte tells us, has *escaped*; it has become autonomous, beyond control of the bourgeoisie—that is, the capitalists who try to master it—exercising domination over all human life. Capital typically appears as a set of contingent but reified social relations—meaning, while capitalism seems to characterize most of social life, there are many moments that seem to be beyond capitalism, at least partially. But today, Camatte suggests, these moments seem to be more difficult to find, as capital appears as social, communal existence as such. Or, we suggest, we can see this "escape" of capital in influencer culture when *capital appears as people*. For Camatte, capital today grounds the very possibilities of being social, and to imagine another world requires rethinking, even abandoning, much of what we imagine to be fundamental social relations. In influencer culture, we can see shimmers of the autonomy of capital, of its existence as that which substitutes for and remakes community. The *Corpocene*, the ultimate concept this book will propose, describes this moment, in which the object we identify with is capital itself—diversified, distributed, and conglomerated.

Our context, which we might term "late capitalism" following the Marxist theorist Ernest Mandel,[52] is a moment in which everything begins to appear as capital and social forces previously beyond the boundaries of capital appear as part of production. "Late capitalism" refers not to a period approaching the end of capitalism but the moment in which possible exteriors of capital seem difficult to identify. The social forces once thought of as human community appear as technology, as *machinery*, designed to commodify all that exists. "Subsumed under capital the workers become components of these social formations," Marx says in the "Results of the Immediate Process of Production," his unfinished chapter of *Capital*, "but these social formations do not belong to them and so rise up against them as the *forms* of capital itself, as if they belonged to capital, as if they arose from it and were integrated within it."[53]

Today, some Marxists see this subsumption (as Marx calls it above) as a necessary point forward to a future communism, arguing for the necessity of complete technological alienation to intensify the contradictions inherent to capital, provoking rupture and collapse. Things must get worse— possibly to the point of a total, dystopian collapse of society—before they get better, this line of thinking goes.[54] Others see the emergence of a mode of production that cannot truly be called "capitalism."[55] Mandel and Camatte see something different. Faith in technology—and the incorporation of life into a technological mode of production—leads to the perpetual wasting of human labor, the generation of extreme irrationality and fatalism, obscuring the points at which we could intervene to stop it. Any hope in technology is misguided. This includes not only the banal belief that technology will save us but also includes the hope that the collapse of capital and society will lead, somehow, to a revolution spurred by perpetually increasing precarity, instability, and crisis.

We can see why this hope is misguided when we begin to look at what is obscured in influencer culture. Late capitalism is a period marked by a pessimism about the possibility of an alternative to capitalism.[56] Yet finding new alternatives and new ways out of capitalism must first acknowledge how almost all facets of social existence have been subsumed by capital, a subsumption that does not—and, most likely, will never—lead to capitalism's collapse through the intensification of internal contradictions. As we mentioned above, influencer culture demands the production of a product called "the self," a product that attains value only through its distinction from others, in which one desires and aspires to become like the luxurious, corporate persons seen online, so there is little hope for unionization or organization—especially if the actual class differences of influencer culture remain unacknowledged.

Our argument is that we can observe the contemporary autonomy of capital, along with how this autonomy has led to a strange context in which people aspire to live as if they are themselves corporations, when we begin attending to the practices of influencers. We can see into the material workings of late capitalism simply by looking at what is indirectly represented on social media, by looking at representational *content*, reading for backgrounds of production—*forms* of capital, as it were—that are certainly not intended to be the focus. In the chapters that follow, this often means looking at where videos were literally shot—in houses, in cars, in thrift stores, storage units, warehouses—drawing out the implications these spaces have for the generation and circulation of capital in influencer culture.

Most of the videos discussed in this book were from around the years 2016 to 2023, slightly predating but ultimately focusing on the years of the COVID-19 pandemic. We've mentioned Jeffree Star, MrBeast, and Emma Chamberlain throughout this introduction, and we will discuss not only these individuals but many who have followed in their mold or predate them in style. We do not examine traditional celebrities who happen to have large online followings, such as musicians, actors, or athletes who are popular on Instagram or TikTok. Everyone we examine seems, to some degree, invested in cultivating a personality, producing a "self," one crafted with the goal of making money either through ads shown during videos or through brand collaborations and sponsorships. Or, at the very least, everyone we discuss makes it appear as if their main job is to promote products through their ability to gain popular attention.

As will also become clear, we believe that YouTube is particularly useful in visualizing contemporary capitalist infrastructures in this moment. YouTube provides an unusual (and unusually large) set of documents through which our "lived culture" is expressed, refined, and archived; YouTube's videos, in acting to document our present, could be said to "correspond to its *contemporary* system of interests and values," to use the words of theorist Raymond Williams.[57] If we are interested in charting how people live through and make sense of what we might term "platform capitalism,"[58] to use one name for the context in which social media and digital technology have reinvented the capitalist base, we must look at the texts made and practices performed within this context—though, we believe that an emphasis on "platforms" only begins to approach one part of our current moment. To provide an immanent critique of contemporary capitalism, we must engage with the products of social media, not just at the level of industry but at the level of subjectivity—especially when subjectivity becomes the commodity into which labor power is fashioned. But this explains why YouTube is a particularly useful archive.

Additionally, in the years covered by this book, it was common knowledge among influencers that, if one wanted to make money, YouTube is where one's efforts should ultimately be focused. As one relatively popular influencer put it in a TikTok video, "the real video monetization is in YouTube and Instagram, and again, unless your content is about you being hot, you're going to find it very difficult to transfer your followers on here [TikTok] to there."[59] We focus on YouTube as the place where the money was.

In looking slightly beyond what we see in the foreground of images and videos on social media, we begin to see the material infrastructures of a capitalism organized around the production of identity, in which the means of production become the means of production of the self, a transformation that affirms an evacuation and undermining of subjectivity beyond what cannot be equated with a saleable commodity. We are seemingly obsessed with identity today because identity has become impossible. And, beyond this transformation of identity into a commodity, we can also begin to see how a major point of identification, of aspiration, is not only wealth and luxury but *imagining oneself as a corporation.*

Before outlining our overall organization and argumentative logic, we'll now turn toward a specific case. We make a claim that seeks to demonstrate our method and approach to influencer culture: *there is no such thing as a selfie, and the belief that there are selfies has served to obscure broader changes in production in which community and selfhood have become subsumed by capital.* We begin by looking at selfies because selfies are commonly understood as a method for documenting and revealing the self, for making oneself visible to others over social media.

Although influencers are not the only people who take selfies, influencer culture begins with practices that show one as a "self" over social media, a revelation necessary to begin the process of manufacturing the self as a commodity to be of interest to others and brands. In looking at selfies, we aim to demonstrate how a logic of commodification has subsumed practices of self-documentation and that we cannot say that there is any authentic "self" being revealed online. In fact, believing in the basic claim *there are selfies* conceals the distinction between the two classes mentioned above; believing that any private, authentic, intimate relation can be revealed over social media distracts from the materiality of capitalism that undergirds social media. Understanding the class politics of influencer culture first requires doing away with the very idea of selfies as a "thing" and, instead, looking closely at what literally appears in the *backgrounds* of images and videos online. It is this turn to the background that guides our arguments and guides the method of interpretation we use in the chapters that follow.

THERE ARE NO SELFIES

Almost anyone writing about selfies refers to the year 2013, when Oxford Dictionaries named *selfie* their "Word of the Year." Canonizing the selfie as an official "thing," Oxford defined this word as "a photograph that one has taken of oneself, typically one taken with a smartphone or webcam and uploaded to a social media website."[60] Selfies were products of social media and digital photography, an effect of the affordances of contemporary technology. This was true. But, if those writing about selfies after 2013 were perpetually referring to a dictionary definition, it follows that selfies were, more than anything, a linguistic trend. Giving primacy to the selfie as a thing—even a thing produced by technology—is, strangely, far too linguistically determinative. The idea that something called a "selfie" characterized photography over social media, that it was something generally new, something specific to its present—these were all products of the act of naming in a dictionary, of saying that, yes, *selfies exist.*

Elevating the act of naming to this preeminent position, even naming to identify something new, undermines historical and material specificity. In the Oxford definition, a selfie, after all, is not *only* taken with a smartphone or webcam—only "typically." This hedge allows for a flexibility and fluidity of usage of the term. The assumed capaciousness of "selfie" as a concept has led to an entire niche of academic and journalistic commentary arguing about the origins of the selfie. Over and over again, we hear that some early photograph should be thought of as the first selfie, a particularly pioneering selfie—daguerreotype pioneer Robert Cornelius in 1839, for instance,[61] or Buzz Aldrin in 1966.[62] Even Adorno, taking a picture of himself in front of a mirror, despite his general disdain for mass culture, engaged in what would eventually be dismissed as a base pleasure of social media self-representation. It seems, then, that selfies were bound together with the entire history of photographic representation, as if we just didn't know we were taking selfies all along, as if we just didn't have the name.

Linguistic determination itself is nothing unique. This historical confusion happened before with the self-portrait, which has been documented for hundreds, if not thousands, of years and is popularly known to have flourished during the Italian Renaissance in the fourteenth century. Art historian Hannah Williams writes that since, "according to the OED, 'self-portrait' did not appear in the English language until 1831—and in France, *autoportrait* did not make it into the Dictionnaire de l'Académie Française until 1928," artists such as Gustave Courbet and Sir Joshua Reynolds were never "painting a 'self-portrait' (or '*autoportrait*'), per se."[63] All "per ses" aside, this isn't true. Language does not dictate technique. Williams assumes that naming precedes material practice or at least that the name transforms practice into something "real." Similarly, when writers argue over what was "the first selfie," their idealism cannot acknowledge material reality unless a word is there to say, *this is new*, to say, *this is old; this is different*, or *this is the same*. And, more questionably, the same word can perform all these functions. Primacy is accorded the name rather than the material practices and techniques through which people develop and locate the daily realities of their existence.[64]

A 2006 article from the *New York Times* demonstrates how we fail to attend to material practice when we focus on specific words. This article is an early discussion of smartphone photography and describes as "the new self-portraiture" what will inevitably be locked in as a selfie by 2013: "To a certain extent new technology is driving the new self-portraiture. Cell-phone cameras and other digital cameras are sold with wide-angle lenses that allow a picture taken at arm's length to remain in focus. Computers are essentially $1,000 darkrooms that permit sophisticated manipulation of images."[65] The *Times* article, published seven years before the canonization of *selfie* by Oxford Dictionaries, highlights how the history of words can distort material history because of its emphasis on material practice. Digital self-portraits—which exist just as oil-on-canvas self-portraits exist, as bronze-cast self-portraits exist, as photographic self-portraits exist, as any self-portrait exists, all with similarities and differences—at some point became better known as selfies. What then is lost in the reduction of all self-portraiture to the selfie? The selfie, it might be said, *subsumes* all representations of the self, a name that comes to stand in for all technological and visual methods for self-depiction.

Yet selfies are dying out today—or, more accurately, are dying in such a way that makes it clear they never existed in any meaningful sense. What we often see online, images that seem to be selfies, are anything but. They are instead artificial selfies designed to look as if they are selfies. This may seem confusing at this point, but we will return to these pseudo-selfies in a moment, when we turn to discuss the "no-mirror mirror selfie," portraits designed to look as if they are selfies taken in a mirror when, instead, they are taken by another camera or by another photographer. These fake selfies reveal how, while the practices of self-portraiture have existed and will endure, remade, reinvented subtly depending on the material support of the image, the selfie, that image of oneself taken at arm's length, is dying a death so strange that it calls into question its very existence as a distinct kind of image. If there ever was something called a selfie, then it was "little more than a blip in a larger history of a mediated production of the self."[66] *Selfie* is a word that delineated a moment more than an object or action and, owing to material, historical changes in digital culture, the way of thinking that differentiated the selfie from self-portraits no longer exists.

What once separated a self-portrait from a selfie was that, in self-portraiture, the act of representing the self inevitably drew attention to *technical means* for representing the self, for producing a self. Parmigianino's *Self-Portrait in a Convex Mirror* (1529) and Velázquez's *Las Meninas* (1656) are notable for how they situate the artist in a particular context, in a particular space, mediated by mirrors. Cornelius, Aldrin, and Adorno's proto-"selfies" are all profoundly aware of the space of the photographer and the technologies on which they relied. In these images, we see Adorno's mirror; Aldrin's selfie was only produced through the technological extensions that permit space exploration; Cornelius's photograph was the first known American photographic portrait, made with techniques developed by the photographer. The selfie, in contrast, seemed to be characterized by the differentiation of a "self" from a background, without direct awareness of this technical ground. The act of taking a selfie produced a "self" that would appear against a background that would disappear to the one taking a picture. Or, when you take a selfie, you tend to focus on your own image as it appears on the screen of your phone or in the reflection of a mirror, a fact that has led to countless lists of "selfie fails," where something embarrassing shows up in an image, neglected by the one taking the picture. Some referred to this operation as "narcissistic," as the material support for the image—the phone, the space in which one is located—disappeared to the photographer as they examined their own visage on the screen.[67] Yet this disappearance, we claim, is no longer the case, or, at least, this claim cannot be so easily made.

An entire set of elaborate production techniques have emerged—techniques barely visible to the spectator, concealed by the photographer—that show how what once appeared to be selfies are, instead, elaborately constructed portraits designed to position the self as commodity. Like the material support essential for the self-portrait, the images and videos we see online only represent "selves" against a range of specific material infrastructure. These backgrounds against which the "self" appears are essential for influencer culture and allow us to turn to a constellation that links political economy, technology, and the cultivation of identity. If we look closely into what once were thought of as selfies, of YouTube videos, of all forms of internet-based self-representation, what we find is an entire, barely obscured, capitalist infrastructure in which the means of production become *the means of production of the self*, a self that becomes a commodity, representative of a society in which community has been subsumed by technological capital.

SELFIES AND SELF-PORTRAITS

Visual artist and performance studies scholar Artemisa Clark captures the shift from self-portrait to selfie and back again in an Instagram story shared on September 27, 2021.[68] The image depicts a white chihuahua and is tightly cropped so that only its head is visible. It's an extremely close shot, as evidenced by the image's primary focus: a delicate snot-bubble emerging from the bug-eyed creature's nose (fig. 1). The dog looks simultaneously unbothered, embarrassed, embarrassing, and beautiful. Above this image is the text, "Even tho I just took this selfie," with the word *selfie* crossed out in red and "self-portrait" written above it in matching red script.

It's an excellent meme, and, because it is an excellent meme, explaining it fully will be impossible. There are many levels of humor at play, many references to get. We will not attempt to capture everything about this image in its entirety, except to acknowledge that the change from *selfie* to

FIGURE 1   "Even tho I just took this self-portrait."

Source: Artemisa Clark (@bustilacaca), Instagram, accessed April 11, 2022, www.insta gram.com/bustilacaca (no longer available).

self-portrait is a humorous one. This doesn't disqualify its truth, of course, but amplifies it.

Obviously, the dog did not produce this image on its own; it doesn't provoke questions about nonhumans owning copyrights or about animals pushing buttons on cameras.[69] One way of understanding selfies is that the act of taking a picture literally serves to produce the self; and to be distinct from self-portraiture, a selfie would need to be taken *by the subject represented in the image*.[70] But there's little evidence that what we call selfies are, in fact, photographs taken by the subject in the image—an argument we will develop as we go along. And unlike a selfie, a self-portrait can be anything: a self-portrait is about *claiming* that *this represents me*. This is how I see myself, mediated through a particular technical ground. It is an act of poetic invention that may involve appropriating others—images, objects, words, animals, even people—and saying, I have produced a representation that is myself.[71] Thus, the snot-nosed dog might be a self-portrait, but it's not a selfie. And once we start examining things that we once called "selfies" more closely, we begin to see that there's an entire system of production intentionally obscured in the fabrication of images of the self, and even understanding what a "self" is today requires not just the foregrounding of identities but this whole system of production. But before we can get to this system, we want to go further: the very qualities that define a selfie in many popular commentaries are blatantly incorrect and serve to further obscure the material condition of production on the internet.

Specific qualities of production are, after all, what some have said separate the selfie from the self-portrait, not just the materiality of production but varied experiential conditions that emerge from the excessive popularity of digital photography on social media. Getty curator Arpad Kovacs states that "the self-portrait and the selfie are two separate, though at times overlapping, efforts at establishing and embellishing a definition of one's self. Qualities like medium specificity, deeply rooted histories, and traditions (or lack thereof) that define these efforts only superficially differentiate the two. What has greater weight is *the selfie's inherently replaceable and even disposable quality*."[72] Selfies are *replaceable* and *disposable*; they are, to quote Kovacs again, "easily forgotten and replaced by a new picture."[73] The selfie is ephemeral. "A portrait lasts," editor Annelisa Stephan concludes based on her discussion with Kovacs, "not because it is better than a selfie but because it is *meant to*."[74]

What makes a selfie a selfie, this line of thinking suggests, is that the *internet is ephemeral*. We already know this to be far too simple. Granted, the images we see passing by on our feed appear to be an endless flow, a stream of constantly updating and renewed content, many of which are never to be seen again; just try to search for a meme you once saw, one that's a bit more obscure than the usual, a specific variant you remember but can't now find. But we also know that the internet appears as completely enduring. We live in a time in which the past seems as if it will never vanish, in which childhood will never go away, in which mistakes refuse to fade, in which years gone will continue to haunt one throughout the rest of their life.[75] This "enduring ephemeral" temporality of the internet, to use a term from media theorist Wendy Chun,[76] means that digital images are both momentary and seemingly eternal, a temporality that emerges from the constant repetition of software and hardware, making endless copies that never seem to fully disappear.

It appears as if the images we see are countless variants of the same, fungible permutations in which no single image is better or worse than any other. Yet the internet is not a differentiated nonspace of immaterial, vague clouds that only take shape when we rest our eyes on them, floating off into the sky as soon as we look away. Assuming as much presumes an impersonal weightlessness to everything we see and do online, as if a distinction between "real life" and "digital life" can be made through the subjective valuation of relations we presume. We might call this "digital dualism," a pejorative coinage by sociologist Nathan Jurgenson to describe the view that online and offline are separate.[77] Equating "online" with something immaterial, or false, or lesser than "reality" is a deeply questionable position. We know that the internet is a space that lives with us and in us, all day every day. What we do online is what we do. The images are meant to last, and they are meant to last online, because they are meant to last in our lives. Because of this, if we want to look to the nature and definition of selfies, if we assume them to be ephemeral and designed to disappear, to be fleeting, then nothing online passes this test now, if anything ever did. If the selfie is disposable, then why not dispose of it?

Of course, not everyone agrees that selfies are disposable or ephemeral. Alli Burness, the founder of the Tumblr "Museum Selfies," argues that, rather than disposability, the difference between selfies and self-portraits involves several other aesthetic and social concerns:

> Self-portraits are created to be read as art, are displayed in museums or galleries, and we are granted permission to view them as texts, functioning independently from the intent of the artist.
>
> Selfies are borne [*sic*] of vernacular photography practices and are brought into museums and galleries by visitors. It is perilous to read selfies in the same way as art, to ignore the context of their social interaction and the intent of the selfie-taker.
>
> It is important to remember *these images are shared as part of a conversation, a series of contextual interactions and are connected to the selfie-maker in an intimate, embodied and felt way.* We are allowed to leave these elements out of our reading of artist's self-portraits.[78]

Self-portraits are *art*, are *institutionally legitimate*, are *public objects* that possess a uniqueness in time and space that is autonomous from the artist and the audience. Selfies are *private*; they are *vernacular*, of the people and by the people, essentially linked to the photographer. The artwork, by its nature, resists interpretation and the gaze of the spectator. The selfie invites the gaze, welcomes voyeuristic spectacle.

Please. Like self-portraits aren't about the people in them. Like the artist didn't want the viewer to look.[79] Like the act of making a self-portrait turns an artist into a document, a monument, not a person at an easel or a person in front of a camera.

Regardless, challenging this view—that the essence of the selfie is its link to the photographer, that it is a "vernacular" form of image making outside the boundaries of institutional visual culture—is more difficult to challenge than the suggestion that selfies are disposable, and it is an argument that characterizes far more commentary on selfies and selfie culture. Do selfies—now self-portraits or, perhaps even better (referring back to the *Times* article from 2006), digital self-portraits—appear different from the disposable, quickly constructed, ephemeral selfies of the early to mid aughts? Not really, but this belies their labored construction. Let us turn to the example hinted at above: *the no-mirror mirror selfie.* This case both undermines the ability to claim the selfie as disposable and reframes what we might mean by "vernacular." If these images come from some form of popular vernacular, then that vernacular is the one spoken by capital.

BACKGROUNDS OF PRODUCTION, OR,
THE NO-MIRROR MIRROR SELFIE

One typical form of selfie was often taken in a mirror, so that the subject, the photographer, would be able to see their image as they capture it with the press of the button on their phone, or so they could capture a better angle of their body than what's possible when holding the camera at arm's length. We still see these images everywhere, with the subject of the selfie, holding their phone, reflected in the gaze of a mirror. Or so it appears. Here we will credit influencer Kara Del Toro, whose popular TikTok video is often cited for "revealing" something unusual about many mirror selfies today.[80] In Del Toro's video, we see numerous, flawless mirror selfies, each hovering behind her using the TikTok greenscreen feature. These selfies all have perfect lighting and are seemingly taken in a smudgeless, impossibly clean mirror. Each photo shows an influencer holding their phone, presumably using it to take their photo in the mirror. But, as Del Toro tells us, "Here's the secret: there is no mirror."

Many mirror selfies today, at least those made by the seemingly more "professional" influencers, have no mirror. They contain the hallmark of the subject holding a phone and looking into it, as if their gaze is merely directed toward the screen and, by extension, the image of their own self—but the phone is a prop. The selfie, Del Toro reveals, is a cheap trick.

The no-mirror mirror selfie follows how literary theorist Sianne Ngai theorizes the "gimmick." A gimmick is a technique that reveals a simultaneous deficiency and excess of labor in production, something that "seems too expensive or too cheap," where "the technology behind it is too new or too old."[81] In a traditional mirror selfie, the phone in the image is the source of the image itself. In the images Del Toro identifies, the subject in the image either has someone else take their photo or they set up a second camera on a tripod in front of them to capture their image. We can see this fabrication at work in fashion blogger Léa-Elisabeth's Instagram post taken on a city street.[82] This would seem to be a traditional "mirror selfie."

Léa-Elisabeth and a friend are looking at their phone, looking at what we, the viewers, assume to also be Léa-Elisabeth and her friend as they take a picture in a mirror. But the context of this image undermines the possibility that what we might presume we see is even possible. Were a wall-sized mirror placed out on the street, it most certainly wouldn't be flawlessly clean. This image was clearly taken by another photographer or another camera—not the camera in the photo.

This revelation, which is very easy to detect once one knows how the image is achieved, especially in photos where a mirror would seem impossible, caused a minor panic across social media and popular websites, with laments over feeling scammed or duped—a panic that affirms how Ngai describes fascination with the gimmick as a "combination of enigma with transparency" regarding "a process of production: . . . a conjunction of what we know, *but also know that we don't or can't entirely know*, or at least not on the same level, about how an object was brought into being."[83] Articles taking simultaneous offense at being tricked and pleasure in revealing the trick's basis could be found across numerous sources of internet journalism. *Dazed* wrote, "Influencers are scamming us with this selfie mirror trick."[84] "This Influencer Conspiracy Will Make You Question Everything," headlined *New York* magazine's blog *The Cut*.[85] "The fakery is all part of the fun: the hoax of the mirror selfie," was the *Guardian*'s take. In the *Guardian*, one influencer, Erica Davies, claimed that she doesn't fake her mirror selfies because "I just don't have the time or the energy. The reason that I do the mirror selfie," she says, "is it saves me setting up a tripod."[86] The distinction, then, for Davies, is the *effort* involved in the construction of the image, a distinction explicitly about an excess of labor involved to look effortless, about the falsity, the gimmickry involved in the fabulation of seeming pseudo-selfies.

So why do others expend their energy in this way? Why take the trouble to construct such an elaborate image, which is often dismissed as "disposable"? There are many practical reasons. Mirrors get dirty, and smudges are "un-aesthetic." It may be difficult to place a mirror in a space with ideal lighting—a condition that could especially affect outdoor mirror selfies. There is simply more control in every way with the fake-mirror selfie, including control over what appears in the background. But why not do away with the idea of the mirror altogether? Why hold the phone? And here the phone *is* the mirror: it shows a false reflection, and, since many of these setups use a second phone on a tripod, the second phone acts as both mirror and camera, literally taking the place of the mirror that we, the viewer, assume to exist. The doubling of the phones and cameras leads to an infinite absence; while we may assume that the image we see is repeated on the screen of the phone depicted in the image itself, this is not the case. Something is there, determining the image; and this "outside" is not a space of pure virtuality or potentiality but an absent presence that signifies the design, the manufacture, the *labor* of influence in constructing a self to be seen and sold.

A traditional mirror selfie is quick and easy to take. But what appear to be mirror selfies are now highly produced, an attempt to recreate a gesture that *seems* to be "authentic," that appears to be disposable, that looks as if it was produced by the person in the picture and them alone. But once we see there *is no mirror*, then we also become aware that the conditions of production involved in these images are both far more complex than often acknowledged and almost impossible for the viewer to identify. The image, its inability to fully conceal that which exists beyond its frame, gestures toward the condition of production; this would, we suggest, make these images *self-portraits*, not selfies. And even if selfies may have seemed to be "disposable," we can begin to see that they've always involved an elaborate, extensive system of production that remains obscured by the image. This is why selfies are not "vernacular" forms of visual culture. We can only say they are vernacular if we ignore the relations inherent in the production of any image,[87] and these relations are surely not "of the people." They are relations of capital, in which sociality and community have been subsumed into production. The moment these images become composed, become an act derived from the labor of the influencer, labor on which making a living as an influencer depends, then they cannot be said to be vernacular. Once we refuse the idea that "selfies" are either disposable or vernacular, we begin to sketch another conclusion about them. Why is it that people put so much effort into the construction of these images? Because they are well constructed self-portraits, not selfies. Because they are representations of a commodity, a representation that produces a commodity, a commodity indistinguishable from a subject, a commodity indistinguishable from an identity.

TRANSPARENCY AND AUTHENTICITY

Michel Foucault's interpretation of Velázquez's *Las Meninas* is cited over and over again. As a good meme circulates because of the slipperiness of its explanation, because it identifies something that cannot be stated succinctly, clearly, Foucault is repeatedly referenced because he identifies something particular about modern visual culture that few others have explained so well. When looking at *Las Meninas*, Foucault sees a particularly modern phenomenon: the technological support for the self-portrait—a self-portrait that doesn't appear to be a self-portrait—explodes the frame, upending the relation between viewer and artist and subject:

> In appearance . . . we are looking at a picture in which the painter is in turn looking out at us. A mere confrontation, eyes catching one another's glance, direct looks superimposing themselves upon one another as they cross. And yet this slender line of reciprocal visibility embraces a whole complex network of uncertainties, exchanges, and feints. The painter is turning his eyes towards us only in so far as we happen to occupy the same position as his subject. We, the spectators, are an additional factor. Though greeted by that gaze, we are also dismissed by it, replaced by that which was always there before we were: the model itself. But, inversely, the painter's gaze, addressed to the void confronting him outside the picture, accepts as many models as there are spectators; in this precise but neutral place, the observer and the observed take part in a ceaseless exchange. No gaze is stable, or rather, in the neutral furrow of the gaze piercing at a right angle through the canvas, subject and object, the spectator and the model, reverse their roles to infinity.[88]

Even further, Foucault draws attention to the mirror in *Las Meninas*, the mirror on the back wall of the studio, reflecting out and depicting not us, the viewer, but those it would seem are sitting for the portrait being painted by the artist in the painting. Who appears in the mirror? It is King Philip IV of Spain and his wife, Mariana, Foucault tells us. But, he also warns, *Las Meninas* is a painting that remains unfixed by these proper names, by royal authority. The sovereign gaze depicted in the painting may be present, but it is undermined, reversed. The painting places the spectator and the artist—not the artist depicted in the painting but the one making the painting (though the boundary between these two is inevitably unstable)—in the position of the sovereign through the mirror in the background. *Las Meninas*, through the mirror, continuously reverses and undermines the very possibility of an "enclosed" representation. "The mirror, by making visible, beyond even the walls of the studio itself, what is happening in front of the picture, creates, in its sagittal dimension, an oscillation between the interior and the exterior."[89] *Las Meninas* opens up a central problem of modern regimes of representation, the reliance on "an essential void: the necessary disappearance of that which is its foundation."[90] That which remains invisible is that which provides the ground on which representation can occur.

For *Las Meninas*, Foucault remarks, one disappearance is that of the king, its royal, sovereign authority—a missing spectator, replaced with the constant oscillation and reversals that invite an impersonal viewing public into the space of the studio. But the spectator and the artist—even though the artist is depicted in the painting—also disappear. The reflections of mirrors are always slightly off. The self-portrait, then, is a form that reflects on the *impossibility* of representing a self, of how the encounter with the foundation—the artist, their ability to know and thus see and thus represent themself—must inevitably fail, must inevitably move outward given the limitations and requirements of the medium. Foundations for knowing the self perpetually intrude, and whatever it is we call a "self" escapes, moving beyond the empirical into the depths of modern knowledge. On one hand, what defines the self-portrait is not the work's autonomy but precisely the opposite: that the composition of the self is an active process that must continue, that searches and reaches away. The selfie, on the other, was supposedly a medium that, rather than demonstrating the artifice of representation, was meant to be *transparent*, to be *authentic*, depicting the "real me" in moments of private spontaneity. The selfie seemed to offer an enclosure, a fulfillment of subjectivity in which the gaze only fell back on one's face. The selfie was for those self-contained moments when one "felt cute" and took a picture but, with a little faux uncertainty, "might delete later." The obvious irony here is, again, the failure of this intimacy, the failure of self-enclosure; these call into question the very possibility of a selfie.

The mis en abyme of *Las Meninas*, its infinite depth, seems completely out of step with our current moment, what philosopher Byung-Chul Han terms our "society of transparency":

> Matters prove transparent when they shed all negativity, when they are smoothed out and leveled, when they do not resist being integrated into smooth streams of capital, communication, and information. . . . Images are transparent when—freed from all dramaturgy, choreography, and scenography, from any hermeneutic depth, and indeed from any meaning at all—they become pornographic. Pornography is unmediated contact between the image and the eye. Things prove transparent when they abandon their singularity and find expression through their price alone. Money, which makes it possible to equate anything with anything else, abolishes all incommensurability, and all singularity. The society of transparency is an *inferno of the same*.[91]

The no-mirror mirror selfie demonstrates how this is a partial account of our transparency. The image is supposed to appear as if transparent; its intent is, in Han's terms, pornographic. But its transparency must itself rely on a set of mechanisms that are concealed. We only begin to approach these mechanisms, acknowledging the lack of transparency of the selfie, once we acknowledge that selfies do not exist. As one journalistic account of the no-mirror mirror selfie remarked, "Celebs and influencers go to a lot of trouble to make their instagrams personal, like an inside peek into their lives. The mirror selfie has a certain, je ne sais quoi, because it's supposed to be taken on a whim, in the moment, a spontaneous second where you look H-O-T," but the realization that there is no mirror would seem to undermine this disposability, this ephemerality, this vernacularity. "That's why it's so interesting that these images aren't being taken in mirrors. They aren't fleeting moments of fab-ness, but actually highly engineered and structured photos with a lot of thought and primping behind them."[92]

Transparency, the dream of being authentic, conceals a simple fact: transparency is impossible, and the perpetual demand both to be "real" and to be a marketable commodity will burn you out, and you will be discarded. Unless you own physical assets and financial investments, influencer culture is a culture in which bodies are consumed in the relentless technical production of a more authentic self, an authenticity that is for-

ever deferred, because this self only exists through the extensive incorporation of commodities, of makeup, of clothing, of real estate, of financial
speculation: transparency for the masses, obscurity for the rich—for one
class a demand to achieve an impossible ideal, for another the ability to
hide behind contracts and business ventures. Living beyond the frame,
once the position of the sovereign in *Las Meninas*, is still the ultimate seat
of power and authority. Transparency is, so often today, presented as the
means to achieve class transcendence, yet it is an ideology that leads not to
upward mobility but to complete and utter disposability.

THE SUBSUMPTION OF SELF AND COMMUNITY

"Digital communication," Han argues, "is increasingly developing into
communication without community."[93] What might this mean? History
generally follows two ways of understanding communication, the first of
which relies on a transportation metaphor. Communication is the movement of information, of "content," of data, from one place to another. The
second, which can be found in the history of religious thought, pragmatist
philosophy, and even descending from Kantian aesthetics, is that communication sustains a community in time. Communication is a ritual that
perpetually reperforms social relation.[94] Rather than deliver information
or content, communication performs social bonds. But, Han suggests,
digital media undermine sociality not only because they transform all
communication into the communication of information, the delivery of
content, but also because the only ritual we have is that of self-production.
All our rituals have become means for producing the self:

> Producing is derived from the Latin verb *producere*, meaning presenting
> or making visible. Like the French *produire* it still carries the meaning
> of presenting. *Se produire* means "to play to the gallery." The colloquial
> German expression *sich produzieren* probably has the same etymology.
> Today, we are constantly and compulsively playing to the gallery. This
> is especially the case, for instance, on social media: the social is coming
> to be completely subordinated to self-production. Everyone is producing
> him- or herself in order to garner more attention. The compulsion of
> self-production leads to a crisis of community. The so-called "commu-
> nity" that is today invoked everywhere is an atrophied community, per-

haps even a kind of commodified and consumerized community. It lacks the symbolic power to bind people together.[95]

One objection to this argument is easy to make: that one is romanticizing the past, that "community" as such never existed in some way, that it always required some form of exclusion or violence. The loss of a primordial agrarian community, Marx's story of so-called primitive accumulation and its role in the foundations of capitalist society, was part fable, part historical account of the enclosure movement, for instance. The enclosure movement usually refers to the historical moment in the eighteenth and nineteenth centuries in England when common land was appropriated by the English government and aristocracy, taken from those who lived on the land who were then forced to rent the land they lived on back from the new aristocratic "owners." In the process, family members had to leave and work in factories in cities, destroying rural community in the name of capitalist "progress" through the theft of resources. To some degree, the narrative of communist triumph suggests that this lost agrarian community will be restored in the future. Narratives such as these defer to some lost wholeness from the past that will then emerge once again in the future, a structure Jacques Derrida memorably termed "hauntological."[96]

We agree that *community* is an amorphous term. Suggesting there ever was some form of nonalienated community is, at best, nostalgia for a past beyond the boundaries of any and all lived experience and, at worst, a backward-looking conservatism that longs for a pure, premodern condition, as if modern history can be undone. But we do consent that, today, in late capitalism, there has been an amplified collapse of social relations that do not conform to the demands of capital, that would otherwise remain beyond the boundaries of capital. Late capitalism, in Ernest Mandel's complex account, is an intensification of the imperialist, monopoly-capitalist epoch, not a completely new and different phase of capitalism, not an exit from capitalism toward something else. Imperial capitalism covered the globe with transportation and communication networks, extracting natural resources from colonies that would be shipped back to the centers of capitalism in Europe. Goods were manufactured in imperialist countries and then shipped back to their colonies, creating dependencies in which the colonies remained partially outside of capitalist "development," remaining impoverished after the devastation caused by colonial conquest. Late capitalism involves, among a range of factors identified by Mandel, exploiting the uneven geographical development produced by imperialism, often through the sale of technologies to "emerging" or "developing" geographical regions as a means to "catch up" to the imperial hegemons after traditional colonial domination has ended, using the tech industry to fill a role that state governments formerly occupied. But this is only one factor in late capitalism, and what is key for Mandel's argument is that this era is defined by capitalism's perpetual ability to save itself from apparent crisis and collapse by taking precapitalist and semicapitalist economic and social relations, relations that would seem to be antagonistic to capitalism, and incorporating these antagonisms into capitalism itself.[97] "The actual movement of capital obviously starts from non-capitalist relations and proceeds within the framework of a constant, exploitative, metabolic exchange with this non-capitalist milieu," Mandel says.[98] Late capitalism is not the same thing as a "postindustrial" or "network" society because technology is only one dimension of the totality through which capitalism incorporates and exploits what was previously outside its limits.

One name Marx used for this incorporation, moving from noncapitalist relations and forming them into capitalist ones, is *subsumption*. Mandel is referencing what Marx called "formal subsumption," the term for those moments in which pre- or semicapitalist relations were incorporated into capitalism, incorporations that often met with resistance. There is nothing intrinsic that links, say, having facial expressions to capitalism. But the moment facial-recognition software identifies your feelings to deliver advertising that supposedly will make you "happy," your emotions have been formally subsumed by capital, transformed from a social, communicative relation into one that generates economic value.[99] There is nothing intrinsic to, say, education that would make it mesh with the extraction of surplus value—or, for that matter, being healthy. Yet both things, today, generate surplus value for someone. Education has become an industry; medicine and wellness are big businesses. Education and health have been formally subsumed, though these subsumptions have not happened without resistance.

Marx differentiated formal subsumption and "real subsumption," in which various social relations emerge from capital itself. The movement

from formal to real, from incorporation to invention—this is how we
should understand influencer culture. Jacques Camatte says that "capital
cannot really develop unless it comes to dominate the society. It must pass
from the phase of formal domination, which corresponds to the bourgeois
society, to the phase of real domination over society, where the community of capital blossoms into being."[100] The conflicts that inevitably emerge
in formal subsumption seemingly evaporate under conditions of real subsumption, where capital is taken as the norm against which social relations
are measured. Everything, rather than appearing as labor—the ultimate
source of value—appears as *capital*, as something to exchange, as a material good to be owned, bought, and sold.[101] To think back to the beginning
of this introduction, we should take Veblen's *Theory of the Leisure Class* as
instructive. The desire for influence is not only a bourgeois value; it is a
form of social relation that assumes, from the outset, that social order and
rank *are* expressions of consumption and waste and that consumption and
waste are activities that have economic value.[102] Around 1900, Veblen saw
this form of social relation as characterizing the rich. Today, with social
media, it is a social relation that characterizes society and community as
such.

Our point is not to long for a lost, unalienated community beyond capital.[103] We seek to demonstrate that the basic presumptions of influencer
culture—of a kind of authenticity, of an accessibility, of a promise of private
access and intimate proximity—is not just that these are illusions, because
to some degree everyone knows these are illusions. Rather, in influencer
culture, we are told to continuously produce the self, and in producing the
self, we will then be *permitted* to enter relations with others—relations of
brand sponsorships, of material goods, of luxury, of wealth, of happy children and happy families. Only through the commodification and sale of
one's own identity is it possible to live an "unalienated" life, this ideology
suggests. Only through complete alienation, in which the last product one
fabricates is one's own identity and body, can one transcend alienation. It's
as if the influencer is, in fact, our Jesus Christ, both god and man, a synthesis of complete autonomy—free of financial burden, free of debt, free of
material limitation—yet still a human being: a pure embodiment of capital
and the material appearance of an unalienated social life. The influencer
is our figure of transubstantiation. This is how the real subsumption of

community by capital appears: as the promise that by commodifying the self one can finally be full and free and real and unshackled from the impoverished social life brought about by capitalism itself.

OBSCURING THE SELF

What would it look like to *not* produce a self? Or to obscure oneself to one's audience? Many artists have worked for the obfuscation or multiplication of the self, a denial that one can be made to speak their name and remain the same.[104] Today, though, we often assume that the desire or demand to be a self is innate, inborn. In the 2006 *New York Times* article on "self-photography" referenced throughout this introduction, we're told by Jim Taylor, a trend consultant, that "self-branding is a big deal for kids, and self-produced entertainment is a big deal," a statement that, in the context of the article, conflates self-branding with self-discovery and assumes that children naturally crave the ability to produce user-generated content.[105] We are told elsewhere in the *Times* article that nothing's really new here, that kids have always thought they're more interesting than they really are, that they always perform for an "imaginary audience," that children always want to be visible and seen. Never mind that contemporary "childhood" is a relatively recent historical invention. We want to be seen, we want to be brands, we want others to love us and like us and see us and share us.

In 2021, the *New York Times Magazine* published a very different article—one ultimately defending a boy punching another in the face. This punch had been documented in a viral video, only eight seconds long, and was described this way:

> A boy and a girl, who appear to be of high school age, are walking into Panda Express when a third teenager with blond hair stops them in the doorway. He brings with him the energy of the hustler or the man-on-the-street interview host, and the couple are temporarily frozen, caught between suspicion and courtesy. It is a space where things could go either way. "Hey, hold on, excuse me—I have something really important to ask you," the blond kid says to the girl. "The moment I saw you, my eyes were just—oh, my God, I love you, please could—*bleagh!*" The "bleagh" is the sound he makes when the other boy punches him in the face.[106]

The author of this piece, Dan Brooks, is both amused but bothered by the video. The blond kid, he thinks, is instigating something for the sake of views on social media: he's being filmed by an off-camera fourth party; there's no authenticity in the setup. It is, Brooks suggests, probably "part of the 'hit on another guy's girlfriend' internet challenge," a viral challenge over TikTok where one becomes part of a loose public by participating in some act, in some gesture, which may involve dangerous or antisocial acts for the consumption of anonymous viewers on their phones. The blond kid is "using other people as props" to generate content, says Brooks.[107]

Brooks, though, makes an interesting move: we can't say, *This is just how kids are*—as if his fascination and horror derive from some misunderstanding of a generational change or as if this video's popularity is the effect of some younger group being more tech-savvy, more digitally "native" than the writer. "As a middle-aged man, I think of such technology as belonging to the kids, but it doesn't. Smartphones, YouTube, TikTok and the like were brought to market by adults and then inflicted on a generation that has had little choice in the matter." The boy who threw the punch, then, is exercising a form of minor, violent resistance, resistance to a culture formed to ensure communication and sociality are always commodified. Brooks continues:

> Our reams of fretting essays about how much the kids love phones tend to ignore who gave them phones in the first place. We are like parents who left the liquor cabinet unlocked and are shocked to come home and smell the children's breath—except we're making money, so maybe we are more like those 18th-century Britons who shipped opium to China. We aren't forcing Zoomers to spend their childhoods watching and shooting videos; we're just giving them the opportunity. Some kids will resist, but most will indulge that opportunity, and those who do will make a little more money for Google, for Apple, for TikTok—all the far-off companies chartered to do business with the digital natives in their new world. It is a world we call barbarous, even as we devote more and more resources to colonizing it.

Brooks seems, to us, to be mostly correct, but his comparison to alcohol and opium is misguided. For middle-class youth, the promise of drugs is often the promise of dropping out, of downward mobility, of escape from bourgeois institutions. Hallucinogens open the boundaries of one's perception, as if the shackles of the world are merely illusions from which one can escape. Opioids—including both heroin and prescription medications—provide a different escape, one that numbs the mind and body from the misery and pain of existence. But opioids, in particular, are bad commodities. They may insulate themselves from the tendency of profit to fall through addiction, but they also kill their consumers. Social media, influencers, and technology, however, are aspirational, their promise upward mobility—not dropping out but fitting in, of being *someone*, of being *valuable*.

Or, what social media offer are different fantasies: the fantasy of fulfillment through self-production in the name of capitalism; the fantasy that there is something called "community" out there that hasn't been subsumed; the fantasy that you can become famous, that you can become rich, that you are unique and special and different and deserve lots of money and expensive things because you exist as an *individual*; the fantasy that you can do these things and feel full and restored, not like a burned-out husk of a person; the fantasy that you can do it all from your own home or seated in your own car; the fantasy that this isn't all an illusion obscuring a new kind of class antagonism, one barely visible, as long as we think that these images we see online are of selves, of identities, of people—and not intricately constructed performances that collapse labor power and identity in such a manner to lead to burnout and exhaustion, a collapse hidden when we assume selfies exist. Transparency for the masses. Obscurity for the rich.

BACKGROUNDS OF CAPITAL

Finally, most research on influencer culture is derived from ethnographic methods, using interviews and observation as evidence of the excessive labor and precarity of those members of the "influencer industry" as they work to produce a sense of "authenticity."[108] Our approach is different and allows us to take an oblique view of influencer culture that results in arguments distinct from what has previously been written. Much of this book is a direct examination of influencer videos, with arguments derived from the actual products circulated over social media. Each chapter looks toward the backgrounds of images and videos online to discover and chart the infrastructures of late capitalist influencer culture—the home, the car, the warehouse, and the "market." These backgrounds were chosen for a simple reason: they constantly appear in the videos of influencers. The backgrounds we examine are not exhaustive, nor are they intended to be. And all of these we take literally, though by "market" we not only mean actual stores but more general spaces of exchange, consumption, capitalist excess, and giveaways and orgies of cash.

Chapter 1, "House," follows the appearance of domestic space in many influencer videos, arguing that rather than only providing an entry into the intimate, private lives of others, the home also becomes a production studio, not a place an influencer lives. "House" begins our discussion of influencer culture because it demonstrates how person and property become interchangeable, where things and persons become intrinsically linked.

If the conflation of person and property charter in chapter 1 derives from a specificity, where seeing into someone's home appears to allow access to a private, intimate selfhood, chapter 2, "Car," examines the opposite: how cars are used as backgrounds in the videos of influencers because of their generic lack of specificity, permitting access to psychological interiority through enclosure in a generic space. The car is also a technology that, historically, has linked domestic interiority with the mobility of capital, extending and connecting the bounds of private space with spaces of shopping, leisure, and work.

So "House" and "Car" explore the contradictions of intimacy and authenticity in influencer culture. Chapter 3, "Market," explores not only videos that deal with traditional "markets," such as thrift stores, but any video that depends on excessive consumption and wasting of commodities: haul videos, unboxing videos, videos where an influencer purchases and sorts through product returns or abandoned storage units. "Market" moves from intimacy toward the essential location of *waste* in influencer culture, where specific commodities lose coherence in an endless stream of more and the influencer becomes the true commodity to be purchased and sold through the differentiation of the self from perpetually wasted objects.

Chapter 4, "Warehouse," places the concerns of the preceding chapters in relation to recent arguments about logistics and supply chains, and it demonstrates how, for some influencers, the warehouse replaces the home and garage, conflating and linking person and corporation. The warehouse, we argue, is the logical end point of influencer culture, a place where self and commodity are linked, where person and corporation become interchangeable.

According to Fredric Jameson, "for Marxism, the emergence of the economic, the coming into view of the infrastructure itself, is simply the sign of the approach of the concrete."[109] Our goal is not merely to describe or inhabit these particular backgrounds. Instead, we use YouTube as a route into the concrete materiality of contemporary capitalism. Thus, we conclude this book by turning toward the totality that we see as guiding all these other infrastructures, the totality we term, with the title of our final chapter, the "Corpocene." The Corpocene is a concept intended to supplement all of the other "-cenes" today by foregrounding the specific demand on subjectivity this book charts. On one hand, we see the collapse of labor power and identity, and on the other, the collapse of subjectivity and the vertically integrated conglomerate corporation. These two conflations, in which self and business are confused and intertwined, we claim, should be understood both as grounding the possibilities of class on the internet and as *preventing* the possibility of class struggle and organization. The Corpocene, following Jacques Camatte, describes the moment in which capital is anthropomorphized. Corporations become people, citizens worthy of rights and abilities under the rule of law. And what were formerly known as "people" and "citizens" become, instead, a mass of potential surplus population, to be used up and discarded.

The spaces we examine in this book are some of the infrastructures that provide the means of production of the self in influencer culture. With our case above, we moved from practices of documenting a "self" toward a range of other concerns, linking visibility, technology, and the commodification of identity. Once we realize that selfies do not really exist, we can then look toward the backgrounds of images and videos, toward an entire architecture that appears in flashes and glimmers in the content of influencers. This architecture links gaudy domestic design with anonymous warehouses, the interiors of cars with ghost kitchens and "lean" start-ups, social media monopolists with the most banal, daily routines of parents and children. And, most significant, it points toward an emerging model of subjectivity in which "successful" individuals understand themselves as living, breathing, talking corporations.

ONE

HOUSE

Where do you live? On YouTube, the ruse of many influencers, maybe even most of them, is that we're seeing into the backgrounds of private lives. We're watching a document recorded in intimate space. We're seeing "everyday" people in their daily routines, as their lives are lived, *au natural.* Yet the idea of "natural" or unmediated living on the screen is quickly becoming a relic of the past.[1] This contradiction is perplexing. We know that most social media images are false, constructed, or at least partial, yet we believe that we are seeing, at times, these influencers in their actual homes. That much is authentic, we may think: the space of the home, where we glance influencers preparing their coffee in the particularly aesthetic way they like or delicately unpacking package after package from Shein or Wish. The influencers we watch speak to us through direct address, talking to us one-on-one as individuals, as if we are not members of an often exceptionally large, anonymous mass. In consuming these videos, we believe we know about quotidian aspects of lives that may otherwise be obscure or invisible. As often as we see Emma Chamberlain order room service in expensive hotels, we also see her wake in her own bed, eat breakfast in her own home, often with her own cats slipping in and out of frame.

Jeffree Star takes us on a tour of his new home whenever he moves. We see how groups of TikTok stars live together in houses in Calabasas or Hidden Hills, nestled among the gaudy, excessive neoclassicist mansions of Los Angeles. We see various residential, interior, private spaces transformed, reborn through upcycling videos, zero-dollar renovations, thrift-with-me hauls, or amazing Amazon hacks. But a specific question reveals the limits of our spectacular knowledge: *Where do you live?* Asking the influencer this question reveals that we may not, in fact, be seeing into another's private life or domestic space. It also exposes the very real distance between audience and streamer, influenced and influencer. An uncanny valley of living and producing emerges: *Where do you live?* It is a question that reveals we are quite aware of the ruse of intimacy over YouTube. It is also a question that, if answered sincerely, reveals one part of the factory that produces selves and identities as consumable commodities on the internet.

The belief that seeing is access, or at least an intimate or truthful access, is an unreasonable assumption. At best we're engaging in a relation that is the total separation of spectacle, a form of social isolation maintained by images, where the only relation that remains is a relation between commodities.[2] These private moments captured in the videos of YouTubers have been staged for our entertainment, not for revelation. They are themselves a media product for consumption. It is, in the words of Jean Baudrillard, *"now impossible to isolate the process of the real*, or to prove the real."[3] Access to the real is forever deferred, even when the promise of media spectacle is presented as that which will, finally, allow us to intrude into the lives of others and form a community grounded on the transparency of knowing, in which the scopophilic pleasures of looking become genuine, dialogic social relations. The idea that media allow us to see into domestic space has long been part of how popular representations make private lives into public interest.[4] So what is different about domesticity when it comes to the products of influencer culture?

One may suggest that the "authenticity" of the domestic is related to the long-standing position of gendered, domestic labor as supposedly "beyond" or outside the space of capitalist exploitation. A range of current feminist writers associated with "social reproduction theory" note that until the 1970s—with the work of theorists such as Silvia Federici, Mariarosa Dalla Costa, and Leopolda Fortunati, among others—the home was regularly overlooked. It was perceived, in the words of Federici, as "a large area of exploitation until then unrecognized by all revolutionary theorists, Marxist and anarchist alike." The capitalist class not only exploits waged workers but extracts surplus value from "millions of unwaged house-workers as well as many other unpaid and un-free labourers."[5] The space of the home, as the primary location of the "private" activities of family life, rest, entertainment, sex, and biological reproduction, is also a space essential for the reproduction of capital. Yet the framing of this space as "private" positions these gendered forms of work as beyond the exploitation of capital, despite their necessity. Because of this link with the private, domestic labor, along with other gendered forms of labor, according to value-critique theorist Roswitha Scholz, is undermined by "value dissociation." It remains disconnected from value and thus "cannot straightforwardly be subsumed under the concept of labor."[6] Perhaps the "authenticity" of the home derives, in part, from how domestic labor is simultaneously necessary for the reproduction of capital and yet perpetually appears as a range of unwaged activities not subsumed by capital.

One way that domestic space can obviously become integrated into machinations of capitalist value and exchange is through *real estate*. Envisioning domestic space presumes access to the private, but, as presented in the videos of influencers, the home also appears as a space inherently articulated with the late capitalist enterprise of property speculation. Of course, long-standing limits permit some the ability to invest in property and prohibit others; the ownership of real estate, in the United States, has long been linked with structures that discriminate on who can and who cannot own on the basis of race.[7] Regardless, foregrounding the *property* that otherwise remains in the background is, perhaps, the most overt entry point into the factory that is influencer culture and how domesticity, when community is subsumed by capital, becomes an alibi for conflating person with property. What we will see, in foregrounding the home, is both the elaborate ownership of production involved in the daily life of an influencer and how the influencer and their home—person and property—have been sutured to assume a coherence between the two. We are not inherently engaging in the pleasure of watching another person and the private intimacy of their body in spaces inaccessible without mediated vision. Rather, we are engaging in the spectacle of consuming images of private property, images of things that have become interchangeable with personhood.

THE HOUSE AS PRODUCTION STUDIO

Mia Maples is a relatively popular Canadian YouTuber.[8] Her YouTube channel, the eponymous "Mia Maples," has, at the time of this writing, around three million subscribers—a substantial number but not remotely in the range of many of the most popular YouTubers. This midlevel success grants her an added air of normie, "down-to-earth" authenticity. Her channel describes itself as a place to "HAVE FUN," which includes "renovating a house, playing with makeup, trying on clothes OR ANYTHING REALLY!"[9] Maples's most popular videos include unboxing "haul" videos, in which the star either tries on a range of clothing purchased online or reviews a variety of seemingly strange products from internet outlets. The haul video is a form popular among many influencers today, a spectacle of excess and abundance that delights in the multiplicity of consumable products available but also cynically laughs at the sheer shittiness of many of these products. Other popular videos include ones in which Maples decorates her home with DIY commodities (especially those popular on TikTok), shops with various constraints such as filters that only allow her to see products in black and white, and tries to pull—extremely mild— pranks on her parents, such as sewing clothes for her mother and suggesting they come from a variety of drop-shipping outlets. Maples also has a second, much less popular, YouTube channel, "Mia Ma-Plays," dedicated to videos about videogames.[10]

In a video from August 14, 2020, roughly eight years into her YouTube career, Maples participated in the popular "AMA" video format. Allowing fans to "ask me anything," she took on a backlog of questions that had been accumulating for years. "So, I think I will start off with probably the second most asked question," she began. "And that is, what in the world is your living situation?"[11] *Where do you live?* Does Maples, who was twenty-one at the time of this video's release, still live with her parents? Does she still live in the same house as when she started her streaming career? What happened to some of the rooms featured in her earlier videos but no longer appear? Why have the backgrounds for her makeup tutorials changed? What happened to the house she renovated for her grandparents? What happened to the kitchen she renovated for herself? What happened to her brother, Tate, who occasionally appears in Maples's videos and with whom she bought yet another house? Where does he live? *Where do you live?* One fan of Maples writes, commenting on an earlier video documenting a house renovation:

> Sounds like Tate's found his own place and Mia's mum helps her with her YouTube channel (probably lots of behind the scenes stuff even when she's not on camera) so they work together on it in the basement of this studio house. I'm guessing Mum, Dad and Mia all live together in the family house (parent's house) and this studio is their "workplace," so Mum & Mia will travel to the "office" (studio house) for work and then go home to rest/unwind/sleep. At the same time, if they're working late they can just sleep in one of the bedrooms at the studio house, which is also handily equipped with a full kitchen and bathrooms etc. It's a very clever way to have a work/life balance as a YouTuber if that's the case. In addition, the renovations will also bring up the value of the property itself, whilst Mia can continue to earn YouTube revenue through her renovation process—genius! This is my favourite series on Mia's channel so I can't wait to see the rest of the reno's and the final house tour. Please say you'll do one, Mia?[12]

It's all very wholesome. This fan imagines the life of a YouTuber as a family business of sorts, with a happy family all collaborating and profiting together. Maples's imagined living situation is one in which she works, sleeps, and eats in a ratio that doesn't exhaust or break down one's body and life.[13] This fan is aware of how being an influencer is often deceptively hard work and applauds Maples's tactics and investments as, this fan imagines, the multiplicity of domestic spaces permits the multiplication of moments to eat and sleep and spend time with others. And we see the fan begging for more content, begging to see more, each glimpse permitting one to get closer to the YouTuber they follow.

These are prying questions that speak to the changing relationship between audiences and contemporary "stars" on the internet. The stars of film, television, and music were, in the past, *images* more than anything—

images linked to but divorced from a "real" person, images produced by the culture industry specifically as marketing tools for generating interest in entertainment. The *culture industry* is the term Horkheimer and Adorno coined to describe tendencies they observed associated with the midcentury American media industries, especially Hollywood, though it refers less to the empirical reality of the media industries than to a general technical standardization perpetuated through mass-produced "culture." The culture industry produces commodified "art," products of entertainment and leisure, inducing conformity in the name of diversity and difference. It rationalizes cultural production intended to amuse, though it also cultivates irrationality, boredom, and dissatisfaction. It promises glamour and fulfillment while it "endlessly cheats its consumers out of what it endlessly promises," thus channeling desire into mass-produced objects that absorb the time and attention of the audience.[14] The *star* is one manifestation of how the culture industry makes people into products designed to direct desire.

The vertical integration of the studio system enabled the controlled management of celebrity image, feeding promotional material through corporate channels of production, distribution, marketing, and more. A star, consequentially, was not a person but a representation of one, a representation intended to attract popular attention, leading to the exchange of money for entertainment, a representation produced by an entire, massive cultural apparatus.[15] This divorce between image and person was essential for the star, a separation that, for instance, fed and continues to feed the gossip and paparazzi industries, industries organized around the knowledge that the image of the "star" conceals the "person" beyond the image. Because the audience knows, to some degree, that the image of the star is itself manufactured, then there is a desire to get to the reality obscured by industry—a reality rife with scandal and abuse.[16] One desires to move past the imaginary to the real, encountering the other as if the interpersonal separation between fan and star is merely an illusion of industry. The "real life" of the star—a fantasy of a life lived that is more full, more salacious, more exciting, more scandalous—promises a fullness foreclosed to the fan.

Maples, however, regularly comments that her private life is *boring*, not something her audience would be interested in, though a brief perusal of the comments on her videos reveals otherwise. Her fans are quite interested in narrating her personal life, of filling in the blanks of family and domesticity that remain only slightly offscreen. The ruse of the influencer is that there is no real separation between image and person. The Hollywood "star" is an image produced by the entirety of the moviemaking apparatus; the Nashville "star" is a product of the music machine. These are alienated commodities distinct from the actor or musician seemingly represented by these image commodities, distinct because of their manufacture by the culture industry. But in influencer culture, the apparatus has been transferred to the influencer. What once was a product of the entirety of the Hollywood studio system, for instance, is now the product of the influencers themselves. Maples must maintain a link between herself and her image, *and* she is the one who must produce herself as the "star" to be consumed. Fan interest in Maples's private life emphasizes that, yes, what we see is a construction: we are seeing an image produced for our consumption. We are seeing a "product," a commodity that is Maples's very identity as presented on YouTube. Because her fans are aware of the disjuncture between image and person, Maples must join the two by revealing personal information, including the details through which her videos are composed.

So, where *does* Maples live? In her August 14 video, Maples reads—extremely elaborate—comments from her fans, such as the one referenced above, which speculate about how many houses she owns, who lives in each one, where their offices are, and where their bedrooms are. These speculations, Maples tells us definitively, are incorrect. She doesn't seem bothered by the seeming intrusion into her privacy. Unlike celebrities who loathe being tailed by the paparazzi, Maples understands her livelihood as bound together with making her private life visible to millions of anonymous viewers. She does not hide behind some belief that she is an untouchable artist, that she deserves privacy beyond what she does for a living. She is merely bothered by the lack of accuracy in these comments (even though some of the comments, like the one cited above, are not far off). Maples is obliging in acknowledging just how confusing her living situation seems to be—her fans are correct. What they've been watching over the years is not a glimpse into a private life even remotely equivalent to their own.

Maples must draw a diagram to explain her actual living situation, as it confuses even her (fig. 2). She explains that she has one house that is a "stu-

FIGURE 2 Confusing, but not boring: Mia Maples diagrams
her home ownership and living situations.

Source: Mia Maples, "Relationship Status? Living Situation? New Dog? Answering Your Questions FINALLY!" YouTube, August 14, 2020, www.youtube.com/watch?v=h5vad7 uQvw4.

dio"—a house for nothing other than filming, editing, and producing her videos; it is also used for storing props and other items Maples has used for production (although, we later learn in a house/studio tour video, she also owns at least one industrial storage unit for this purpose). Maples bought this "studio" house with her brother, who used to live in its basement but currently lives in a different house, which he rents. Maples is now the sole owner of the studio house, a house in which no one currently lives. Maples still lives with her parents, and her parents own two different houses, all of which are used for filming. Laying it all out like this isn't too confusing. But for dedicated followers of Maples's videos, the shifting backgrounds *are* confusing, as they've seen family members, domestic interiors, various home renovations, all at different times, all presented with the alibi that, to some degree, these are spaces in which Maples lives. The sheer multiplication of space is confounding, and explaining the spaces glimpsed in the background of videos requires an account that, until Maples's description and diagram, verges on conspiracy theory.

Maples's property acquisitions do not rival other influencers with higher numbers of followers, though the buying, renovating, and selling of property is clearly an interest that emerged through her videos. Maples, as revealed in one of her videos, has been working toward obtaining a real estate license.[17] What is unusual about Maples, however, is the willingness she displays in divulging the details about production. In another video, from June 11, 2021, Maples goes into even more detail about her "studio" house. In an explanation more confusing than the one of her living situation, she states that she is giving this tour because she will soon move into another studio. Her plan is then to renovate the "studio" house, both to make house-renovation content for her channel and to sell the house as a "normal" house; she would later promote the renovation content as "un-making over my house." Maples then takes us behind the scenes of her studio, and we learn that most of this house is used for storage. About halfway into this video—which is nearly forty minutes long—Maples finally tells us that, while we've mostly been seeing how much of the house is ultimately *unused*, a space for random objects and things, "Upstairs is where the magic happens. That is where all the filming 'sets' are. Now, I know a lot of YouTubers don't have filming sets, but for me, it was just really hard to keep a nice tidy filming area in my room whilst having all the lighting and microphones and audio equipment that I wanted. So, this works well for me. I love my filming area." Maples takes us into the upstairs bathroom: "You can really tell this is a studio, because in the bathtub there is only one thing—filming equipment! And wigs, in the corner here." The walls of every upstairs room are covered with ring lights, flood lights, acoustic panels to absorb sound, all attached to walls in a seemingly haphazard fashion, a bizarre chaos to manage sound and vision (fig. 3). There are different rooms for different kinds of videos, one for sitting down behind a table that is used for shots in which Maples talks only to the camera, a craft and sewing room for videos in which Maples does more than talk but only requires mostly up-close or midrange camera shots, a room for "try-on" hauls that require shots of Maples's entire body, and a room—well, closet—for gaming, set up for Maples's gaming YouTube channel. The basement of the house is an office space, used for editing videos and containing three full computer setups. Maples says she works a normal office schedule—Mondays to Fridays, nine to five—which allows her to produce two videos a week. The infrastructure and schedule she's developed helps avoid both procrastination and a drift into constant work.

Maples is remarkably willing to let us all in on a (barely concealed) secret: that successful influencers are media professionals who have developed elaborate production techniques, reliant on "domestic" stages that convert houses and apartments into media studios. These techniques and sets are not inherently those of "traditional" media production, however. The presence of *so many* ring lights, for instance, demonstrates the strangeness of these production techniques. Anyone trained in traditional

FIGURE 3   The revelation of not a home but a studio:
Mia Maples shows her recording rooms to viewers.

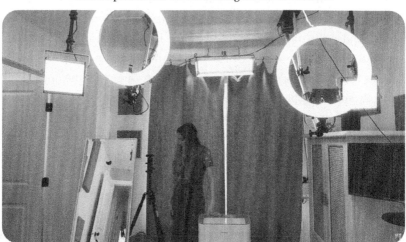

Source: Mia Maples, "STUDIO TOUR !! *House Transformed into a Complete YouTube Studio*," YouTube, June 11, 2021, www.youtube.com/watch?v=ZxLX1Tgivig.

methods of media production will know, this is an absurd process to light a room. But paying close attention to the videos of YouTubers—looking closely into the eyes of those we watch—reveals the constant and ever-present reflection of the ring light in the iris of the influencer. Maples's setup allows her to maintain a particular look and style of YouTube video in almost any situation and angle she might need. Any amateurism in these videos is deliberately cultivated, advancing a style that is read by viewers *as if* it is simple, lazy, or slapdash when it is anything but.

The home, when it comes to the influencer factory, is not a location for living. The home is a set, a soundstage, a studio. The home is a place where the star-making activities of the culture industry are transferred to the influencer, who, rather than permit the "star" to exist as autonomous image, must constantly work to ensure the correlation between the image of the influencer and the person that image supposedly represents. Richard Dyer, in his book *Heavenly Bodies*, focused on how specific stars—Marilyn Monroe, Paul Robeson, Judy Garland—ultimately resisted or protested the labor of the star, the culture industry's absorption of person in favor of image. They refused the subsumption of personhood by capital, the replacement of person by image. Other stars, however, fully embraced this capitalist logic of performance and stardom. Dyer mentions how stars like Fred Astaire and Joan Crawford were notable because of their willingness to reduce their entire existence to the mastery of their craft. But the star that Dyer discusses that seems to be most relevant for the contemporary context is Barbra Streisand, who demanded control over both her performance and the conditions of production, producing and directing the products in which she starred.[18] Streisand the person asserted control over the industry designed to produce the image of Streisand the star. Today, rather than an entire industry designed to generate and police these images—the profits they generate, their use as public relations and marketing, ensuring the articulation of person and image—these tasks are outsourced and embodied in the domestic architecture found in the background of YouTube videos. The model of celebrity characterized by Streisand—both star and manager of the capitalist infrastructures for producing stardom, both image and industry—has been transferred to individuals and their homes.

The moment that one realizes that these homes are not places for living but places for generating content, generating brands, generating identities—filled with techniques for generating detailed and yet occasionally (often purposefully) rough-looking images—we can see the problem posed by a seemingly simple question. *Where do you live?* Somewhere else. The distance of the star reasserts itself, indicating that the closeness and intimacy we may feel toward these people we watch is false; it is a closeness and intimacy produced only through the real subsumption of sociality by capital.

DOMESTIC INTERIORS AS EXPRESSIONS OF SELFHOOD

Mia Maples's decision to reveal her space of filming speaks to a brilliant maneuver on her part, that her brand (which is very wholesome, very friendly) is strong enough that any shattering of the spectacle, rather than emphasizing her difference from her audience, makes her seemingly more relatable. Perhaps this is because—while quite successful—Maples is still a more midlevel YouTube celebrity. Perhaps this also is because Maples is a bit younger than many of the most popular YouTubers, and we've come to simply accept any possible social relation as always-already subsumed by capital. Thus, even when she turns the cameras and we see just how constructed her persona is, there's no hint of anyone criticizing her for "selling out" or being "fake." This is not the case with Elsie Larson and Emma Chapman, sisters behind the popular lifestyle blog *A Beautiful Mess*, which features home renovation, DIY fashion and crafts, recipes, and even business and life advice. Predating the rise of YouTube celebrity, Larson and Chapman have been influencers for more than a decade, millennial pioneers of today's influencer culture now seen on YouTube, TikTok, and Instagram. While their blog is still the center of all *A Beautiful Mess* content, the sisters also have a YouTube channel, accounts on most popular social media websites, a podcast, several books, and in the past have developed two different photo editing apps linked with the blog and its visual style,[19] among a range of other business- and publicity-based ventures that rarely last for long (including several brick-and-mortar shops).

Given the longevity of their internet careers, it shouldn't be too surprising that *A Beautiful Mess* emerged not purely from an attempt to become famous on the internet but from an endeavor to promote the vintage clothing store owned by the sisters. In 2009, Larson opened a small boutique in

Springfield, Missouri, named Red Velvet. (Her initial capital to open this store came from success in the scrapbooking community with a line of mass-marketed scrapbooking accessories.) By 2010, her blog had garnered wide success, and her sister, Chapman, had moved from Los Angeles to work with her. The two acquired a fully stocked vintage store in Springfield to expand their business. The blog itself, around this time, focused on themes related to their store, like the styling of vintage clothing and recipes for baked goods Chapman sold in the store's dining area. Over time, the sisters began to realize that the idea of a storefront in a city like Springfield is not particularly profitable and moved their business almost entirely to creating online content. They purchased several houses in town, including one that they converted into office space for their growing staff, and began building infrastructure for internet-based clothing sales and houses to renovate for blog content. Much like Mia Maples's videos, some of the most popular features on the *A Beautiful Mess* blog and social media channels are those of home renovations. Because of this, the question of where one lives constantly intrudes—especially since, unlike Mia Maples, Larson and Chapman are often hesitant to reveal their "secrets" about property ownership and living arrangements, instead filtering personal life through business suggestions and financial management advice. And while Mia Maples frames owning multiple homes as a mere accident of being an influencer (a deferral belied slightly by her training to become a real estate agent), *A Beautiful Mess* positions home ownership as deeply linked with personal achievement and selfhood.

The sisters of *A Beautiful Mess* regularly tell stories of property and home ownership that rely on a kind of city-versus-country divide, opposing, for instance, Los Angeles with Springfield, positioning home ownership as a natural desire. Chapman, the first of the sisters to purchase residential property in Springfield, links home ownership with the very centrality of her life narrative as a blogger:

> After college I had moved to a bigger city (Los Angeles) for adventure and to pursue other things. This is when I got really into food blogging, and after a few short years decided I'd rather live near my family and work with my sister in our little Midwest hometown. As I packed and planned for my move home, I started dreaming about buying a house.

I couldn't afford to right then, but the possibility was much more real
than thinking about buying a house in LA. The cost of living between
LA and Springfield, MO is . . . very different. But I also felt intimidated
about trying to buy a home. What if I applied for a loan and got rejected?
Would it hurt my chances because I was single and only 24 years old? It
felt like a far fetched goal, but I kept dreaming—and occasionally looking
at houses for sale online. 😶[20]

Homeownership, in the American popular imaginary, was defined as a
"duty" for "good citizens" around 1945, after decades of governmental campaigns and programs. Propaganda for property defined homeownership as
an act that would ground an individual as a member of a community, directly opposing homeownership with imaginary fears of socialistic, anar-
chistic, or communistic forms of collective ownership and the destruction
of private property.[21] This ideal of citizenship, however, was articulated in
terms of time: the time to take care of a house or take care of a family
would absorb the amount of time one has for other causes. In the words
of Helen Hester and Nick Srnicek, "Owning a home . . . precisely meant
being too busy to think or act politically—too much free time might lead to
communism!"[22] In midcentury America, homeownership became a central
example of the formal subsumption of community by capital, a form of
subsumption that persists today, in which the time required for the reproduction of capital absorbs all other possible uses of time, in which home
and family become temporal barriers that prohibit resistance to, among
other things, the economic domination of daily life. The desire to own a
house is a desire shaded by the destruction of free, unallocated time that
exists beyond productivity.[23]

In Chapman's narrative, the divide between country and city becomes
one in which this achievement of community, citizenship, and selfhood is
either possible or prohibited, with community, citizenship, and selfhood
articulated entirely as an effect of investment in property: one can buy a
home in particular geographic regions but not in others. The relation between country and city, as Raymond Williams says, is a relation "active
and continuous: the relations are not only of ideas and experience, but of
rent and interest, of situation and power; a wider system."[24] Los Angeles—
fully in line with its usual interpretation as a city in which glitter and

glamour obscure seediness and corruption[25]—becomes a space in which appearances may glisten but dreams ultimately die, where the presumed duty of citizenship has become impossible. Springfield, the Midwest, the "country," becomes the realization of "true" fulfillment, the achievement of property ownership—albeit only because the country has now become linked to urban centers through the networked circuits of commodity exchange via eBay and other peer-to-peer marketplaces. But the ideal of having time to oneself, having a self beyond property, is forever ignored; the only time one has is to be spent on personal business ventures, on the cultivation of means to generate profit.

Larson and Chapman are, in some ways, at the vanguard of millennial anxieties about homeownership. Mainstream shills of global capital, like *Forbes* and *Bloomberg*, regularly report on market concerns about millennials either priced out of homeownership or lacking the desire to own homes, among other reasons regularly reported.[26] Yet at the same time, we hear of how—in the wake of the COVID pandemic—millennials were at fault for the 2020 housing shortage and surge in demand for real estate, a surge that effectively priced millennials out of the housing market, yet again.[27] The early stories that Larson and Chapman tell are very much in line with these millennial worries. They cover being denied for home loans, being unsure of how to deal with taxes when one's income is contingent, precarious, and otherwise dependent on sporadic forms of employment. Posts cover recommendations about how to approach accountants and mortgage brokers.[28]

After their blog and assorted ventures—their apps, a book, and so on—became successful, the sisters closed Red Velvet to focus on online content.[29] Larson and her spouse decided to move to Nashville, buy one house, then move into another, from which they very quickly moved again into a much larger house, one bordering on a modern McMansion rather than the seemingly modest, older homes mostly covered on the blog.[30] During this time, the sisters began to purchase and renovate a series of Airbnb-based rentals, including two in Florida and one in Springfield they named the "Holiday House." These rentals were not particularly successful, and the sisters, while maintaining ownership of the "Holiday House," began to purchase houses to renovate for content and then donate to Habitat for Humanity.[31] While these houses continued to supply renovation content for the blog, readers began to question the seeming "relatability" of the sisters and the ruse that the constant purchase and renovation of houses is, in fact, "normal" behavior, even for a lifestyle blog. Larson had to defend the size of one of the houses she has purchased,[32] a defense that at least one reader of the blog did not accept.[33] *Where do you live?* The question emerges yet again, now, with an additional question: *And how much did your house cost?* The entire pretense of *A Beautiful Mess* and its renovation content emerged from the fact that, say, Los Angeles is too expensive, and renovating a run-down house in Missouri is not. Nashville, in contrast, is an exceptionally expensive city, and, like Los Angeles, is a center of the culture industry (Larson's spouse, a studio musician, works in music recording, something which occasioned the move). In response to the question, "How much is your budget?" readers received the following response:

> Eh. That's probably a bit personal and does it really matter anyway? I will share our budgets on makeovers and individual purchases though, because I think that can be helpful.
>
> I don't want to go into detail on exactly what location we live in for our children's privacy. So if you recognize the area or just know for some reason, please keep it to yourself. Each time we have ever moved some asshole has posted our new address publicly. Please don't be *that* asshole. If you want to gossip about a blogger or be a jerk, that is one thing, but posting their private information is not OK—please respect that![34]

User comments both applauded the refusal to divulge personal details and demanded closeness, intimacy, in the name of knowing more about property. Wrote one reader, "I am SO SO SO GLAD you did not give more info about your new address. For your family's privacy and safety that is a great move. I know the audience wants all the info (maybe they can buy the house down the street?) but you should have a home that is a haven for your family and keeping your address private is a great start! Kudos and Congrats!"[35] Other fans of *A Beautiful Mess* described the moves in terms of "mourning," of a loss because of how they "fell in love" with past homes.[36]

A Beautiful Mess reveals two contradictory trends. On one hand, there is the demand to continuously generate "content," which, in the case when home renovations are a featured and popular focus, involves a constant churn of purchasing houses and figuring out what to do with them. The audience demands more; capital demands more. On the other hand, this "more" must be articulated with some sense of genuine "real life." This is not only because the link between image and person must be maintained but also because *the house*, as part of the image of the influencer, *becomes that which represents the person*. Thus, there is a need to purchase and offload houses that both are and are not intimate, domestic spaces. The donation of houses to Habitat for Humanity is explained in a somewhat perplexing fashion, addressing obliquely some audience comments: "So, we wanted to find a way to makeover a smaller home, but how could we do this? Could we just invade someone's home? Or buy one? We didn't want to buy a house that would ultimately just sit empty, and we didn't envision ourselves in the house flipping business."[37] The sisters were criticized for owning houses too expensive and too large; readers could not identify with or see themselves living in these houses. But business ventures, especially in Springfield, were not successful. They could not pivot renovations to rentals; they could not make physical retail profitable. The artifice that separates image and person, here, cannot be fully acknowledged.

Where do you live? becomes a question not only about the "reality" of domesticity but about the very attachments the audience has with the object of their attention. And the demand for *more*—for that *more* to be "authentic" and linked to the person—is exhausting for the influencer, tasked with the labor of making image and person cohere. On an episode of the blog's podcast, Larson revealed that the constant demand to renovate houses was deeply tiring, that, despite being some of the most popular parts of the entire *Beautiful Mess* industry, she simply could not continue remaking and redoing domestic interiors.[38] Responding to the demand to see inside—the demand for *transparency*, to recall the arguments of Byung-Chul Han[39]—is a demand that burns one up and burns one out.[40]

FROM BODIES TO HOUSES

On December 11, 2002, the American television network ABC premiered the reality television show *Extreme Makeover*, one of the most notable examples of the relatively short-lived genre we might term "cosmetic surgery reality television." These television programs featured participants and sometimes contestants (for the variations of these shows that were competitions) all going through extreme forms of plastic surgery, often framed through narratives in which technological modification would allow the "birth" of a real or idealized self.[41] Plastic surgery—and reality TV—allowed for a realization or revelation of one's true identity through the modification and reinvention of one's body. Transformation, these shows suggest, is necessary because one believes their self to be fundamentally at odds with one's body. The judgment of a proper body, however, requires a gaze that simultaneously derives from the doctors on these shows, there to make "corrective" judgments about surgery, and that of the television audience, delighting in their scopophilic pleasure and disgust at what appears onscreen.[42]

Of course, the body under capitalism becomes the final thing the worker owns. The worker, the "possessor of labour-power, instead of being able to sell commodities in which his labour has been objectified, must rather be compelled to offer for sale as a commodity that very labour-power which exists only in his living body."[43] One way of interpreting plastic surgery is that under conditions of spectacle, in which an idealized image becomes something that adds value, surgery is an act designed to make one's body a commodity with a greater exchange value. Implants, augmentation, and other forms of medical enhancement become practices that enhance one's labor power when one's visual appearance is part of the labor one performs. In the end, however, plastic surgery is also inevitably about suturing self and body. It may rely on technologies and techniques that are "artificial" and make one into an augmented cyborg of sorts, but in both the legitimation from television producers—that the show is designed to reveal and give birth to a true self—and its critique—the show exists to reify a particular spectacular, economic social relation in the very foundation of the body and its capacities as a visual commodity—these shows involve an articulation that happens at the level of a specific person and image. As with stardom, the goal here is to articulate image and identity, making sure this link between image and person is worthy of attention and therefore profitable.

On December 3, 2003, ABC premiered a spinoff of *Extreme Makeover*, which would go on to become far more popular than the original show. *Extreme Makeover: Home Edition*, instead of detailing invasive plastic surgery operations, revealing a "true self" hidden behind a body that refused

this truth, would identify a specific family seemingly worthy of aid because of economic and social hardship. This aid came in the form of an
extravagant, massive house. The show—as revealed in leaked production
documents—intended to attract "people bravely living with rare and incur-
able diseases, victims of hate crime and vandalism, and parents grieving
children killed in drunk driving fatalities," among other seemingly tragic
figures left behind by the lack of any reasonable American social safety
net.[44] *Home Edition*, rather than working to link (self) image and body, used
property as a reward for social trauma. The personalities and stars of the
show were not its contestants but a set of designers who would craft and
shape the massive home, personalizing it for the episode's chosen family.
While each episode delved into details about these families, the property
we see remains fundamentally disarticulated from the stars of the show.
The television network HGTV began following this model around 2011,
organizing television shows around particular stars and personalities—
for instance, the *Property Brothers*, Drew and Jonathan Scott, or Chip and
Joanna Gaines, who flip houses in Waco, Texas, on their show *Fixer Upper*.
Since 2018, HGTV has ranked number 4 in cable television ratings, following only Fox News, MSNBC, and CNN.[45] In each of these examples, the
star of the show is fundamentally disarticulated from the houses seen on
the show. *Home Edition* and any of the HGTV celebrities simply move on to
another property, another house, at the end of every episode.

For an influencer, however, the house becomes the person. We have
gone from watching a transformation of a body to a transformation of a
home, in which body and home are ultimately representative of the same
thing. The renovation of the home is, inevitably, perpetual content to be
consumed. On HGTV, there is no intrinsic connection to these houses and
the people who appear episode to episode. Whereas the original *Extreme
Makeover* worked to suture person and image, revealing the "real" person
through technical augmentation, influencer culture sutures home and
person, suggesting the two are intrinsically linked. Homes are billed as
"forever homes,"[46] and fans get obsessed or invested in particular spaces
and places. On the *Beautiful Mess* podcast, we are given advice if we "feel
unsettled and not 'at home' in a new house," with tips on how one can
"bond" with a house.[47]

At the same time, these "personal" connections are almost always di-

rectly framed as business connections. Private lives—family, selfhood, relationships, identity—are irrelevant unless they can be mined for content,
attention, and profit. Larson and Chapman give tips on diversifying content, maintaining multiple revenue streams.[48] We are told that personal
enjoyment and passion are almost always subsumed under the ability to
make a profit, like when Larson, discussing her hobbies, says, "But then
in the end, it turns almost like poisonous when I can't make money from
it. And it isn't sustainable. It's, you know, sad. It becomes like really, really
sad. So I try to focus on that. Just, you know, find projects that have a sustainable way to make money. And then I know that I can always get more
excited about a project and think of more ideas within a category."[49] We are
told that, in becoming a successful blogger, we'd need to pay for a professionally developed website, which "could be like 20 grand," though we're
also warned to not spend that much initially and, instead, focus on calcu-
lating risk.[50]

With Mia Maples, looking into the background reveals the house as
a stage. With *A Beautiful Mess*, this stage is conflated with personhood
and with a potential for profit. The home becomes part of the influencer's
image, part of the self as constructed by the influencer for consumption
by others. To some extent, Maples, Larson, and Chapman all perform a
persona that isn't truly wealthy, extravagant, or excessive—hence, the
pushback by fans when Larson moved into a seemingly gigantic home in
Nashville. When we turn toward some of the most successful influencers—
people like Emma Chamberlain and Jeffree Star—the home remains part
of an influencer's personhood, performing both excess and private authenticity, revealing how the home is central to the influencer's reinvention of
the traditional logic of stardom, of the simultaneous articulation and dis-
connection between image and person in the name of intimate closeness.

THE HOMES OF ELITE YOUTUBE STARS

As we have mentioned, Mia Maples is a solidly midlevel YouTube celebrity, while Elsie Larson and Emma Chapman are, first and foremost, bloggers. What then, of the homes and living situations of the YouTube elite?
Those with millions upon millions of subscribers? *Where do* they *live?* This
change in object manifests an entire ecology of video content. There is, for

example, the highly produced and popular series on *Architectural Digest*'s YouTube channel, "Open Door: Inside Celebrity Homes." The series, which provides a tour of the homes of the rich and famous given by the rich and famous who live in them, is by far the publication's most popular YouTube series, and views often double or triple the actual number of subscribers of *Architectural Digest*'s channel. (YouTube metrics usually work in the reverse, with fewer views than subscribers for the most popular YouTube stars.) *Vogue*'s popular "73 Questions" series provides a similar service, being largely an excuse to gaze inside celebrities' living situations while they guide the viewer (and interviewer, who always remains behind the camera, a first-person surrogate for the audience) around in an extremely staged manner. While these videos make use of old forms of media—produced, as they are, by print publications with histories that extend over a century—they demonstrate how even "legacy media" are turning to social media content for their revenue streams, part of the transmedia reinvention of, in this case, print.

There are also offshoots of these videos that exist entirely in the realm of YouTube, with influencers commenting on the homes of other influencers. One especially odd but self-contained instance is the video entitled "PewDiePie Reacts to Emma Chamberlain's $3.9 Million Dollar Home."[51] This video, from June of 2021, uses existing content from the YouTube channel AnyHome, a channel devoted to detailing specifics of the houses purchased by ultrawealthy celebrities. Over the AnyHome video, the controversial—and exceptionally popular—YouTube star PewDiePie *reacts*, commenting with asides and jokes—reaction videos, of course, being a staple of the platform, with ironic commentary and seemingly spontaneous responses recorded for viewing enjoyment. AnyHome's initial video is cheaply produced, with stock real-estate photos and video of Chamberlain's properties panned over, a generic voice-over providing details on location and price, offering gossipy assumptions about how Chamberlain will complete renovations. PewDiePie, seen in an extravagantly lit space designed for the game streaming for which he is known, comments from the corner of the first video, pausing it every few seconds to say something complimentary about the décor or disparaging about himself.

The existence of AnyHome—and the mere fact that one of the most popular YouTubers in existence can "react" to the house of another extremely popular YouTuber, turning this reaction into popular content in and of itself—signals a slightly different spectacular economy than what we've been describing so far in this chapter. Chamberlain, unlike Maples, Larson, and Chapman, does not need to answer questions about where she lives. Others will answer for her. We still get videos about domestic space, in which house and person are, to some extent, conflated. The home— and seeing its interior—is still presumed to permit intimate closeness, presumed to allow us to be closer to the person, not only their home. The home PewDiePie reacts to is eventually labeled a "starter" home. Chamberlain moved into an even more expensive home in Beverly Hills,[52] which AnyHome documented around the same time as the PewDiePie reaction video.[53] We hear of the prices of these homes: the new one is $4.3 million; Chamberlain sold her previous home for $4.1 million, and she's living in a rental ($35,000 per month) on Sunset Strip until renovations to her new home are completed.[54] Chamberlain's video describing her new house, titled "I MOVED . . . ," was written about in *Vogue Australia*, as was her "starter house," both houses described and detailed for their architectural value, with one as "the epitome of Zen" and the other "an architectural showstopper."[55] Los Angeles appears again as a city of dreams, of aspirational gleaming modern architecture and taste, where one house is exchanged for another—a larger, more glamorous, more excessive one.

Chamberlain—rather than appearing "relatable," as she so often does, at least when it comes to real estate—occupies the space previously occupied by the traditional celebrity and star. The possibility of achieving her level of wealth and success is impossible for all but a few; the apparatus of the popular press, in which the homes of the stars are in and of themselves newsworthy, suggests the functions of these domestic interiors are different. We presume likeness and identification from Maples, Larson, and Chapman, and that identification comes from how the home is conflated with the person. We may still feel that Chamberlain is "friendly" and "relatable," but the home—still sutured to the person—becomes a space of aspirational otherness, signifying both identification and disidentification. As a result, truly successful influencers do not need to worry about answering any questions about where they live, even though they'll gladly supply some sort of commentary and evidence of their private, intimate, daily life. The real answer, when we get to the truly elite, is provided by *Vogue*, by *Architectural Digest*, by *other influencers.*

This journey of trading up homes as one's fame and bank account climb is not by any means new. The deeply controversial influencer and makeup mogul Jeffree Star taught his followers about the finer points of Los Angeles gated communities when he moved from his extravagant home in Calabasas to an even more extravagant home in Hidden Hills near the end of 2019. As with Chamberlain, and most celebrities, one could find the estimated value of these properties quite easily from any number of gossip websites (or from AnyHome videos). Star demurred about the price and simply explained the reason for the move was space. "Me and Nathan [Star's partner at the time], we've outgrown this house right here two years ago, bitch. . . . I look like a hoarder, there's been no room."[56]

Star's tour of his new home is particularly fascinating for our purposes here. Just as Mia Maples is willing to detail her production tricks and techniques, built into her home, techniques and tricks otherwise obscured, Star is completely willing to show the film crew he uses to produce his videos. His crew literally live with him in his massive house; there is an entire wing of his home for his personal assistant. We again see how the "domestic" space of the influencer becomes a studio, set, and stage for the recording of video. Of course, the scale is completely different. Star doesn't have to do his editing himself—the showing of production is not just about equipment or bedrooms that have become setups for a particular kind of video—though it's common for even moderately successful influencers to have others do their editing. Rather, Star directs our gaze toward those media workers who otherwise remain behind the scenes. In showing his employees, Star, like Chamberlain, like Maples, allows us to "see" into the private, domestic space of his life, but the specific content we observe asserts his difference and otherness to his audience. Star asserts his existence as a "star," a separation of image and person, in which access to what appears to be intimate, private space uses the excess and expense of the home, its size and scale, to reassert distance while simultaneously permitting access.

Having purchased one of the larger, gaudier homes one can purchase in California, in one of its priciest neighborhoods, Star made a move that is becoming increasingly popular with the super-famous and super-rich: he bought land in Wyoming. Like RuPaul and Kanye West, Star purchased a ranch. He left Los Angeles at the beginning of the COVID pandemic, like a modern Marie Antoinette escaping Versailles. His videos shifted from covering haute couture and makeup, trying out the latest Gucci foundation, to sitting in a truck showing off the salsa he picked up from his local farmer's market. Star's crew dropped away, some of his business deals were criticized, and he finally seemed to be "cancelled" in the popular internet imaginary—something he had otherwise avoided throughout a decade of making provocative, racist, and otherwise offensive comments.

We will return to Jeffree Star and his move from Hidden Hills to Wyoming in chapter 4. With Star, the backgrounds of his videos speak not only to the unsteady suturing and separation between person and image but also, quite literally, to supply chains, warehouses, and manufacturing. Star's backgrounds point to something larger and more complex than what we've documented here. For now, however, a more basic conclusion: in influencer culture, the home, when viewed as a background against which the influencer appears, is a stage to produce content, a stage that is also conflated with the very identity performed in the videos we watch and images we see. The house becomes part of a broader apparatus, part of the means of production of the self that is the influencer factory. Not a space of domestic intimacy, in influencer culture the home reveals how the self is subsumed by capital. The home is fashioned into a material expression of personhood, a realization of a dream begun in midcentury America, apprehended materially not just through mortgages and debt but through videos of home makeovers.

Our next chapter turns to a different background, the background of the car. If houses express one kind of intimacy, then cars provide a different set of articulations between the production of the self and the subsumption of community and identity in contemporary capital. With the car, intimacy emerges not from specificity, not from condensing property and person, but from a generic and interchangeable *lack* of specificity that performs intimacy through heterogenous emptiness.

TWO

CAR

For some of those discussed in the previous chapter, the home is, in actuality, a secondary location. Instead, the *car* appears as the primary background of their videos, a setting for content that appears as much, if not more, than any other interior. Emma Chamberlain, for example, frequently films vlogs in which she takes her viewers along to run errands. Since Chamberlain lives in Los Angeles, her daily life usually involves extensive time in her car. She uses this time to talk about her life and her feelings, as in the video "GROCERY SHOPPING CURES BOREDOM," where she explains that she hasn't left her home in more than seventy-two hours. On her way to Trader Joe's, Chamberlain, set against the beige leather interior of her otherwise unspecified vehicle, monologues while driving. She tells us, "I've been spending a lot of time alone, and I choose that. . . . But I'm not gonna lie, I do get a little bit lonely. . . . I just kind of want to exist in silence a lot. I know I need a vacation; I know I need to get out. . . . But I also don't want to go anywhere. And see, this is why I have issues—I know the solution to my problem, but then I don't have enough energy to do the solution."[1] After finishing her shopping trip, she sits in the Trader Joe's parking lot and does an in-car shopping haul, ripping into various packages she purchased. In a different video, "ugg season," Chamberlain takes us along in her car as she gets gas, drives to Whole Foods, and does another parking lot food-haul review.[2] In "haunted," she makes yet another trip, to Whole Foods (trips to grocery stores such as Trader Joe's, Erewhon, and Whole Foods are frequent vlog pastimes for Chamberlain, always necessitating a filmed car trip). As she sits in the driver's seat of her vehicle in the parking lot of Whole Foods, she tells us, "Grocery shopping just makes me feel safe and happy. I do not think there's anything I love more than the grocery store. . . . It feels like time doesn't exist, [and] problems don't exist. It's just you and the produce."[3] Yet the location we see for these shopping excursions is not the interior of the store itself (though we do see inside the store occasionally) but Chamberlain's car. Chamberlain has made videos in which she compares fast-food breakfast items, entirely filmed while in her car. She has documented several road trips from her car. In one road trip video, "i lowkey crashed into someones car (plz don't tell my mom)," Chamberlain even documents, as the title suggests, a car crash in which she was involved.[4]

Chamberlain may seem to be exceptional, as she is one of the most excessively popular influencers today. Yet filming YouTube videos in one's car is exceptionally common, often performed in a manner like Chamberlain's. As a background, the car is a liminoid space between point A and point B where content will be found and documented as one navigates the necessities of daily life. The personality speaking may change, but the background has little variance: a car seat in a neutral color, windows showing small glimpses of the moving scenery as it passes, or the static snapshot of a parking lot. The car may provide a space of "privacy" as one makes their way to work—which includes not only the labor of making content but content that may be produced as one drives to an office or a warehouse. It may provide a space in which one can honestly talk and reveal personal opinions while on a break for lunch.

Or, on social media, the car is a background for monologues, dialogues, commentary, and criticism or simply going through the motions of one's day for the benefit of an audience. If the house is a space of personal intimacy, where property is conflated with personhood, where the details of interior design become signifiers of specificity, of personality as such, the car is *generic, fungible*—devoid of personality, devoid of specificity. Yet even as the car seems to reverse the specificity of the home, it ultimately becomes a background deployed for similar ends. Where the home allows access to the apparently private through the visualization of domestic interiority, the car permits access to psychological interiority through its appearance as something nonspecific, interchangeable, placeless.

Furthermore, the car represents how the dream of the house becomes entrepreneurial and mobile, escaping the bounds of a specific building and its fixity by way of the garage. The garage is another liminoid space, a construction adjacent to the home that turns away from the domestic to the generic mobility of capital. In the garage, the private turns outward toward the city, toward shopping, toward work; the garage is an interface that overlaps and intrudes through its permeable boundary, remaking the domestic into the entrepreneurial. As the precarity of contemporary life regularly makes homeownership an impossibility, the garage wanes away, and the car itself becomes an object that links domestic privacy and capitalist mobility, displayed on social media not only through #vanlife, the Instagram hashtag characterized by glamorous nomads, but also #carlife, a hashtag in which otherwise unhoused individuals frame their precarity as attention-getting content as they dream of an upward mobility that culminates not in a home but in a van, mobile and "free." The car—and the garage—are, like the other locations we survey in these pages, components of the factory that is influencer culture: backgrounds, machines, spaces deployed in the entrepreneurial production of the self.

THE FREEDOM OF THE CAR CAMERA GUY

Some of the most notable examples of car videos do not emerge organically from social media. (Although what, if anything, can be said to organically emerge from social media?) These videos are sometimes billed as talk shows, or segments on talk shows, and the most notable ones feature extremely popular and recognizable celebrities. In them, or more accurately, in the controversies they create, we can see how the car is a space between public and private, a space in which the self is imagined as authentic, not just a product crafted in the service of spectacular consumption. For instance, take Jerry Seinfeld's *Comedians in Cars Getting Coffee*, a "roving talk show" that originally premiered in 2012 on the digital streaming service

Crackle.[5] In it, one comedian drives another comedian around in a vintage car to—as the show's title explains—get coffee. Another example is the regular, pretaped "Carpool Karaoke" segment on James Corden's *Late Late Show*. Popular on YouTube and on Corden's show itself, "Carpool Karaoke," which first aired in 2015, features the host encouraging some celebrity to sing along with him while playing songs (sometimes the celebrity's own) in a car. These productions rely on digital video, appearing amateurish despite the famous hosts and guests that appear on them, even though the car is known by many to be a location for social media filming characterized by relatively excellent acoustic qualities. Obviously, these videos attempt to mimic the form and style of social media influencers, a mimicking perpetuated by the culture industry to provide some modicum of authenticity to what is otherwise an obvious product. The subjects of these videos, ideally, appear not as traditional celebrities but as everyday people, reinvented through their placement in an intimate venue in which an audience can approach celebrity with a closeness usually prohibited.

On January 22, 2020, tech entrepreneur (and former *Shark Tank* contestant) Zoli Honig posted to Twitter a video of Corden and Justin Bieber filming a "Carpool Karaoke" segment, revealing—surprise, surprise—Corden was not driving during these videos as the finished product would have one think. Instead, the car was towed around by a truck.[6] Anyone paying attention to the backgrounds of the "Carpool Karaoke" videos should be at least somewhat aware of this artifice; it's often obvious that Corden is "driving" his celebrity around a single city block or a space that requires slow speeds. The segment is introduced as an artificial joke, anyway; Corden may explain that he needed someone else in his car so he could use a carpool lane on the highway or, if in another country, that he needed a local to help him with directions. Even a modicum of attention reveals these excuses to be false, so why assume anything about "Carpool Karaoke" to be something other than artifice? Honig's Twitter post reveals that, like much of what we've seen throughout this book so far, there's an elaborate production apparatus involved in the crafting of videos that otherwise seem amateurish or spontaneous.

But the "revelation" that "Carpool Karaoke" was staged generated a significant amount of social media outrage. Corden even responded on his show to Honig's post, pleading with a blend of sincerity and irony: "I've recently been the victim of a scandal in the media, and there have been some very, very serious allegations made against me." The towing of the car, Corden joked, was because the host was infatuated with Bieber. Corden "just kept getting lost in his eyes."[7] Despite these deferrals, Corden's response divulged just how concerned he was about any "revelation" of a production apparatus otherwise invisible, how much he *actually cared* that the audience believed the videos to be, in some sense, *real*. The Bieber video, Corden claimed, was one of only a handful in which he was not actually driving. Corden then listed the specific stars who appeared while he was using the towing rig—Meghan Trainor, Chance the Rapper, Migos, Cardi B . . .—a listing intended to legitimize the belief that, in almost *all* other appearances, Corden *really was* driving himself and his guest around a city. Corden, therefore, seemed genuinely worried that his segment had some perceived "authenticity"—that, as members of his audience, we believe our gaze is merely one of a hidden camera watching a celebrity and a television host belt away while sequestered privately in a car.

More than the home, the car is a mobile and flexible encapsulation of privacy, a singular space that "represents freedom because: it is . . . a place to be alone, as a mobile apartment, a place where your children can misbehave without embarrassing you and themselves in public, a place for sexual activity; you can pick and choose your companions; the car waits for you; waiting at a bus stop is far less comfortable than sitting in traffic jams."[8] Today, along with these other functions, the car becomes a space to film oneself, a space where, through one's social isolation, a camera can reveal one's true beliefs and feelings while one is otherwise hidden from view (aside from the view permitted by the smartphone and social media). In the online magazine *Mic*, writer Shaun Cooke noted that Corden's somewhat surprising defense of "Carpool Karaoke" and its amateurism (and hence naturalism) reveals a hidden desire: "Everyone secretly wants to be a car camera guy, even if they don't have the moral fortitude to admit it."[9] Being a *car camera guy*, to use Cooke's excellent phrase, refers to a populist desire shared by Corden, Dale Earnhardt Jr., and Jeremy Renner, as well as with politicians across the political spectrum, including Marco Rubio and Bernie Sanders. All of these "car camera guys" are united in their tendency to use smartphones to shoot videos while driving—videos in which they lecture, converse, or, in the case of Corden, sing about whatever might be on their mind that day.

For Cooke, the promise of the car camera guy is the general promise of "democratization" over social media: "Even as fame has established itself as the most crushing cultural force, the tools for recording shoddy phone videos while driving remain pretty fundamental. . . . Anyone from sitting U.S. Senators to vloggers and SoundCloud rappers will produce the same quality as you might in your own car."[10] Echoing countless past arguments about the internet and its democratic potential, its ability to generate "prosumers" or "produsers," its "collective intelligence" in which the anonymous mass of users online generate "truth,"[11] the car camera guy seems to be a remnant of the fading dream where the internet acts as a means for undermining and leveling barriers of public discourse. But there's clearly a twist here: the idea isn't so much that shooting in one's car actually does this but that the reliance on everyday consumer technology *appears* as populist, as democratic. That filming in a car is a predominant form of video among celebrities and politicians suggests something strange about its claims to democratic equivalence over social media.

Cooke argues that the desire to film oneself driving is intrinsically masculine; its implicit danger requires an internalized masculinity, a fantasy of mastery over machines, a fantasy that presumes a coherence among one's ability to drive, one's ability to be inattentive and negligent about one's location in time and space, and one's aptitude in controlling the manifold technologies in use: "Car camera guys—they're almost always guys, and for the sake of argument over 40—require a certain level of comfort with mortality, but also a brazen confidence in the driver's ability to drive safely independent of other cars suddenly eating shit. It's also the most ridiculous aesthetic for asserting this sort of tossed-off masculinity, and makes the video an afterthought to wherever they're going."[12] The car camera guy, as a particular kind of person, draws attention to the implicit recklessness of driving while filming, which, to be sure, descends from the lengthy genealogy of masculinity, bridging fantasies of domination with idiocy and self-assurance. Its democratic, populist appeal can only be made through a form that, quite directly, does not give a shit about the safety of either oneself or others. To shoot a video while in a car is the epitome of distracted driving. To be like others, to be "democratic" or "populist," in the capacity to record and share requires one to not care about one's effect on the lives of others.

We want to suggest something a little different from Cooke, though. Filming in cars is, certainly, a form of narcissistic oblivion in which one's voice and one's desire to communicate, to generate information, to have a voice all supersede a concern for safety, a care for others. It requires the extreme confidence that Cooke describes *but also requires a belief that one's primary purpose and significance is to generate content.*[13] While Corden's defense of "Carpool Karaoke" and its authenticity could be seen as a fear of his own emasculation, not all those filming videos in cars are the car camera *guys* Cooke describes—something obvious in our foregrounding of Chamberlain and her car. As we will describe, many of those who make videos in their cars are not always moving and thus not intrinsically reckless. At the same time, while the car video is not always as easily gendered as Cooke suggests, we can link the car and its private mobility with a transformation in the gendering of private space, sexuality, and technology that occurred in midcentury American culture.[14] Above all, we suggest, the car is a background central for the factory that is influencer culture because it permits anyone access to a space that is equally intimate, an intimacy that emerges from particular techniques for *isolating* oneself, thereby producing oneself as a commodity.

In other words, the "democratic" ruse of the car video is grounded in the fact that the car is another background for intimacy, much like the home. But instead of an intimacy determined by specificity, in which the house becomes a metonym of the influencer, conflating the two through the appearance of private space and the assumption that to *own* is to *be*,[15] the car is a space for intimacy premised on the generic and the fungible. The intimacy of the car appears "democratic" and "populist" only because this democratic populism presumes that the primary measure of citizenship and equality is, today, a generic exchangeability of information that seems "intimate" because of its detachment from specificity. The car suggests that each and every one of us can successfully produce the self as commodity, a self that can appear both as product and as "authentic," as "real." The self can emerge more fully, more directly, because of the blandness of the background against which it appears. The car video, thus, is another sign of the real subsumption of sociality by capital.

THE CAR AS A GENERIC SPACE

When we see into the homes of influencers, the intimacy we feel is based in the privacy of the domestic. The use of media to see into private, domestic space has characterized visual spectacle since at least the time of television.[16] The visualization of the private sphere through media is a transformation foundational for the proliferation of spectacle in contemporary culture,[17] a remaking of private intimacy into public intimacy.[18] The intimacy of social media, as we've been suggesting, is one in which, as Guy Debord wrote, "Everything that was directly lived has receded into a representation,"[19] where our visual social relation becomes one of separation through the appearance of closeness, through the appearance of access.

If there is an awareness that the home has become a stage, that the interiors visible on social media are constructed, manufactured, all while appearing as if interchangeable with the influencers themselves, then the car is a strange, unstaged space shorn of personality and, as such, becomes peculiarly more personal, more intimate than the privacy of the domestic. Videos in which we see influencers carry out their daily routines include lengthy digressions and discussions in which, for instance, Emma Chamberlain drives around, stops at stores, gets fuel for the vehicle that transports her, all as we ride along and see the banal details of Chamberlain's daily life. MrBeast provides us with many car-based videos, in which he may act as an Uber driver,[20] or may even purchase a used car lot to give away all of its cars,[21] all with the seeming goal of generating an orgy of emotion from the subjects who wittingly and unwittingly appear in his videos, intensities that signify the release of hidden, interior desires and feelings. Even more ubiquitous are videos in which someone, anyone, is simply talking to the camera, digressing on one of any number of possible topics, be it their personal feelings about whatever is on their mind that day or an application of the Lacanio-Marxist film criticism of Slavoj Žižek to the Netflix series *Squid Game*.[22]

At first glance, the locations used for these videos are completely pro-saic. As with social media and contemporary entertainment, American urban space is dominated by cars. American cities regularly devote more than half their land toward uses dedicated to cars—roads, highways, park-ing lots, garages. In some cities, like Los Angeles, the amount of land de-voted to the car can reach upwards of two-thirds of total urban space.[23] The car, after all, is often physically larger than the cubicles in which people work, so parking a car quite literally requires more space than one's desk.[24] This isn't even to mention how the car itself has become a working and living space for many since the 1990s, at least, transformed not only into a means of mobility but into a hybrid space filled with internet access and television screens, a space in which one can move through the city and still remain "productive" for capital.[25]

The car, thus, is a key element of what French anthropologist Marc Augé memorably described as "nonplaces," physical locations that do away with the idea of "culture" as grounded in practices bound by specific lo-cations in space and time. Nonplaces are characterized by "installations needed for the accelerated circulation of passengers and goods (high-speed roads and railways, interchanges, airports)," as well as "the means of trans-port themselves."[26] The car, it would seem, is indicative of how most urban space has been remade as a physical infrastructure that moves a person from one location to another, a conduit rather than a "place."

Yet, when we look to the background of influencer videos and find the interiors of automobiles, we don't find "nonplaces," at least not quite. Iron-ically, we find not only a space to move through but a background that gen-erates a new kind of intimacy, an intimacy that is simultaneously personal and impersonal, specific and nonspecific. In stripping down the details of personality and place—details that characterize the specific intimacy of the domestic—we see how cynical we have become about the intimacy of social media. The car shows us how intimacy can be obtained only by shedding details that, today, we believe to be fabricated and therefore false. The dialectic of intimacy we see with cars is that "personality" and "speci-ficity" can only emerge when the material details of personality and spec-ificity are annihilated.

THE CAR AS AN INTIMATE ENCLOSURE

In the second half of the twentieth century, theorists of urban space regularly lamented the transformations undergoing the city through "modernizations" revolving around cars. Architectural theorist Albert Pope, for instance, in his influential book *Ladders*, decried how "the vast parking lots, continuous or sporadic zones of urban decay, undeveloped or razed parcels, huge public parks, corporate plazas, high-speed roads and urban expressways, and the now requisite *cordon sanitaire* surrounding office parks, industrial parks, theme parks, malls, and subdivisions are spaces that have failed to become the focus of systematic investigation."[27] In the failure to examine these new features of urban "planning," Pope claimed that the city was, in effect, becoming concealed not only to architects and developers but to those residing within the city itself. A range of structures had been invented to explicitly and surreptitiously direct movement and, at the same time, remain invisible and unacknowledged by the vast majority of the city's inhabitants. The car—and the range of environmental reinventions it requires—has been central to these transformations, ensuring a route that directly connects one place to another, ensuring a life permeated by work and little else. Urban planners in the twentieth century, Pope tells us, have been instrumental in producing a form of urban space that encloses and directs people to be "productive." "While the development that ties the housing tract to the freeway, to parking garages, to tunnels, and to office slabs is relentless,"[28] Pope suggests, some planners have attempted to negotiate this demand to enforce automotive pipelines between home and work with an illusory appearance of *freedom*. The avatar of this illusory freedom is the car.

Although the car was often a major symbol of "freedom" and "mobility" throughout the twentieth century,[29] Pope, along with numerous other theorists of urban space, demonstrates how the car has been essential for the increasing control and management of daily life, restricting the possibilities for self and society by parceling out bodies through the management of movement. With the loss of the city, the car became the primary means to experience space. The experience of "mobile privatization"—the phrase Raymond Williams coined to describe the intertwined reinvention of urban space and the rise of televisual spectacle[30]—shows us how the car is necessarily conjoined with a complete reframing of public and private life. The public life of urban space, in which the street, the sidewalk, the park, and the pub are physical spaces for chance encounters of friends and strangers, is replaced with the simulacrum of sociality given by the televisual gaze into the lives of others, with personal privacy mediated as bodies are shunted from home to car to work and back again. The car becomes necessary for the enclosure and impoverishment of social life, for the loss of public interaction in favor of, at best, scopophilic, spectacular intimacy granted only through visual media.

Yet the car has seemingly become the ideal space for intimacy today—though, again, not because it permits freedom but because it permits enclosure. Its liminality—that it is neither home nor work nor school but a medium for transport from one enclosure to another—seems to demonstrate that people are more "real," more "authentic," in their cars than elsewhere. Being "real," being oneself, requires imprisonment in a moving vehicle, where one is simultaneously mobile and shackled by seatbelts into a chair. One (somewhat odd) location we can see this assumption at work is in parenting advice. "Cars are the best place to have tough conversations with kids," proclaims the parenting website Fatherly, sponsored by the insurance company Geico: "Cruising down the road with your child is a surefire way to find out what's really going [on] in their life. There are fewer distractions, kids can't squirm away (at least physically), and there's a limited amount of time to tackle the topic at hand."[31] For parents, it would seem, the car becomes a place to ensure that children *cannot escape*; in a time of technical, social enclosure, there's always somewhere for one to hide or sneak away. Even in a city characterized by panoptic surveillance, even in a home fully optimized with smart sensors and video, the child can always slip away unseen.[32] The car, doors locked, speeding down the road, offers no escape. The car becomes control perfected and even adjusts for the "problem" of looking another in the eye and the difficulty one might have in being "honest" when gazes are held steady. According to Fred Peipman, a psychologist cited in the Fatherly-Geico article, "People say things in a car that they'd never say to someone on the street because there is a perceived separation," and removing eye contact highlights "the power dynamic more than facing someone else. When the child is beside or behind the parent, it is a bit easier to talk freely. . . . You are moving together which can lead to the psychological or emotional concept of moving toward something together."[33]

Peipman, a major advocate for car conversations with children, suggests four reasons that cars provide a space for increased intimacy and honesty. Not only is the passenger held captive (his first reason). But, when people are seated next to each other or even beside each other, the lack of eye contact permits one to be "honest" because it may feel "less intimidating or less threatening" to have a genuine, potentially confrontational conversation (the second reason). Car rides usually have a clear and defined end (the third reason), and even though there may be phones, radios, or other mobile technologies in the car, these distractions are often easier to minimize than they are outside the car (the fourth reason).[34] Parents referenced independently of Peipman seem to agree. For example, "a mom of two in South Portland, Maine" cited in a CNN article, "said quick car trips tend to be a successful way to get a little bit of information from her children. . . . 'Teenagers may call that a trap, but I call it parental opportunity.'"[35]

The car video is a perplexing reinvention of this parental structure. The person behind the wheel is free to revel in their discursive authority, free from intrusion by others. The car becomes a space of banal, fungible luxury, in which the contingencies of daily life are eliminated, an "elaborate form of mobile body-armour," a secure cocoon "against the (perceived) risks of the wider urban environment."[36] By insulating one against others, locking the doors, driving away, the car becomes a libertarian paradise, a space in which others are finally disposed of and one's voice can truly be heard. In the car, it would seem, one's sovereignty is never in dispute. With children, the car becomes an interrogation cell, a confession booth, in which the discomfort of being locked up with a parent incites the child to discourse. I'll lock you in a car to make you tell me who you are. But the point of parental discussions in the car is to let the "honesty" of the automotive trap force the child to speak. When an influencer (or politician, or celebrity) is given a smartphone, the car's incitement to discourse expands out elsewhere. In its sequestering from the outside world, the ability to feel free, to feel like one can finally speak one's truth, is transferred from other spaces of confessional enclosure toward a space of confessional broadcasting.

Even beyond the car as an apparatus of discursive power, its intimacy emerges from its existence as a contained, confined, generic space. Glimpses into private, intimate space carry with them a risk—that something truly private will be revealed. Think of any listicle of "Selfie Fails," photobombs, YouTube humiliations, in which something in the background of a video, ignored by the photographer, makes itself known after the fact: a dog defecating, a toilet, a dildo, a naked partner in a mirror, a mirror revealing that the photographer isn't wearing pants. . . . Unless one presumes the home to be a stage, the intimate privacy of the home is, in fact, risky. The car, in contrast, is boring and generic—off-white, beige, or gray, maybe a little dirty. The specificity of a car is easily obscured. In a car you do not have to worry about what will be in the frame. One wants a banal, generic car because one wants a banal, generic background. "Cars are everywhere on YouTube, and they look really, really boring," writes Inkoo Kang, a television critic for the *Hollywood Reporter.* "Viewers likely have no idea what brand the automobile is, nor is anything in the cabin worth a second glance. In contrast with, say, a video recorded in a bedroom or a living room, these car-set videos lack the revealing details that give those homey vlogs a sense of raw authenticity, as most cars look the same from the inside."[37]

Kang's observations, which resonate with what we've been arguing so far, should be extremely strange when positioned against our argument from the previous chapter. In the home, intimacy emerges from personal details that allow glimpses of specificity, something completely missing in a car video. Yet the absence of the "raw authenticity" of the home can make the car video *more* "authentic." This contradiction takes us further into the dialectical contradictions of authenticity when the self becomes subsumed by capital. Personal detail and interchangeable genericness can *both* lead to an increased sense of "authenticity," but the detail and specificity of the home is "authentic" precisely because of its inauthenticity, because of its necessary staging, because of its necessary production. The car video is "authentic" because of its lack of detail, its lack of staging. Yet this lack of staging is completely controlled; the car is explicitly chosen as a background because of its necessary negation of contingency, because of its innate hermeticism.

THE GARAGE AND THE REINVENTION OF DOMESTIC INTIMACY

The reinvention of the link between home and city, where the car remade urban geography, keeping bodies separate, enforcing pathways directly from the bedroom and living room to the cubicle and boardroom, also required the remaking of domestic architecture via the garage. "Built for the car," write artist Olivia Erlanger and architect Luis Ortega Govela, the garage "exists as a space where the rules and relations inherent in the suburban home are seemingly absent."[38] Pioneered by Frank Lloyd Wright, the garage was a particularly important element in an architectural dream that synthesized man and machine, domestic and industrial. In 1901, Wright gave a speech in which he announced that "a hope has grown stronger with the experience of each year, amounting now to a gradually deepening conviction that in the Machine lies the only future of art and craft—as I believe, a glorious future."[39] The garage was Wright's attempt to integrate the car into the ideal of the family, an integration he proposed in 1908, prior to the public availability of Henry Ford's Model T.[40] Wright removed places in the home designed for socialization, like the front porch and the parlor, along with spaces for storage, like closets, replacing them with an attached garage, central features of Wright's monuments of architectural history like his Robie House in Chicago. The Robie House was concealed from the neighborhood, hidden behind brick walls, invisible to those walking by on the street. Thus, Erlanger and Ortega Govela explain, "the garage was a new threshold that could be closed off or opened at will, a ritual in which the family and home were no longer connected to the neighborhood outside; rather, the garage and the car opened the home to the modern city."[41] In doing so, it also opened the home to the flows and movements of capital. The garage would come to dictate which houses would qualify for mortgages and which were deemed overly risky, differentiating between mostly white suburban neighborhoods, defined by new construction, and urban spaces. So the garage was a feature of a house linked with the structural racism of redlining.[42]

In the 1930s, during the Great Depression, Wright reinvented his own plans for houses and garages, moving from the urban bourgeoisie to the middle class. Wright's *Usonian* projects, a term he invented to describe a utopian model of suburban, futurist housing, removed the garage and replaced it with a *carport*, a term Wright coined to describe a roof without walls designed to house a car, rendering it visible rather than concealed behind a door. Followers of Wright perpetuated this utopian model in the development of their midcentury suburban modernism. Yet legal restrictions on mortgages, restrictions motivated by racial segregation, designed to differentiate suburban from urban, white from Black, carried with them wasteful architectural excess that remained: Wright was forced to build homes with both carports and garages, a feature his followers maintained.[43] A house needed a garage to be respectable, to be suburban, to be white.

Consequentially, the car was often placed under the roof of the carport. The garage became not only a liminoid space connecting home and city but something akin to what philosopher Gilles Deleuze termed an any-space-whatever: "Any-space-whatever is not an abstract universal, in all times, in all places. It is a perfectly singular space, which has merely lost its homogeneity. . . . It is a space of virtual conjunction, grasped as pure locus of the possible. What in fact manifests the instability, the heterogeneity . . . is a richness in potentials or singularities which are, as it were, prior conditions of all actualisation, all determination."[44] The carport, in allowing for placing the car elsewhere, made the garage a place of heterogeneous abstraction—generic, but not homogeneous, because its function became undefined. But one function, linked with the garage's history as an interface that remade the home, integrating it with the city and divorcing it from community, was predominant: the birth of entrepreneurial selfhood. The garage became a site of subjectivation linked with the development of creative projects, illicitly or surreptitiously produced in hours stolen from the family and from one's day job. From Hewlett Packard and Apple to countless Silicon Valley start-ups, we hear repetitions of the mythos of the garage as this unbound space of entrepreneurial invention. The birth of late capitalism's reliance on technology, software, and information can be found in the space that pushed beyond the boundaries of the domestic toward a room undetermined and undefined by traditional roles of the family and work. Yet rather than pure potentiality, the garage was quickly subsumed by the logic of capital as a space of entrepreneurship that, we will see later in this book, has also become a space for the corporatization of selfhood.

The classical liberal model of subjecthood might be thought of through the term *homo economicus*, economic man, who imagines himself and his relations through the supposedly innate capacity to barter, truck, and trade, to rationally evaluate his self-interest and make decisions and investments accordingly. This, however, is not the subject who we find in a garage. Instead, we find something closer to what Michel Foucault describes in his lectures collected in *The Birth of Biopolitics*, his description and discussion of the emergence of neoliberalism. "In neo-liberalism," Foucault says in a lecture from March 14, 1979, "there is also a theory of *homo œconomicus*, but he is not at all a partner of exchange." Exchange, the capacity to barter, truck, and trade, has been replaced with the ability to *craft oneself as capital*. In neoliberalism, "*homo œconomicus* is an entrepreneur, an entrepreneur of himself."[45]

The garage is part of the architecture that invents this subject. In it, we find not someone working on producing a product, per se. We find someone producing their self as a commodity to be sold. Capital fills the vacuum produced by the garage's openness after the car is removed; where family and domesticity are left behind, the self as capital emerges. The entrepreneur in Silicon Valley does not sell their product to the venture capitalist. They sell their capacity as one who has ideas in which capital invests and which it cultivates.[46] Even if the product is vaporware, failing to manifest as a real thing, value is produced through a range of fictitious financial investments as long as the next Uber or Airbnb generates enough hype for its IPO. But there's still a material commodity produced here. The "person" becomes capital to be bought, sold, and exchanged. The garage is the workshop for this subject. And today, as many cannot even accumulate the capital to invest in their own house, their own garage, the car itself has taken on the qualities of an any-space-whatever, a generic heterogeneous background against which the subject produces their own self as a commodity to be bought and sold.

If the interior of the home is gendered feminine, the garage reinvents domesticity as masculine, a portal that permits the intrusion of "public" life into "private" space by way of the car. *The garage is a portal that opens the house to the space of work, of capital.* As Paul Preciado has argued about *Playboy* and its representation of architecture, in midcentury American life, modern design reinvents the domestic as a space of masculine domination and control, opening the house through an intertwining of architecture and media.[47] If envisioning domestic interiors carries with it some sort of "authenticity" because of its links with forms of labor that are "private," and thus supposedly beyond the space of capitalist exploitation, when the domestic is exposed—both through technology and through automobility— the public intimacy of the house becomes an intimacy in which the interior self can mold itself into a product, bridging interior and exterior, allowing car and camera to assert a control over self and environment.

REPLACING THE HOME WITH THE CAR

The garage, as a relatively undefined space for creative labor, was regularly converted into home recording studios, a space for bands to practice and record. Today, YouTubers tell us the best GoPro and microphone setups for cars.[48] We are told that "cars have amazing acoustics. . . . It's a cheap and easy way of getting studio like quality sound with no studio setup."[49] *Carpool Karaoke*, of course, even works to visualize the articulation of the constrained acoustics of the car with the intimacy of enclosure. But the turn away from the garage to the car is not merely a turn determined by acoustic fidelity. We conclude this chapter with one final suggestion: not only has the car opened the home and remade domesticity and its seeming "authenticity," but, for some, the car has completely replaced the home. Yet this is not quite in line with the images of wealth, waste, abundance, and luxury we'll be turning toward in the remainder of this book. If one direction for the car is a space of generic authenticity, a "democratic" equivalence falsely accessible to all, another is toward extreme precarity obscured by this equivalence, in which the promise of entrepreneurial selfhood and the "freedom" of influencer automobility leads toward constant work and constant struggle.

One YouTuber, Nikita Crump, whose channel is titled "Life in a Vehicle" (with nearly seventy thousand subscribers), gives advice about how she lives completely in a car, how she stays warm or cool, how she cooks and eats, where she showers, how she insulates her vehicle. "I feel like this is something I need to do," she tells us. "I feel like it would be out of my character not to do this. And, I just want to. I want to live in my car. I wish I had done this sooner. I'm happy I'm doing it now."[50] In this video's description are Amazon-affiliate links advertising the products Crump has described using and a link to a company that sells diffraction lenses that generate rainbows, complete with a coupon code for viewers of Crump's channel. Crump tells us about how she can now afford rent by living in her car. The car, in replacing the domestic space of the home, permits Crump a way into a kind of entrepreneurialism that avoids the trap of real estate, rent, and other usurious machinations of contemporary capitalism. Yet, Crump's stated "happiness" may conceal just how difficult this life of freedom is.

Alyssa Vanilla, whose YouTube channel has nearly fifteen thousand subscribers, tells of similar things—how to stay warm in the winter in a car, how to stay cool in the summer in a car, how to cook food in a car, how to pee in a car, how to date in a car—along with videos that tell of her sadness, loneliness, and anxiety. "I don't know what my plans are for the future," Vanilla says in one video; "it'd be really nice . . . so if you guys can make me famous in some way . . ."[51] Vanilla's #carlife looks radically different on her Instagram page than it does on YouTube.[52] One is filled with well-lit, glamorous pictures of nature, of camping, of travel; the other is filled with videos where Vanilla talks about her feelings, the lack of a future in America, her car (meaning her home) getting totaled, her emotional and psychological struggles. Crump's Instagram and YouTube pages display a similar difference—a set of Instagram images intended to represent freedom and liberty as one lives cheaply and independently across America,[53] a set of YouTube videos talking of hardship and precarity.

Highlighting the anxieties of #carlife requires us to rethink the so-called democratic potentials of the car as background in influencer culture. When the house becomes an impossibility, when spaces of private intimacy become a financial liability, the generic openness of the car becomes an apparent background that allows for access to mobility, access to intimacy, access to seeming "authority" as one sits in the sovereign position behind the wheel. This, of course, both conceals and reveals the lived precarity of many of those streaming from the car but is nonetheless presented as a route of mobility elsewhere. The car may become a house, if only one can sell themselves.

THREE

MARKET

We have examined two backgrounds of influencer culture, homes and cars, and what these backgrounds reveal about personhood, property, and intimacy under the real subsumption of community by capital. In our contemporary conjuncture, a "self" is reduced to that which can be crafted into a saleable commodity, a commodity that appears to be a "real" and "authentic" expression of one's personhood. Yet this "self" defines its specificity and uniqueness through its interchangeability with property; this "self" is generic, mobile, fungible, exchangeable with all others. In the next chapter, we will examine a transformation that may seem perplexing but is completely logical: in the videos of numerous influencers, homes and cars are increasingly replaced by *warehouses*. The warehouse, a space for the storage and circulation of commodities and, in influencer culture, an outgrowth of the garage that replaces domestic space, tells us something more about how domesticity, intimacy, and identity have been subsumed by capital, about how backgrounds that signify intimacy and private identity can be reinvented through spaces designed directly for the circulation of commodities. The warehouse is the end point of all culture and all sociality after the real subsumption of community by capital. When capital absorbs self, society, relation, being—then we will all be living and working in warehouses.

But before we can turn to the warehouse as the ultimate background of influencer culture, we must make a detour through a setting slightly more diffuse and abstract than those we describe elsewhere in this book: the *market*. By *market*, we're not referring to the general capitalist market, where assumed equals barter, truck, and trade; we're not talking about the abstraction imagined as a gigantic information processing machine that "knows" better than any individual, better than any human collective.[1] We're also not thinking exclusively about stores and shops, the quotidian "markets" we visit regularly—though sometimes these spaces can be located under this heading. By *market* we mean spaces of capitalist *excess*, of giveaways, orgies of cash, spending and buying—spaces of exchange specific to YouTube, documented through videos of endless commodities. Some of these commodities are luxurious and costly, but most are cheap and disposable. By the end of this chapter, it will become clear why we must make this detour, as it is through the market that we move from house to warehouse.

A market is an infrastructural background of contemporary capital, much like the house and the car. It names a material technique of creating and producing a self as commodity. What we're interested in is how the function of exchange, in influencer culture, becomes a background in which *people* become commodities with value—*not* the objects in videos that would seem to be, traditionally, the commodities represented. The representation of exchange is a background against which an entirely different process of exchange emerges. YouTube is the factory where influencers work to forge themselves, but it is also the marketplace where those selves are traded. The influencers themselves are both product and producer, worker and widget. For this chapter, we will, among other things, discuss how any other commodities beyond the self are only bought and sold in service of enlarging the power of the self as a commodity. The representation of exchange on YouTube is an alibi to produce a different commodity that is exchanged: a self. At the same time, things and objects, traditional commodities that are bought and sold to appear on YouTube, are, in fact, *wasted*. The self appears only against a background of waste, of trash, of useless excess, as objects are rendered valueless beyond their appearance as one part of an infinite, everlasting series—a series that only ends in complete and total exhaustion.

We know a market can be a place where people gather to purchase and sell commodities, an arena in which commercial dealings are conducted, a means of promoting, advertising, selling anything and everything. On social media, a market might be defined as a relational configuration of people, platforms, and environments where excessive exchange happens— something like eBay or Etsy, for instance, or any number of the newer, more niche versions of these peer-to-peer online marketplaces (Poshmark, Depop, thredUP, etc.). But on YouTube, a market always contains *more*— more things to buy, more money to spend, more objects to circulate, more excess to discard. A market may be a thrift store, where we watch a camera attached to a shopping cart pan over racks of vintage and used clothing. It may be an Amazon return center, where boxes and bins are filled with countless semianonymous objects. It may be an apartment that becomes a "market" through an unboxing video, in which an influencer pulls myriad products from a container or advertises their Depop page under the guise of a closet cleanout; it may be a backyard where a child pulls seemingly ineffable objects from giant eggs. It may simply be a place where vast sums of money are given away, in which "exchange" becomes unlinked from traditional norms of capitalist value.

A market, in all these examples, is intrinsically *wasteful* or, at least, appears as such. That a space of exchange has been remade into a space of waste indicates how the "market" on social media has become something other than its traditional existence as a nexus of liberal capitalism. Or perhaps social media has realized the true essence of consumer society all along. "The consumer society needs its objects in order to be," says Jean Baudrillard. "More precisely, it needs to *destroy* them. . . . Only in destruction are objects there *in excess* and only then, in their disappearance, do they attest to wealth."[2] The use value of a commodity is not in its specific utility as an object. Rather, use value has become the capacity of a specific thing to *lose* its specificity, to become a negligible part of a gigantic mass.

This is slightly different from how objects have been valued in the past. In the time of mass production, the critical theorist Walter Benjamin argued that there was a transition away from objects possessing "cult-value." Objects like religious artifacts or fine art had a specific value because of their exclusivity, because of their singularity in time and space, something Benjamin termed "aura." Something had value because it was difficult to see, because it was unique, because of its provenance, because it had been touched by its creator, because of its historical specificity. This is still the case with things like antiques, with collectible goods. Something is expensive because it is difficult to obtain, because the object has a singular existence. But with mass production, endless copies of the same object can be made. The object loses its exclusivity, its aura, and instead its value comes from its ability to be seen, its "exhibition-value."[3]

And today, in influencer culture, an object's value comes not only from its capacity to be seen but also from its capacity to be forgotten, destroyed, ignored, discarded. Beyond Benjaminian arguments about mass production and the commodity's loss of aura, the excesses of the market on YouTube lead to the annihilation of all values other than those derived from an object as one among countless others, exchanged with others, infinitely replaceable. Value emerges from sameness, from a spectacle of the constant appearance of differentiated yet indistinct objects over and over and over again. Value comes from the remaking of an object into *content*. As we might hear, delivered semi-ironically by some popular influencers, "Is this content?" The transformation of the commodity into a general, fungible element in a massive spectacle of excess suggests something else is at stake in these "markets" than a capacity to barter, truck, or trade. On YouTube, the exchange of commodities becomes a background from which a subject emerges and understands *itself* as a commodity, exchanged on a market distinct from the one represented onscreen.

THE LIQUIDATION OF ONE'S PAST

In a video titled "My Childhood Bedroom," from November 8, 2021, Emma Chamberlain takes us on a banal tour of forgotten objects from her past in the video's eponymous childhood bedroom. From a closet, Chamberlain pulls toys, earrings, a Blockbuster Video coupon, a plastic recorder from an elementary school music class, old artwork, and a multitude of other nostalgic personal remnants from her upbringing. Digital culture is often characterized by a tendency toward memorialization through hoarding. However dated various critiques of a "digital dualism" are today, physical objects are still prized in their seeming resistance to the ephemerality of the digital, the persistence of a Benjaminian "aura," especially through their registration of physical traces. These traces come to signify people, experiences, memories of the past and thus saturate the material with the metaphysical.[4] The trace inscribed is evidence for the continued presence of what is otherwise no longer.[5] To some extent, Chamberlain appears involved in one of these rituals, examining physical things and noting their material connection to herself, her past, and her family.

Yet, for Chamberlain, this ritual of memory is continually undermined by capital. While the tour through her former bedroom is rife with commentary about childhood memories, Chamberlain keeps making asides about *reselling* the things she's finding. "This is actually really cute," she says of one discovery. "I feel like I could sell this online for a lot of money. I don't know why I keep thinking about different ways that I could sell my old things on Depop."[6] Nostalgia is cut with the desire to sell, to profit, to liquidate one's own past in the name of its ability to be exchanged. The indexicality of the trace links *this* object and *this* person; nostalgic longing for childhood necessarily resurrects an auratic articulation between person and thing. But the desire shifts, without a second thought, into the dispersion of memory for profit. The ritual leads elsewhere: Chamberlain's video is a performance that transforms her childhood bedroom into content, while the objects we see are converted into waste.

We begin with the example of Chamberlain and her childhood closet to point out two things. On one hand, we have a video that follows our earlier arguments about the house in influencer culture. The things that Chamberlain pulls out of her closet are intended to represent her, as a person. These objects visualize something about *who she is*, about *who she was*; they provide a glimpse of intimacy recorded only by *seeing* the commodities that represent the person, the influencer, and her childhood. In seeing these things, the viewer seems allowed access to the private space of the influencer, in which property is conflated with personhood. But, on the other hand, whenever Chamberlain mentions the peer-to-peer fashion marketplace Depop, invoking a speculative plan to resell her childhood belongings, she's transforming this connection between person and property to something else. These objects are, effectively, *not* connected to the influencer, at least essentially. Unlike the "forever home" in the background of

A Beautiful Mess, these objects are temporary, and the link between person and property is tentative (of course, the links sustained by a "forever home" are, in practice, also temporary and tentative—no property, no possession is forever). Were these objects purchased with the specific connection to the influencer in mind, then the reselling of the object allows fans of the influencer "access" to being *like* them, to *have* them, though in a way that can never actually approach intimacy because the shedding and sale of these otherwise "useless" commodities indicates not their connection but their distance from the seller.

This is, of course, a foundational inequivalence between use value and exchange value found in any and every commodity, in every act of exchange. "Profit" can only be extracted from exchange when the lack of equivalence between use values is manifested in quantitative form, in money, in exchange value.[7] As sociologist Georg Simmel put it in his *Philosophy of Money*, "The economic form of value lies between two limits: on the one side is the desire for the object, arising from the anticipated satisfaction of possession and enjoyment; on the other side is the enjoyment itself, which is not strictly speaking an economic act."[8] This doubling of limits is further doubled: both parties in exchange desire something related to the object and something related to enjoyment. One party desires the object, as well as an imagined enjoyment from the object. The object becomes that which will finally satisfy. The other party desires to rid themselves of the object, exchanging it for another object—money. Their imagined satisfaction emerges from the belief that the sale of the object will return an excess, a profit. All exchanges are based on the presumption of inequivalent use values, that the desire for the object differs, in some way, from the desire to rid oneself of it. Money adjudicates subjective differences, both liberating the individual from social bonds and destroying relationships that cannot come to be quantified.[9] The contradiction between use value and exchange value here reveals the impossibility of human relation through the purchase and sale of belongings, the impossibility of an object maintaining a "trace" of another beyond synecdochical trope. The object is exchanged because it matters to one but is generally meaningless to another.

This all presumes that Chamberlain does, in fact, sell these belongings on Depop. If she does, and she more likely does not, the transaction is surely not a significant part of her existence as an influencer. Chamberlain makes far more money from her videos than she ever would selling trinkets online. Thus, the reselling of personal belongings—or, even more minimally, the mere *suggestion* of resale—reveals at least two different economies, one of which requires that the objects Chamberlain finds in her closet are, essentially, useless to her. Some of these objects are ultimately waste—of value to nobody beyond the connection to the influencer. Some may possess value to someone, hence the possibility of resale online. This is a very traditional understanding of exchange, which follows how most of us judge the value of our own possessions, if we've ever had a garage sale or sold things on a peer-to-peer marketplace online. But this entire understanding of exchange is not the point, bringing us to the second economy. The first economy is an alibi for the real commodities produced, the real exchanges occurring in the making and viewing of Chamberlain's video. The use value of the objects Chamberlain finds in her childhood bedroom is found in their ability to become *content* for the influencer, and this content depends not on Chamberlain's ability to feature one or a couple of *specific* objects but in her ability to pull out different objects and things from her closet for around twenty minutes (most likely, she did this for much longer, but this specific video has been edited to twenty minutes). The things that Chamberlain examines do not matter, really. Their importance is in the attention they attract, which emerges only through their ability to be incorporated into an infinite series.

Content is a particularly ironic term to describe whatever it is we see on YouTube because what the market reveals is the primacy of a particular *formal* economy. Any specific instance of content—that we are looking at a specific object or a specific commodity—is subsumed by the infinite perpetuation of *more content to come.* In the market that is YouTube, *the specificity of content never matters*, only the formal perpetuation of more, more, more objects that, at a level of individuality, are thus "de-formed" beyond their ability to become subsumed in the overarching stream of more.[10] And it is on this indistinct stream of more—this stream that is the embodiment of the market on YouTube—that the "real" commodity appears: the influencer as a particular subject and a particular "self" that can be exchanged for profit.

INTERESTING CONTENT

The irrelevance of specific instances of content has specific economic implications. Since communication scholar Dallas Smythe's classic analysis of the political economy of advertising, published in the 1970s, it's been widely accepted that the "consumers" of ad-subsidized, "free" media are mislabeled. With commercial television and advertising-sponsored newspapers and magazines, Smythe argues, audiences are not consumers of media. The newspaper article, the television show—the "content," in other words—is not a product that is consumed. Rather, audiences and readerships are themselves the commodities, manufactured through a complex set of factors that relies on content as a lure (the ability of television, newspapers, and magazines to attract attention). The audience—or more accurately, the audience's attention—is fabricated into a salable commodity through marketing research, which demographically sorts the members of an audience as a statistically generalizable and predictable mass of people with shared interests and tastes. This "audience commodity" is then sold to advertisers. "The material reality under monopoly capitalism is that all non-sleeping time of most of the population is work time," Smythe tells us. This "work," which involves the fashioning of audience attention into "products" to sell to advertisers, is not performed by "workers" themselves, if we think of workers as "people" who make up the working class. Smythe continues: "Who produces this commodity? The mass media of communications do by the mix of explicit and hidden advertising and 'programme' material, the markets . . . which preoccupy the bourgeois communication theorists."[11] Or, as more simply and directly stated in Richard Serra and Carlota Fay Schoolman's 1973 work of video art, *Television Delivers People*, produced several years before Smythe's essay, "The Product of Television, Commercial Television, is the Audience. Television delivers people to an advertiser."[12]

As more recent critiques of social media have argued, the "audience commodity" as defined by Smythe has become the dominant economic model of the internet and of social media in particular.[13] Sometimes termed "surveillance capitalism,"[14] the political economy of the internet depends directly on the extraction and sale of data to advertisers, "innovating" new ways to identify and predict human activities and spending patterns, enforcing the rule that Smythe proposed about entertainment and leisure: almost all nonsleeping time is put to work, as it were. And, of course, even sleep time is valorized as "productive" for capital today. Rest either results in a stream of data (if one keeps their Apple Watch on all night, for instance) or is optimized to ensure the continued ability to labor.[15] Social media platforms compete for audience attention—perhaps, more accurately, "user" attention, given that the mass formerly known as the audience has been disaggregated through varied means of data extraction designed to create predictable, cybernetic profiles assumed equivalent to a "person," even though this equivalence is questionable and partial at best.[16] As an oft-repeated aphorism goes, one that descends from Smythe, Serra, and Schoolman, "If you aren't paying for it, then you are the product."

Yet this relationship between "product" (users, audiences) and "consumer" (advertisers, marketing firms) cannot fully explain the function of influencers such as Chamberlain. This is especially true in videos where content appears to explicitly represent traditional understandings of exchange. Chamberlain, certainly, is a lure. Her sifting through endless objects that appear "meaningful" but are more or less interchangeable is a means to attract audience attention. The generation of content, for the classical media industries described by Smythe, relied on a range of assorted media professionals, including writers, editors, producers, publishers, and actors, among countless others. The "democratization" of social media, however, transformed these jobs into ones performed by everyday individuals, a form of "democracy" that led to increasing precarity throughout the culture industry. Thus, from this process, successful influencers like Chamberlain must constantly work to *valorize themselves* as lures. YouTube, as a platform that bundles users and sells their attention to advertisers, does not care that Chamberlain is the *specific* route through which attention is captured, at least beyond the influencer as a means to direct and "effectively" place specific branded content and ads. Chamberlain only matters insofar as she can continuously and consistently capture attention. Whereas users and viewers sitting at home are passively, unconsciously made into a commodity sold to advertisers, a commodity possibly termed "attention" or "eyeballs," Chamberlain must *consciously* labor to make herself "interesting," producing herself as a commodity that is both visually consumed by audiences and economically consumed by advertisers through the labor of capturing and absorbing the time of us sitting at our computers or scrolling on our phones.

Chamberlain is, effectively, not selling her labor power but herself as a fully formed commodity, a stable and coherent "identity" that acts as a channel for conducting attention, a conduit that must perpetually generate more and more "content" in the name of ensuring the influencer's continued existence as one who attracts attention. The perpetual work of self-valorization is essential for the precarity of the vast majority of contemporary influencers. Chamberlain—like those we will discuss in the final chapters of this book—avoids some of this precarity by vertically integrating her identity (she owns a coffee brand, and her videos can be interpreted as lengthy advertisements for coffee; rather than an intermediary, Chamberlain is both lure of attention and the one purchasing audience attention). But for now, we can see how the need to produce oneself as a saleable commodity requires the constant generation of *more*, necessary for the maintenance of interest and attention, and—as we will discuss further momentarily—the constant generation of waste in the name of interest and attention.

The "interesting" is, in the words of literary theorist Sianne Ngai, "an aesthetic about difference in the form of information and the pathways of its movement and exchange."[17] To be interesting requires one to foster a minimal difference, a minimal distinction—to be different enough to attract attention but not different enough to attract a more significant (usually negative) aesthetic judgment. The judgment of "interesting," for Ngai, depends on the seriality of mass production and how that seriality began to shape aesthetic expression after World War II. *Interesting* signifies a distinction much like that denoted by Gregory Bateson's well-known definition of a "bit" of information as a "difference which makes a difference."[18] The labor of the interesting, then, both embraces the fungibility of the commodity and the self after the real subsumption of community by capital, but it also seeks to maintain one's distinction—and therefore value—by perpetuating some form of spectacular difference to be worthy of attention. Bizarrely, this means that what may appear as "too much" (as too many objects, as too much spending) is framed as only "just enough" to maintain a stream of *more* (more content, more videos, more to see, and more to buy).

The specific differences enabled by the market on YouTube are perplexing—the difference leans on the seriality of "interesting" content. What is truly valued is not difference as such but difference's inclusion in a generally homogeneous stream of information, a stream of constantly differentiated yet substantively identical commodities. What is valued is the mere fact that there's always *more*. Chamberlain must negotiate the specificity of personal content, of intimacy, with the demands of exchangeable, impersonal excess. It is this negotiation—of the personal with the impersonal, of the indexical with the exchangeable, of the meaningful with the meaningless—that defines the "market" we see on social media.

INTERESTING EXCESS

Throughout 2020 and 2021, at the height of the coronavirus pandemic, most traditional media industries had difficulty adjusting to the demands placed on work, entertainment, and life itself. Release schedules for film, television, and videogames were continuously restructured depending on varied challenges of production under quarantine, often related to wishful desires that particular movies could be watched in theaters at some point in the near future. The demands of production, for the traditional routes by which content was generated for the culture industry, often proved insurmountable, reliant, as the process is, on a massive number of individuals performing a wide range of different, distinct, coordinated tasks. At the same time, hours spent watching YouTube exploded during the pandemic, with 2.3 billion users worldwide watching over one billion hours of video per day.[19] By January of 2023, Nielsen reported that YouTube was the most popular streaming service viewed *on television*, besting all other streaming services like Netflix, Hulu, and HBOMax.[20] YouTube, like social media more generally, with its "user-generated content," shifts all roles of the culture industry, the entire division of labor it requires, onto individuals who are expected to perform previously distinct production roles. While this has often been thought of as "democratic," a major theme we've been noting so far is just how elaborate the production methods of contemporary influencers actually are—even though what was formerly a product of massive media conglomerates has today become a product of individuals, families, and small groups. When we look to the elite of influencer culture, the *cost* of these productions on YouTube and social media, shockingly, can equal or even exceed the amount of money spent by traditional film and television production. Instead of paying salaries for media professionals, this excessive cost is used to generate more, more, more, to generate constant waste, which appears as an "interesting" stream of commodities.

The highest earning "star" of YouTube in 2021 and 2022 was Jimmy Donaldson, better known as MrBeast.[21] Donaldson, at the time, was a twenty-four-year-old living in Greenville, North Carolina. Greenville is a city of around ninety thousand located about an hour east of Raleigh, the state's capital. Raleigh is one of three cities that make up North Carolina's "Research Triangle," a location known for its prevalence of universities and technology companies, a center of the "New South" and its varied investments in technology and finance. (In the next chapter, we will return to this specific location and the importance of the New South discourse today; like the opposition of Los Angeles and Springfield articulated in the *Beautiful Mess* videos, it exemplifies the implicit and explicit distinction between city and country in the work of many influencers.) Many of Donaldson's videos are filmed around Greenville and eastern North Carolina, using, for instance, East Carolina University's athletic stadium, or repurposing a fast-food restaurant in the town of Wilson to launch the massively successful MrBeast Burger delivery-only fast-food chain. While Donaldson got his start as a videogame streamer, today, across his numerous YouTube channels, he has more than 155 million subscribers, and his videos have accumulated more than seventeen billion views. The most popular of his videos are spectacular and gimmicky feats that involve him spending or giving away large amounts of money—"Anything You Can Fit in the Circle I'll Pay For," "I Bought Everything in a Store—Challenge," and "If You Can Carry $1,000,000 You Keep It!" The "MrBeast Philanthropy" YouTube channel features videos such as "We Fed Five Cities in 30 Days!" and "Giving $300,000 to Students,"[22] reframing the excess and waste of many of Donaldson's videos as charity. Perhaps the most extreme stunt of Donaldson's is his recreation of the popular Netflix series *Squid Game* (fig. 4).[23] While, at the time, the Korean television series was Netflix's most popular show ever, reaching 142 million households, MrBeast's YouTube recreation of the show reached 142 million views after its first eight days on YouTube. Netflix's show cost around $21.4 million to produce, which av-

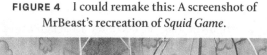

FIGURE 4   I could remake this: A screenshot of
MrBeast's recreation of *Squid Game.*

Source: Jimmy Donaldson (MrBeast), "$456,000 Squid Game in Real Life!" YouTube, Nov.
24, 2021, www.youtube.com/watch?v=0e3GPea1Tyg.

erages out to $2.4 million per hour of television. Donaldson's video, which
was twenty-five minutes long, cost $3.5 million, meaning that, minute-to-
minute, it cost more to produce than the show it emulated.[24]

The motivation and appeal of Donaldson's stunts appears simple: pure
excess. Cash is squandered, and every stunt must be larger and more extravagant than the preceding stunt. Donaldson's videos almost seem to
enact a contemporary form of potlatch—the Indigenous American term
appropriated by anthropologist Marcel Mauss in *The Gift* to describe a
total system of competitive, excessive giving and waste, where gifts serve
as a material means for marking social interrelation and social debt.[25] Yet
instead of a mutual exchange of gifts between two entities, gifts that get
ever larger and ever more wasteful, the only entity with whom Donaldson would compete would be himself. Rather than reciprocity, giving and
waste are unidirectional. Whereas the competitive, agonistic giving described by Mauss indicates a kind of relationship among equals, Donaldson's waste repeatedly performs his difference from—and as we will later
see, his control over—others. Whereas waste, as described by Mauss and
some of his followers, can be deployed to perform an egalitarian social
relationship—competition in the service of performing a mutual equiv-

alence and obligation, waste in the service of competitive sharing—what we regularly see when the market becomes a background for influencer culture is how waste becomes a means to highlight difference, to highlight the otherness of the influencer and, therefore, their existence as an "interesting" commodity to attract attention.

Donaldson's income from YouTube in 2021 was estimated at approximately $54 million, overtaking the highest earner for the previous two years, the ten-year-old toy reviewer Ryan Kaji.[26] Both Donaldson and Kaji's videos are archetypal of what we mean by the market as a background for influencers; their videos depend on the depiction of excessive exchange, excessive spending, excessive products. When we see Donaldson spending money, giving away countless things—which include not just cash but food, cars, and pretty much anything that can be commodified—we can tell that, in some way, his value as a broker of attention is worth far more than even the vast amounts of capital his videos require. Kaji, whose videos of toy reviews may seem to be entirely about evaluating and reacting to commodities, shows us something similar: that the spectacle of excess on YouTube gets attention, is "interesting." This also tells us something more about how the influencer, at least at the levels of people like MrBeast, Ryan Kaji, and Emma Chamberlain, has reinvented its past existence as an "influential" or "opinion leader."[27] As we mentioned in our introduction, influencers descend directly from a particular kind of person, one often identified in marketing and communications research, who was imagined as a holy grail of persuasion. Influentials, or opinion leaders, were important for brands, advertisers, and marketers of all stripes because they were more trusted by community members than ads were; influentials and opinion leaders could be more effective at moving messages and persuading everyday people than could the propagandistic mechanisms of the culture industries alone. This is, still, the logic behind most sponsored content on social media. Brands sponsor influencers because they seem more "personal" and more "intimate" than ads alone. But the spectacle of excess here indicates that the point is often not to market specific products—even though this marketing role cannot be completely discounted—but to keep people watching through infinitely *more* images, *more* objects, *more* waste.

GIANT EGGS OF CRAP

In January of 2022, shortly after MrBeast and several other YouTubers dethroned ten-year-old influencer Ryan Kaji as the top moneymaker on YouTube, the *New York Times* profiled Kaji in its magazine. Kaji is best known for his "toy videos," as the author of the profile, Jay Caspian Kang, describes them. In each video, Kaji is shown purchasing or receiving a new toy. He frees it from its packaging, and then he plays with it. These videos are a version of any typical unboxing video, almost all of which follow this same structure. Kang notes how the sheer popularity of Kaji—and the "toy video" more broadly—"has spawned many toy-video variants: Some feature adults; others, kids. Some have even been deliberately packaged to hide their true content from concerned, but perhaps less than vigilant, parents."[28] Kang wonders about the difference between allowing his daughter to watch videos of, say, *Peppa Pig* or *Paw Patrol* (which he does) and videos of children playing with *Peppa Pig* or *Paw Patrol* merchandise (which he does not). "What's the difference between watching the Anglophone silliness of Peppa, a show that exists only to sell toys, and a video of someone playing with the toys themselves?"[29]

Within the market of YouTube, while there exists a back-and-forth between consumer goods and their representation—all these videos are ultimately ads; the goal is to dictate and fixate the desire of the child on the purchase of a toy—what is truly being marketed on YouTube is the *act* of presenting *oneself* as an object of consumption, not the toys themselves. In his videos, Kaji is the product. He ceases to be a human boy playing with toys. He becomes a brand that exists over several YouTube channels, spilling over into merchandise and television content that make up "Ryan's World," raking in more than $250 million dollars a year for his branded merchandise.[30] *Peppa Pig* and *Paw Patrol*, the "content," the shows themselves, are manufactured by the culture industry and delivered to sell toys, to sell products. While the viewer's attention may be the product sold to the advertiser, the program nonetheless interpellates the viewer into the subject position of consumer,[31] desiring to buy commodities with the belief that these products will, in some way, satisfy. For those who watch Kaji play with the toys, the point of identification between the child at home and the child onscreen is less about fostering the desire to consume a particular toy than the desire to *become Kaji*—not Kaji in particular but a generic position where one's self-commodification renders one worthy of social relations or, more directly, worthy of *more*. The point of identification reflects a desire for a constant stream of commodities, where the fulfillment delivered by any specific toy is known, in advance, to fail. It's as if the lessons of Lacanian psychoanalysis and its interpretation of the death drive have been internalized in a particularly novel way.[32] The object itself, we seem to know from the outset, will inevitably fail to satisfy our desire, fail to make us whole again. What we really want is to perpetually desire; and the influencer, appearing against a background of waste, of a stream of endless commodities, is the realization of this desire. We know commodity culture will perpetually fail to make us happy; but we also know of particular kinds of people, particular kinds of subjects, who may never be satisfied but who always can get *more*.

One may object that Kaji's videos are, still, little more than ads to sell toys. If they weren't, then toy companies would not pay him and his parents to let us watch him play with toys. Yet the best example of how little these toys matter in his videos, how little the representation of specific material goods motivates his popularity as an influencer—the proof that Kaji's popularity depends so little on any singular, specific plastic monstrosity that children are seeing—is the video that first made Ryan Kaji a breakout star, a video from July 1, 2015. Kaji had, at the time, been making videos for several years, each showing him buying or playing with singular toys. This video, "GIANT Lightning McQueen Egg Surprise with 100+ Disney Cars Toys,"[33] which today has more than *one billion* views on YouTube, was his first foray into this consumption of excess, his first attempt at content as a stream of *more*, thus shaping himself into a consumable that is valued by how much he consumes. (We might add for specificity, Kaji did not do this himself. Kaji's parents did this. As a child, he had little to no choice in his own self-commodification.)[34] According to Kaji's mother, he wanted to take part in a popular YouTube video trend at the time, the "egg" video, in which someone would whack open a papier-mâché egg filled, ideally bursting, with toys. Yet, at this early stage in his career, Kaji's parents had limited how much he could spend on toys per week for his videos, so they loaded up the egg, covered in designs from Pixar's *Cars*, with old toys—plastic cars representing the characters from *Cars*, stuffed cars, and other cars that had nothing to do with the Pixar film. This video launched Kaji's meteoric rise to fame, and it never mattered what toys were in the egg, just that there were many of them, an excess to spill forth.

This video remains Kaji's second most popular on his YouTube channel today. On April 13, 2016, Kaji released another egg video, this time titled "HUGE EGGS Surprise Toys Challenge with Inflatable Water Slide," a video in which Kaji searches around an inflatable water slide in his backyard for multiple eggs, each containing toys from *Cars* and *Paw Patrol*.[35] The second video has accumulated more than *two billion* views, a truly staggering number approximately equivalent to the number of users there are on YouTube itself (which is also more than a quarter of the world's entire population). Kaji's videos usually rack up between one and twenty million views, with only a few surpassing one hundred million. The popularity of Kaji's egg videos, his most viewed by a significant margin, indicates precisely what we are suggesting: the true pleasure of these videos is in their representation of excess, in which constant, mediocre objects emerge from nowhere and are discarded for the next thing, videos in which it is the stream of more that attracts attention. These videos are "interesting" in the sense described by Ngai, though the interesting nature of the video is necessarily excessive. They depend on the spectacle of seriality, in which the "sale" of a commodity—a toy, in this case—is so much less important than the stream of objects, in which the real commodities produced are both the audience and the influencer who brokers their attention. The audience is commodified unconsciously, but the influencer works to become a commodity, to become worthy of exchange, worthy of interest.

In his *Times* profile of Kaji, Jay Caspian Kang searches for a specific meaning as to why Kaji's videos are popular. But his explanation focuses on the specific objects represented in the videos themselves—as if the toys were the point: "Why do children want to watch happy children playing with toys they can't have? Are they responding to the toys or to the images of a happy family? Are they envisioning a life they already feel may be out of reach? And at what age does aspiration turn into resentment? I imagine my daughter will grow tired of these toy videos when she learns to feel real jealousy, which I suppose is a good reason to hope she just keeps watching them."[36] Kang presumes the desire to watch is one in which the viewer experiences a vicarious fulfillment of desire that, nonetheless, leaves one

empty and desiring. The viewer watches, Kang suggests, because they want
what Kaji *has*. Yet, he admits, "there's something a bit unsatisfying about
this explanation," because, were it true, "the most popular videos would
show kids watching *Paw Patrol* on an iPad," a representation that recreates
what children seem to want to do with their time.[37] Our argument, however, is that what really invites attention is the stream of interchangeable
commodities—the spectacle of excess, the spectacle of more. The things are
merely a background against which the real commodity appears, against
which the real desire of the audience is directed: one desires to make oneself into something that can be sold, something that has economic value—a desire defined less through ownership, less through a desire fulfilled
by possession, than through a desire fulfilled by waste. Kaji represents a
subject—a subject interchangeable with a commodity—who emerges only
against an endless stream of wasted excess. The desire his videos represent
is a desire in which one can still be useful—to make money, to have a job,
in a sense—and in which once can endlessly squander. It is a desire for the
utmost luxury and yet a refusal of the true uselessness of the luxurious.

LUXURIOUS WASTE

On social media, images of excess are thus understood as *aspirational*. We
see images of extreme wealth, and we desire the things we see—things that
we cannot possibly afford, things that are beyond our ability to obtain.
Excess is something to aspire to. This is especially true with the main
predecessors of influencers like Kaji—excess, rather than framed entirely
as a constant stream of interchangeable objects, is *luxurious*. The link between excess and luxury is perhaps most obvious when it comes to influencers such as Jeffree Star, whose videos regularly feature expensive cars
and houses. They highlight costly haute couture and cosmetics. We see
videos of Star "Buying Myself a NEW $700,000 McLaren!"[38] "Trying the
World's MOST Beautiful Makeup,"[39] and even "Getting Rid of $1,000,000
of Makeup."[40] These are only a few of many videos in which Star revels
in extreme wealth and the pleasures of consumption that emerge from
having lots of money to waste.

YouTube videos reveling in excessive luxury—defined through the depiction of expensive, often gaudy, consumer goods, houses, cars, and so

on—descend from television shows like *MTV Cribs*. This show has aired sporadically over a wide range of media from 2000 to the present—most popularly on MTV but also on CMT and, briefly, on the social media platform Snapchat's "Discover," which promoted ad-supported, short-form videos from commercial media companies. *Cribs*, ostensibly a documentary reality television program, depicted celebrities showing off their houses and their belongings, a clear precedent for much of what we've been describing throughout this book. The explicit point of *Cribs* is the spectacular consumption not only of domesticity, of privacy, but of wealth and excess. The pleasure of *Cribs*, like the pleasures of Star's social media persona, like many of those we see reveling in wealth and luxury, would seem to derive from an aspirational desire to be wasteful, glamorous, excessive in the consumption of extremely expensive objects and experiences. One potential interpretation is that we watch these shows because we aspire to be like those we see—and not just to be, but to have the same things and to waste the same things; to treat personal belongings like they don't really matter, like they can be trashed without a second thought. We, too, want to be wasteful, to be excessive, to seem like we can live a life of glamour and luxury free from the apparent drudgeries of work, free from the disappointments of our own daily lives, free of the cares and anxieties that characterize the necessity of working to be paid. The potential of excess, of money, appears as that which fulfills the desire to be free of obligation to others and, perhaps paradoxically, to be free of the requirements of material possession.

Excess as luxury—and therefore a signifier of status, wealth, and social standing—has an exceptionally long history and, despite different interpretations of what excess and luxury might mean, never truly suggests a pecuniary freedom. In Veblen's *Theory of the Leisure Class*, especially its famous chapter "Conspicuous Consumption," excess and waste are necessarily articulated with bourgeois ideals of idleness and uselessness, in which the capacity to be wasteful, to be excessive, signifies class distinction and elite privilege—an idleness that must be properly maintained to perform aristocratic class privilege correctly. Being rich means not having to work, spending extravagantly without lowering oneself to the "indignities" of labor.[41] This vision of wealth manifests itself not only in the purchase of luxury goods for oneself but in events, in parties, orgies of excess whose social function is to perform class difference through waste and indulgence, performances designed to highlight and make visible one's proper location as a member of the elite:

> Conspicuous consumption of valuable goods is a means of reputability to the gentleman of leisure. As wealth accumulates on his hands, his own unaided effort will not avail to sufficiently put his opulence in evidence by this method. The aid of friends and competitors is therefore brought in by resorting to the giving of valuable presents and expensive feasts and entertainments. Presents and feasts had probably another origin than that of naïve ostentation, but they acquired their utility for this purpose very early, and they have retained that character to the present; so that their utility in this respect has now long been the substantial ground on which these usages rest. Costly entertainments, such as the potlatch or the ball, are peculiarly adapted to serve this end. The competitor with whom the entertainer wishes to institute a comparison is, by this method, made to serve as a means to the end. He consumes vicariously for his host at the same time that he is witness to the consumption of that excess of good things which his host is unable to dispose of single-handed, and he is also made to witness his host's facility in etiquette.[42]

The excesses described by Veblen are not only about competition through extravagance but about a competitive giving—the perpetuation of potlatch among the bourgeoisie.

The nature of extravagant waste, which for Veblen is evidence of bourgeois decadence and thus deserving of condescension, is also central for French writer Georges Bataille's arguments about waste and luxury. Instead of condemnation, Bataille places this kind of competitive giving, so criticized by Veblen, as essential for a kind of "communism" beyond an economy of monetary value. Bataille's "general economy," which proposes an economy not of capital, purely speaking, but of exchanges and flows of energy, elevates the squandering and destruction of energy, of resources, to the highest value; this squandering and waste is, for Bataille, the very principle of "luxury." It is impossible for economic exchange to maintain its efficiency; some aspect of economic energy is inevitably "doomed," inevitably wasted, in any act of exchange: "If a part of wealth . . . is doomed to destruction or at least to unproductive use without any possible profit, it is logical, even *inescapable*, to surrender commodities without return."[43]

Waste becomes evidence of a collective giving—again, the perpetuation of the potlatch relation. For Bataille, this "general economy" includes not only the giving of expensive commodities and goods but a range of experiences—many of which are transgressive and potentially extreme, such as non-procreative sex and human sacrifice—that lead to an inherently collective "wastefulness." Uselessness—wasting one's life and one's money, renouncing labor in favor of collective spending—becomes evidence of individual "sovereignty" that is nonetheless oriented toward collective existence rather than individual, competitive being.[44] The gift, even if seemingly competitive, is ultimately a waste that serves the greater whole through its expenditure.

Veblen and Bataille could be said to be dialectical counterparts, describing identical phenomena but coming to opposite conclusions. For both, the squandering of wealth and the wasted expenditure of energy and goods are essential for the luxuries afforded to all. For one, these wasteful luxuries are signifiers of class opposition and social competitiveness; thus, waste has a specific "use," a specific utility. For the other, waste is a universal human principle, an inherently collective experience of sovereign revelry, evidence of a uselessness that comes from sheer expenditure to the point of complete exhaustion of resources. How might this understanding of luxury and waste describe influencers and the backgrounds on which they appear? Or does the waste and excess of influencer culture demonstrate a radical reinvention of what both Veblen and Bataille suggest about luxury?

Alice Marwick describes the performance of luxury on Instagram with a description that could be said to characterize Jeffree Star:

> Luxury Instagram accounts function as catalogs of what many young people dream of having and the lifestyle they dream of living. Decoupling extreme wealth from fame, they pull back the curtain on lifestyles typically unavailable to and unseen by most. Notwithstanding the expectation that people on social media will be more "authentic" than traditional celebrities, who typically are separated from fans by a layer of managers and agents . . . this authenticity contradicts the photographic "truth" of an endless parade of luxury goods, in that it enables the audience to ask, "How can you afford that?" There *is* a difference between traditional celebrities and the highly followed. While most rich people

are not famous, and many famous people are not rich, income inequality is deeply obvious when the wealthy person is brought into intimate high definition through his or her personal pictures.[45]

Marwick's description of luxury and its relation to "Instafame" suggests a potential *illusory* performance of wealth, defined, in part, by an "endless parade of luxury goods" such as expensive cars, expensive fashion, expensive food, expensive travel. Star, throughout most of his social media career, faced constant questioning from fans, who could not comprehend his seemingly extreme wealth. Yet this emphasis on closeness, intimacy, and authenticity distracts from the key part of Marwick's quote, which is, we want to suggest, the *endless parade* of commodities. It isn't just that there is a specific instance of waste—or even that this waste is or is not genuine—but the representation of a potentially *infinite waste*. In this sense, Bataille hits on the essence of luxury and expenditure in a way that Veblen does not—that true "luxury" resides in the complete expenditure of *all* energy. Bataille makes it clear that there is only one limit point to this expenditure: death. The endless parade has only one end, which is the complete exhaustion of capital, of natural resources, of life itself. Because of luxury's necessity of constant, infinite waste, its only real outcome is total destruction. Simultaneously, Veblen understands that this expenditure, rather than a complete squandering, has a potential use: the visible display of class distinction and privilege. Showing, on Instagram or YouTube, deceptively or not, that one is excessive and wasteful is an act that *has value*. As one manufactures oneself as commodity, waste becomes a background out of which a saleable identity emerges.

Thus, it is through this double articulation that we must understand waste and luxury on YouTube. What we see in the market of influencer culture is a conjunction in which social class and distinction—the act of making oneself "interesting" and "different" and thus worthy of brand promotions and audience attention—is directly articulated to an embrace of wastefulness that only concludes in complete exhaustion, in death. This may seem an extreme conclusion, but this link between class distinction and death characterizes contemporary luxury more broadly. Luxury, in general, is a deeply questionable and contradictory concept, a word that derives from the Latin *luxus*, or "abundance." Its etymology suggests not only indulgence, but *"vicious* indulgence." A careful study of the history of what is considered "luxurious" at a particular time, John Armitage and Joanne Roberts argue, "offers productive grounds for a discussion of minds turned toward extravagance—the conscious pleasure in and enjoyment of rich, comfortable, and sumptuous living—and toward things considered luxuries rather than necessities."[46] Not all historical contexts share the same definition of luxury, and, for Armitage and Roberts, contemporary luxury is characterized by at least three contradictory dimensions that, as we see it, also characterize the contradictory dimensions of the market as a background on YouTube. First is the growth of a global "super-rich," whose wealth is often concentrated in royal families (those of Brunei, Thailand, Saudi Arabia, and Swaziland, among others) and the families of billionaires. This class of "super-rich" use their wealth to invest in hotels and contemporary art, among other "luxury" goods and services (Maybachs, McLarens, and Lambos, ornate and gaudy mansions, makeup and wellness products). Second, contemporary luxury finds everyday consumer goods branded as "luxury" items to indicate their commitment to "social responsibility" and "community." Third, contemporary luxury embraces the collapse and destruction of the world, reveling in excessive spending and waste, embracing the finitude of all life, with existence as such framed as a resource to use up and annihilate.[47]

On social media, aspiration (the desire to appear and live as if one is a member of the "super-rich") realizes itself in the contradiction between social responsibility and wasteful annihilation—a seeming synthesis of both Bataille and Veblen. Social responsibility, the second dimension of contemporary luxury, hasn't featured much in our discussion so far, but contemporary luxury "saves" itself by pretending that excess can be a social good, though the pleasure of luxury is one of total annihilation. Luxury is, in this context, the willingness to represent excess, to show excess—which, as we will see, is often deployed to strangely undermine the seeming "wastefulness" of luxury. There is a simple solution to this seeming "problem" of the visualization of excess and luxury, of the contradiction between extreme wealth, social responsibility, and the pleasure of annihilation—not the route taken by Star but one closer to people like Ryan Kaji and even Emma Chamberlain (at least in the videos described above). One must embrace the stream of excess as, from the outset, always-already trash, always-already garbage, always-already waste. This embrace, while seen in glimmers when Chamberlain unpacks her bedroom closet or when Kaji bursts open an egg filled with toys, becomes a central feature of another kind of video that begins with waste: the purchasing and display of the contents of storage units, of lost cargo, of Amazon returns. These videos, which begin with waste, operate under a pretense in which "garbage" is "saved" by the influencer. An alchemical reaction, the lead of other people's trash becomes gold—to be resold on peer-to-peer marketplaces like Depop or, at the very least, donated to a thrift shop for a tax write-off. This permits, on one hand, a view of excessive luxury as socially responsible but, on the other, necessarily relies on the belief that all physical commodities, in some way, start and end in a landfill.

WASTED LIVES

In a MrBeast video from December 1, 2017, we watch Jimmy Donaldson travel from his base in Greenville to Raleigh. The video is titled, "1 Bought an Abandoned Storage Unit and Found This . . ."[48] Donaldson and his crew are going to a storage unit auction (which, we hear, they were not allowed to film), purchase the contents of an abandoned unit (which, we hear, cost $350), and then show us, the audience, what was inside. That's it. That's the premise of this video, which has garnered more than thirty-five million views.

On entering the unit, Donaldson finds dozens of boxes of shoes, almost forty pairs, which he and his crew line up on the sidewalk outside of the unit, a virtual store aisle worth of product, an image reminiscent of someone selling knockoffs on Canal Street. "We just have so many [shoes] we don't care at this point," Donaldson says. He and his friends goof around with a hula hoop they find; they jokingly smash a printer to the ground for laughs; they make fun of some art left in the unit—an admittedly kitschy print of a child angel kissing a baby angel. They find piles of clothes, some in boxes, some in plastic bags. As they tear into the cheap protection for these goods, Donaldson asks, "Are these clothes worth anything?" This question, about the exchange value of the objects in the storage unit, as evidenced by the destruction of the printer, is ultimately meaningless. The value of these objects is beside the point. Value is eked from these material goods as Donaldson and his friends speak these words and record them, as they throw piles of seemingly worthless clothes (at least worthless to them) outside the unit, heaping them on top of the shoes, making an even more ludicrous display of excess and destruction (fig. 5). The video cuts to black and the words "ONE HOUR LATER" (a reference to the television show *SpongeBob SquarePants*) flash on the screen, showing the "hilarious" time their excessive haul has taken to go through. We, the audience, are enrapt by not only material excess but temporal excess as we watch Donaldson and his friends rip open box after box. We applaud the hundreds of used socks we are shown, the costume jewelry that these influencers throw at each other. We delight when they look up items on their phone, finding monetary values of the things they've purchased, the sale of which they will most likely never pursue.

Even if Donaldson throws all these goods in the trash, they have served the purpose of creating more commodities: those of content and identities. Even the destruction of these objects is valuable. Asks Jean Baudrillard, "*Does not affluence ultimately only have meaning in wastage?*"[49] And even

FIGURE 5 I could own this: Jimmy Donaldson displays goods he found in a storage unit he won at auction and the aftermath of his exploration.

Source: Jimmy Donaldson (MrBeast), "I Bought an Abandoned Storage Unit and Found This . . ." YouTube, Dec. 1, 2017, www.youtube.com/watch?v=yUXIx2l8kko.

more important, the more excessively objects can be wasted, the larger and more spectacular their destruction, the better the display of affluence. "At any rate," Baudrillard continues, "it is clear that destruction, either in its violent and symbolic form . . . or in its form of systematic and institutional destructiveness, is fated to become one of the preponderant functions" of our current capitalist order.[50] But Donaldson is, in a sense, not actually "wasting" these objects, at least not completely. Their wastage becomes a background from which Donaldson emerges as a commodity named "Mr-Beast," a commodity whose use of physical objects signifies his difference and distinction from the flow of things against which he appears.

As the video continues, a fact becomes inescapable: Donaldson and his friends cannot simply treat the objects they are unpacking and wasting as fully detached, alienated commodities. These objects refuse to reside completely in the background. The shoes, clothing, toys, jewelry, it becomes painfully clear, were at one point owned by *someone*. The influencers, in unpacking their unit, find dozens of debit cards. What better haul? What better content for our late capitalist society? Never mind these cards, inscribed with the name of a person unable to pay the monthly rental fee for their storage unit, bear witness to the precarity and tragedy of financialization and debt. The influencers find a series of business cards for shoe stores. The goods in the storage unit attest to a real life obscured through capitalist alienation mediated by commodities, mediated by spectacle. Donaldson realizes he is digging through the remnants of someone's life. "I feel horrible," Donaldson says while smiling. "I don't see how this is legal to just, like, steal stuff like this from people." It is only a brief commentary on the real implications of this video before Donaldson goes back to ripping open more boxes. The storage unit is a grave, a monument to loss and death indexed by the presence of so many, too many objects, all marked with the trace of one who couldn't afford to maintain the rent, who couldn't maintain the financialized relations on which their life was otherwise based. Yet we want to watch the exhumation of this grave of capitalist loss. At the end of the video, the influencers assess their excess and say they will give it away; it is all a tax write-off. This happens with two more units they have purchased. Repetition. The video ends with them driving to a thrift store; tax write-offs are discussed further. The property of another becomes tax-deductible waste, foisted onto a charity.

In this MrBeast video, we can see sketches of how the three-part understanding of luxury and waste above informs the market on YouTube—luxury as a signifier of elite class distinction, luxury as social responsibility, luxury as destruction. While the name-brand excesses of someone like Jeffree Star are nowhere in sight, the idea of class distinction is performed in the very setup of the video. Donaldson can purchase something that someone else has sacrificed as a result of their inability to maintain rental fees. The point is not in the specific value of any one object but in the appearance of many, many objects. Additionally, the destruction and wasting of these objects is essential. Neither Donaldson nor any of his friends need—or even can use—anything from the storage unit. But the nihilism inherent in this destruction, the pointlessness of the acts to which we are witness, cannot be fully embraced. Donaldson feels bad about the video, even suggesting that, in some way, these goods have been stolen from their rightful owner. Yet the video exists. This bad feeling is not enough to prevent this "theft" from becoming content, from these belongings becoming waste. Rather than total destruction, these objects are reabsorbed into a chain of circulation through their donation to a thrift store. Waste is made into a form of social responsibility—not a pure squandering—through the assumption that a donation means that these objects will return, in some way, to someone who "really" needs them. Regardless, the real product, above all, is the content, is MrBeast himself, is the promise of more to come in the future.

WASTED CARGO

The problem of MrBeast's foray into storage unit archaeology—objects inherently speak to the life of another; the abandoned storage unit is a grave, not an impersonal archive of complete disposability—is corrected in the videos of other influencers, such as those of Hope Allen, an influencer better known as HopeScope. Like Mia Maples, Allen is a moderately successful influencer who has, at the time of writing, around 1.3 million subscribers to her YouTube channel. Most of Allen's videos relate to her perfecting the kind of content MrBeast attempts above: lengthy unboxing videos of lost cargo, Amazon returns, Target returns, used clothing, and so on, all which Allen purchases without knowing exactly what she is buying.

Where MrBeast's attempt at purchasing an abandoned storage unit failed to embrace the impersonality of exchange, approaching, if not ultimately reaching, the acknowledgment that the "waste" in the video is not waste to all, Allen turns instead to objects and products more likely to be *corporate waste*. She thus begins with the implicit alienation of mass culture as a backdrop for her content.

Allen's most popular video, with around 2.7 million views, is from March 9, 2021, titled "I Bought Amazon RETURNS for CHEAP! *disaster*."[51] In it, Allen claims that she intended to buy a single box of Amazon returns, a box that, while still large, was small enough for an individual to pick up and carry. Instead, she found herself the owner of a 423-pound pallet, requiring a forklift to move (fig. 6). Allen discusses the auction website she used to purchase these returns; how, while she spent $575 on the returns, their estimated value was around $9,764. She discusses the expensive shipping costs to transport the returns, the listing of specific brands that led to her purchase (brands such as Lululemon and Adidas), the manifest that comes with each box or lot (which, she claims, she did not read; otherwise she would spoil the excitement and mystery of unboxing). She tells us, if without much detail, of the entire economy of returns and liquidations, of the rise of auction websites, of the potential profit that comes from this entire network of relations produced through Amazon's waste. "I'm pretty sure most all of us have, at one time, bought something from Amazon," Allen says. "When I send it back, I just assume that item got put back on the virtual shelf, but a lot of items end up in huge liquidation facilities, and then the website that I found this box on, it's someone who went to the facility and picked out all this stuff to actually run their own individual auction on."

Throughout the video, Allen unboxes things like Adidas jackets, an Ugg robe, Adidas leggings, a Calvin Klein dress, many of these items with tags and each of which is individually wrapped (most likely by the liquidation facility or auction website). But for every fashionable find, Allen discovers and unwraps many, many, destroyed, dirty, or otherwise unusable items. Some of the items smell horrible, some are flecked with body hair, some are wet and moldy. The impersonality of exchange is subtly questioned through abjection. The presence of other items is disgusting, a barrier to the resale and circulation of objects. Beyond clothing, Allen unboxes more

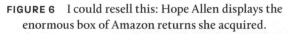

FIGURE 6 I could resell this: Hope Allen displays the enormous box of Amazon returns she acquired.

Source: Hope Allen (HopeScope), "I Bought Amazon RETURNS for CHEAP! *Disaster*," YouTube, March 9, 2021, www.youtube.com/watch?v=H_U29oAqsiw.

than eleven coffee makers, toys, furniture covers, pillows, a sous vide machine, and so on. She opens box after box after box, with dozens and dozens of items in each. Together, she claims, the many parts of her unboxed haul add up to thousands of dollars of random commodities. Nonetheless, most of what she finds is still junk, is still in poor condition. Allen keeps some of the items but ends up donating most of them. As with MrBeast's storage unit, the things found end up as a tax-deductible donation given to a thrift store.

Allen's videos—while they fail to undermine the logic of alienation inherent in commodity exchange—bizarrely feature their own infrastructural imaginary, in which the influencer regularly uses stock footage to represent the supply chains that permit her videos to exist.[52] "People are online shopping and mailing merchandise all over the world more often than ever," Allen tells us in a later video, from January 1, 2022, "which means more packages are getting lost and going unclaimed more often than ever . . . but liquidation auction warehouses and those wholesale bargain shops are popping up everywhere in our communities and online so we can buy that for a steal of a deal."[53] Allen states these lines over images of warehouses, cargo ships, and freight trucks, along with video appropriated from other influencers doing their own return-type unboxing videos in warehouses.[54] The HopeScope videos visualize and dramatize the real relations of shipping and returns required under the dominance of Amazon. This visualization is almost always framed pedagogically; the "point," supposedly, is to teach the viewer of potential profits to be made from waste squandered by contemporary capital. The "accursed share" comprising product returns—to use Bataille's name for the "part" of exchange that cannot be reabsorbed by the economy and is, consequentially, destroyed[55]—becomes, here, an innovative source for profit and income. What becomes waste began as waste. Of course, this is not the point of these videos. The point is to revel in this excess, revel in this waste. There is a tendency in contemporary media theory to suggest that the mere depiction of contemporary infrastructures of capital—server farms, shipping containers, cables and wires—performs a critical function that unmasks a hidden materiality of media, labor, and infrastructure obscured by the digital.[56] "Amid the complexity and, for the most part, illegibility of global finance, the infrastructure and economy of logistics serve as diagnostic devices," says Ned Rossiter. Foregrounding processes of shipping and logistics management are essential to understand the politics of contemporary technology.[57] We certainly do not disagree, but we would hesitate to suggest that this move is, in fact, either critical or even an "unveiling" of much of anything today. Allen's videos reveal that popular culture is, in fact, well aware of at least some dimensions of this infrastructural and logistical economy. *We just do not care*, or do not care as long as this economy underpins the potential to generate *more—more* waste, *more* content. Socially responsible, critical pedagogy is only an excuse to permit one to delight in economies of waste that are, otherwise, destroying the planet.

Despite her critical, pedagogical role of showing the infrastructural ground of contemporary logistical capital (fig. 7)—Allen remains interested mostly in how this infrastructural arrangement permits an opportunity to generate capital. Yet, at the same time, the *showing* of infrastructure permits a broad gesture toward the claim that she is, in fact, refusing the economy of waste implicit in contemporary shipping. In a video where Allen purchases around four hundred pounds of Target returns, she marvels at how everything she received appears new and, since a lot of the goods have clearance tags on them, were never sold prior to their liquidation.[58] Allen suggests that this is a way to "rescue" products from being trashed: "If you're in the resale business you could probably make a killing from boxes like this." But because she is in the *content generation* business, she cannot figure out what she is supposed to do with all these items. She makes snow angels in piles of secondhand underwear (fig. 8) and suggests that she'll make mystery boxes to sell on the resale website Poshmark for her fans. The ruse is that the influencer can "save" trash, turn it into excess, and then still waste it; but because the wasting of this trash takes the form of a donation, or a "mystery box" for fans, then it is not *truly* wasted but, instead, is reused, perhaps even "sustainable."

Safiya Nygaard is another relatively popular YouTuber (with more than nine million subscribers to her YouTube channel) who has several notable Amazon "haul" videos like those of HopeScope. Nygaard got her start making videos for Buzzfeed and is the source of some of the video repurposed in Allen's depiction of infrastructures—in part, because Nygaard is even more explicit about the specific infrastructural demands charted in these videos. Nygaard was based in Los Angeles until 2021, after which she moved to Raleigh, North Carolina (making some of her videos, like Donaldson's, a particularly strange charting of Raleigh's specific infrastructures of commodity waste). In "I Went to an Amazon Returns Store," from October 14, 2021,[59] Nygaard and her husband, Tyler Williams (another former Buzzfeed employee and YouTuber, who appears in and helps produce many of Nygaard's videos), go to an Amazon liquidation store in Raleigh named "Treasure Hunt Liquidators." There are shots of a large, generic, warehouse-like space filled with rolling table-sized bins, all of which are crowded with countless consumer goods, dozens of people digging in each bin, grabbing at these products, desperately finding an apparent "deal." The

FIGURES 7 AND 8 I could never use all this: Hope Allen discusses Amazon warehouses before making snow angels in a giant pile of returned items.

Source: Hope Allen (HopeScope), "I Bought LOST Cargo Packages for CHEAP," YouTube, Dec. 23, 2021, www.youtube.com/watch?v=AXv4Y87ocLY.

kinds of products represented are likewise excessively diverse: there are dog treats, drones, Christmas sweaters of a weight-lifting Santa. Of course, this diversity inverts into an indistinct homogeneity; "products" become a singular category of interchangeable items, not a series of truly distinct things. Nygaard describes and depicts the specific details of the cultural patterns this store has produced: the demand for the "best deals" relies on a particular temporal, weekly structure. On Wednesdays, an Amazon truck full of liquidated items arrives. Each truck drops between fifteen and twenty thousand items. On Thursday, the store closes for restocking. Store management discards trash and any obviously broken items. Management then performs a rough categorization and accounting of things that may deceptively appear to have been returned. (For instance, unopened Apple watches and computers are clearly the pride of the store owners, but often what appears to be a watch or computer is simply an empty box returned without the product.) On Friday, when the store once again opens, there is a long line. Camping out overnight seems to be required.

The Amazon haul video, in the form taken by Nygaard and Allen, is quickly becoming a concretized genre of influencer video. In a YouTube video posted to Nygaard's channel on June 25, 2022, she teams up with Allen to visit a lost luggage store.[60] The store buys vast amounts of assumedly abandoned luggage from airlines. Toward the beginning of Nygaard's video, she recaps her past videos in which she purchased Amazon returns and visited the Amazon liquidation center in Raleigh; she claims they are part of a new "alternative secondhand purchasing experience arena." Later, she refers to these types of videos as "hustle-tok ventures."[61] Rather than a critical revelation, the influencer shows these things to tell us not how to fix consumer spending and waste, not how to take action but, inevitably, how to profit and, more directly, how to transmute waste into content through the excuse of "charity." Nygaard distances herself from this "hustle" for profit; her point, she's suggesting, is *identifying* the rise of videos that depict new forms of internet-based entrepreneurialism. Her videos have little direct interest in explaining ways to hack or profit off resale. Yet her videos inevitably tend toward the educational, illuminating something about contemporary capitalism through the depiction of infrastructures, of waste, of landfills, without ever leading toward the larger implications of an economy based on the constant circulation of waste. There is no critical function to this infrastructural unveiling here, merely a palliative belief that one can be simultaneously wasteful and socially responsible. As Nygaard and Allen unbox their hauls, we can contrast them with the other people Nygaard depicts in her initial Amazon returns video, waiting for Treasure Hunt Liquidators to open. "I think with the rise of 'hustle culture' more and more people are interested in eBay reselling stores or just in finding really good deals," she says at one point. Picking through trash can be profitable, she seems to suggest.[62] Allen is explicit about this profitability at times. Yet neither Nygaard nor Allen—like Chamberlain above—rely on the profits from picking through and flipping trash. They merely start and end with waste, waste that appears only as a background against which the influencer appears as a commodity.

THRIFTING IN A WORLD OF WASTE

That the world is increasingly covered with an endless flood of waste is all too clear. The images and videos we discuss in this book are almost entirely North American and are thus somewhat isolated from the true global damage of a luxury that requires a steady stream of objects only ending at complete exhaustion. But the last decade or so has seen countless examples of popular journalism or contemporary art depicting the impact of consumer waste on countless regions across the globe. One only needs to look at an Edward Burtynsky print, or open the *New York Times*, or even watch a HopeScope video to see a depiction of waste and its damaging effect on the planet. Some of this damage is even done in the name of being "socially responsible." Senegal, a hub for plastic recycling, is covered in waste that never arrives at recycling centers. "Despite all of the efforts to recycle, much of Senegal's waste never makes it to landfills, instead littering the landscape," the *Times* reports. "Knockoff Adidas sandals and containers that once held a local version of Nutella block drains. Thin plastic bags that once contained drinking water meander back and forth in the Senegalese surf, like jellyfish. Plastic shopping bags burn in residential neighborhoods, sending clouds of chemical-smelling smoke into the hazy air."[63] Cajetan Iheka, in his book *African Ecomedia*, explores the impact of consumer waste via media production and discusses how the "promise of [media] infrastructure is undermined in Africa by the ecological consequences of its ruins," while also advancing an ethics for how these ruins might be represented via "alternative media practices suitable for an era of ecological precarity."[64] In one case study, Iheka explores Agbogbloshie, one of the largest e-waste dump sites in the world. Located outside Accra, the capital city of Ghana, Agbogbloshie, which was once a wetland area, is now occupied by laborers collecting scrap metal—primarily copper, which is harvested by burning automobile and electronic wiring. This makes the area both environmentally damaging and extremely harmful to work in. Iheka draws on Lisa Parks and Nicole Starosielski's concept of "infrastructural disposition," as well as on Mark Andrejevic's call to align online worker exploitation with the labor occurring in sweatshops and landfills to reimagine what immaterial labor may mean today.[65] Iheka writes:

> The manual labor that powers Agbogbloshie is crucial to the functioning of the global digital network and thus deserves to be understood as digital labor. . . . Digitality has always been associated with smart, geeky, labor, so it is easy to discount manual work that is nevertheless pertinent to digital processes. . . . This emphasis around being "on" the internet favors "immaterial labor." . . . It can easily overshadow the heavy and dirty work involved in electronic waste disposal and recycling. Furthermore, the location of Agbogbloshie in Africa, far away from the cities driving the current global order, contributes to its marginalization in discussions of the digital sphere and labor.[66]

Iheka suggests that classic theorizations of "immaterial labor," in their privileging of relationships, communication, and knowledge, must be expanded to include economies of waste and production in the Global South too often ignored.[67] We agree, though the videos of Nygaard and Allen, which demonstrate an awareness of the global supply chains necessary for their "content" to even exist, reveal how acknowledging the global interconnection of a wide range of labor is not nearly enough to combat the destructive effects of consumer waste. The many meanings of waste and the market as background open a space in which one can simultaneously be aware of the damaging excesses of contemporary capital, its reliance on global exploitation through waste, and also spectacularly consume the visualization of a constant stream of wasted objects. Knowledge is not enough because the drive for luxurious annihilation cannot be overcome through a "critical" unveiling in this context.

The knowledge that even attempts to recycle cannot fully do away with the "accursed share" doomed to waste is implicit in the visualizing of these global infrastructures of trade and shipping. Thus, we find influencers placing themselves in the very location that MrBeast and HopeScope deposit their waste: the thrift store. Even though none of those we've discussed throughout this chapter rely on reselling any of their waste for their own income, this also returns us to the very beginning of this chapter and Emma Chamberlain speculating about the value of her childhood belongings, were they to be sold on Depop. In 2019, 90 percent of Depop's users were under twenty-six years of age, and much of the platform's appeal seems to derive from a particular logic of social responsibility. Depop was acquired by Etsy in 2021 for $1.6 billion, specifically to target younger demographics.[68] In an article on Depop and thrifting, the fashion website Refinery29 interviewed notable sellers on the site, who all refer to the belief that thrifting is, in some way, socially responsible, an act that prevents clothing waste from ending up in landfills. One of those interviewed, Hannah Valentine, who runs the Instagram page @shopghostsoda, which focuses on the "handmade original pieces + vintage clothing" she has "curated,"[69] states that she started thrifting for its serendipitous thrill. But, today, she continues, "I thrift because I want to help save clothing from being thrown away, while also providing an easy and accessible way for people to shop secondhand so that they're not instead shopping on fast fashion websites."[70] Another Depop seller, Monique Miu Masuko, would seem to agree: "[Thrifting] is more affordable, accessible, and eco-friendly—all three of which go hand in hand with sustaining Gen Z's future."[71] In the *New York Times*, a high school student from Cary, North Carolina (a suburb of, again, Raleigh), notes that "I prefer thrifting to regular shopping for two main reasons: one, I don't want to give in to fast fashion, and two, I am very money-conscious. Thrifting is a wonderful solution to both dilemmas because it's usually very cheap and helps keep perfectly fine clothes out of landfills!"[72] Of course, the irony of Depop—much like the distinction between "vintage" and "thrift" stores—is that the products sold via these marketplace websites are expensive, and there is a premium charged for the labor of those willing to sort through the massive stream of waste and find specific objects to "curate."

This turn to Depop is an adjunct to everything we've discussed so far. The existence of the actual economies of peer-to-peer resale is parasitical on the existence of the massive, endless waste that is the expenditure of luxury. Thrifting, here, is "sustainable" or "environmentally friendly" because it manages to reabsorb some of the endless stream of waste and return it to economic circulation, to revalorize waste through a symbolic act of differentiation that refuses the commodity's subsumption into the endless stream. But these people we mention—Valentine, Masuko—are not influencers of the variety charted in this book. Their social media accounts are less involved in selling themselves as commodities than in literally selling the products produced through their labor. But this brings us to influencers such as Jenna Phipps. Phipps is probably the least followed of any of the major influencers discussed in this book (her channel has around 333,000 followers). She regularly posts videos about knitting, resizing clothing, cheaply renovating rooms in one's house. Phipps, for us, is particularly notable with her series of "Thrift with Me" videos, which feature the influencer going to a thrift store and purchasing clothes and home goods. These trips are inevitably paired with videos in which Phipps must clean out her closet, making room for more thrift hauls, selling her previous purchases on Depop or a similar peer-to-peer marketplace, like Poshmark or thredUP.[73]

Phipps's "Thrift with Me" videos follow a consistent structure. She begins with a set of shopping goals—a wish list, a craft project, or a room she wants to decorate—or explains that she is thrifting explicitly to make mystery boxes for her viewers. She visits several thrift stores, with most of the video shot in first person (fig. 9). Phipps pulls out items from clothing racks, shows them to us, discusses what she likes about them as her hand brushes over the fabric, points to the tag, the brand, tells us why she may or may not buy it. Sometimes the video moves beyond this first-person perspective, and we see Phipps in the shot holding her thrift-store finds up for our inspection (we must imagine she has a camera rigged to her cart). Phipps loads her cart up in store after store; then, if it is a clothing video, she will take us back to her house and try everything on, explaining her motivation behind her specific purchases. Sometimes Phipps doesn't even go home. She instead shows us her haul in her car, which sits in the thrift store parking lot, returning us to some of the themes from our last chapter. The phrase "Includes paid promotion" flashes in the corner of almost every one of Phipps's videos, which are often promotions for brands such as web design and hosting service Squarespace, the jewelry company Ana Luisa,[74] or the compostable phone case company Pela.

We are obviously in a different space than we have been in the earlier parts of this chapter. Nothing seems truly "wasted." The demand for *more* must be filtered through a seemingly contradictory demand to be "sustainable." Luxury, especially the luxury of total expenditure and waste, is seemingly prohibited. Yet the demand for luxury and excess inevitably intrudes. This might be in videos where Phipps shops for other people; these appear as any other "thrift with me" video except that the excess can be visualized because it is inevitably offloaded to a paying customer elsewhere.[75] But more often it is in videos where Phipps must clean out her closet, clean out her house, so she has more space for the things she purchases. She has several videos that deal with Phipps ridding herself "of half my clothes."[76]

FIGURE 9   I could reduce waste: Jenna Phipps
shows off clothes at a thrift store.

Source: Jenna Phipps, "Thrift with Me for Some Trendy Y2k Clothes \\ Thrifting Value Village in Vancouver, Canada," YouTube, Jan. 17, 2021, www.youtube.com/watch?v=l6Vo PXcJsxM.

The fact that there are multiple videos in which she must rid herself of so many of her belongings demonstrates how sustainability cannot truly conceal the economy of waste inherent in YouTube's market. In one of these videos, she tells us that "I have a lot of clothes that I've already accumulated and I'm only halfway done filming them, so I need to start getting rid of some of the clothes in here in order to get the clothes, you know, that I just thrifted in here after because there's no room for them."[77] The necessity of content—of the endless stream of commodities to attract interest, that the market must always contain more—is inevitable. "I just feel like they [Phipps's clothes] need a new owner, so I'll be putting them on my website and selling them." Sustainability becomes yet another lure obscuring the endless churn of market exchange, the endlessness of market potentiality, which requires more, more, more.

Phipps is not the only influencer to produce these kinds of "Thrift with Me" videos. They are made by people such as Lone Fox, a slightly more popular influencer who focuses more on home renovations than clothing, for instance.[78] The videos of Kim Ebrahimi include scenes in which the influencer throws many, many pairs of jeans into a cart and then tells us of selling them on Depop: "I had to get it and if I end up not liking it I can sell it."[79] Alexa Sunshine has a "Thrift with Me" video in which she attends a specific sale in Los Angeles, the Jet Rag $1 Sunday sale, a sale every Sunday in the parking lot of the vintage store Jet Rag,[80] depicting a chaos of bodies grabbing and clawing at specific garments.

Even Jeffree Star engages in some of these kinds of videos—well, not videos that depict Star shopping at thrift stores but videos in which he cleans out his closet. We don't see Star literally cleaning out his closet, but we do hear him complain about the problems of simply having too much stuff, about his need to physically and spiritually "cleanse." Star keeps his clothing in a "SECRET Black Vault" and, in a video in which he leads us on a tour of this clothing vault, from October 30, 2021, we hear him comment: "I can't believe how much stuff I have. . . . I almost feel embarrassed. No one ever put me in check . . . and it's no one's fault, it's my own . . . but this is a lot of shit, it's overwhelming. It's almost like another lifetime ago." This waste isn't just going to the landfill. Star tells us, "I've also donated a lot of clothes today to Goodwill."[81] The squandering of designer goods is inevitable, but the waste cannot be performed without some sense of social responsibility—of a philanthropic donation, of a gift that, unlike potlatch, signifies not a competitive equality but class distinction and difference out of a stream of interchangeable waste.

The occasion of the Black Vault tour is Star's brief return to Los Angeles, to his massive house in Hidden Hills, to retrieve his dogs before they all make their way to Star's ranch in Wyoming. Star apologizes about the lack of content on his channel during the pandemic while he's mostly been in Wyoming. But he's briefly returned to LA to "cleanse." "We're getting rid of things, we're cleansing before I move." "Excess" has become an issue. "This is obnoxious, no one needs this many purses. . . . I think before I move officially to Wyoming . . . I need to get rid of some bags. . . . I'm busy riding yaks, sucking dick, I don't have time for 1,000 purses anymore." But then Star admits that, perhaps, he is feeling like he should turn toward sustainability, too. "Now that I'm a Wyoming girl I wear Wrangler, things like that as well. It's nice to not always be in designer [jeans]. . . . It's cool to be in four dollar jeans now and cowboy boots and just like, laying in the field with animals." The uneasy articulation of wasteful excess and social responsibility, here, turns into a fetishizing of "heritage brands," clothing that will endure, will not wear out, will not be wasted.[82] But, of course, without waste there can be no luxury. And without *more*, without a market, there can be no content.

DEMONETIZED WASTE

What happens when objects refuse subsumption into a stream of infinite luxury, of infinite waste? Demonetization. The market on YouTube values exchangeability above all else. All objects must become content; all content must lead to more content, content to attract attention, attention that leads to an influencer's own self-valorization and exchangeability as a commodity with value. For a video to be *monetized*, attention, measured in terms of thousands, millions, billions, of views, becomes reason for the influencer to be paid. Monetization names the exchangeability of attention with money, in which the influencer has successfully been commodified, has successfully been valorized. Monetization says that yes, this influencer can be bought and sold on the market of YouTube, the market that may not appear onscreen but is the real process of exchange happening behind the scenes. Demonetization, then, names the moment that the influencer's exchangeability fails for one reason or another. As Robyn Caplan and Tarleton Gillespie describe it, the debate over monetization and demonetization is part of the economies and governance of the YouTube Partner Program, or YPP, which rewards particularly popular YouTubers with a share of revenue from the ads shown during these videos. But with inclusion in the YPP comes a set of often amorphous rules and regulations that an influencer must follow regarding the "acceptability" of their content to advertisers. "Demonetization is usually imposed as a penalty, for videos that violate YouTube's 'advertiser-friendly' content guidelines, specific to videos in the YPP; videos might also be demonetized when the terms for participating in the YPP change."[83] Demonetization is the moment that the market collapses: objects are revealed in their specificity; the influencer fails to individuate as an exchangeable commodity. Streams of capital venture elsewhere.

In Safiya Nygaard's "I Went to an Amazon Returns Store,"[84] one of the products found and purchased is an "herb and spice grinder." Nygaard, apparently, was under the impression that this product was, in fact, just a grinder for fresh or dried herbs. After doing a little research online, and after looking more closely at the grinder's packaging and instructions, she discovered that it was a product designed very specifically for grinding marijuana, along with easily filling and forming joints. "For this video's monetization sake," Nygaard says, "which is already hanging in the balance just by bringing this up, I'm not going to try it." Nygaard will tell us about the grinder but will not use it. Discussing products designed for drugs—and certainly, using them, even if not with any intended use in mind—is one way that Nygaard has found her videos either demonetized or threatened with demonetization. The influencer is subject to a set of moral judgments about proper and improper behaviors and content. The weed grinder exceeds the judgment of interesting and becomes too much, too different, too distinct. Another encounter between Nygaard and these operations of demonetization includes a lengthy livestream in which she and her husband, Tyler, are, as the video's title lets us know, "Testing Out More Bizarre Kitchen Gadgets from the Internet."[85] One gadget they try out is an automatic peeler, but instead of vegetables, they attempt to peel a mango, a twinkie, some cheese, some soap, and, most significant, a salami (fig. 10). In a pinned comment, Safiya informs us that this stream has been "demonetized (because of the sausage i think), so leave us a like & comment if you feel so inclined so we don't get suppressed in the algorithm!!" The sausage had been mistaken, it seems, for a penis.

And yet this video has not been removed, despite YouTube's apparent criticism of its content; it is still part of YouTube's algorithmic capture of attention that inevitably leads to the viewing of more video, of more content.[86] Demonetization, instead of removal, highlights how videos on YouTube are, really, owned and controlled by the platform, not by the content creators who made them. And more significant, demonetization is not about rendering videos nonexchangeable but *rendering influencers nonexchangeable*. Because the objects in the video—a weed grinder, a salami—refuse subsumption into an incoherent stream of waste, then the influencer as a commodity fails to emerge. The demonetization process is the complete accumulation by dispossession of the platform; it's in the interest of the platform to demonetize since videos still get attention, clicks, and views, but the platform doesn't have to pay, along with imposing a moral system of judgment enforced by algorithms.

FIGURE 10   I could get demonetized: Safiya Nygaard
and Tyler Williams attempt to peel a sausage.

Source: Safiya Nygaard and Tyler Williams (Safiya & Tyler), "Testing Out More Bizarre Kitchen Gadgets from the Internet," YouTube, August 10, 2021, www.youtube.com/watch ?v=k6YDStI9veI.

The market, then, must make every object an indistinct part of a total-izing stream, a stream that must endure and turn from the "sustainable" to the "luxurious" as we demand more, more, more. We've already seen how dealing with this excess leads to waste, to sales, to thrift-store donations and giveaways. And if one builds up a large enough business out of resell-ing things, then it might make sense to give up one's house and instead invest in a space for the storage and movement of this constant stream of waste. It might make sense to purchase and move into a warehouse.

FOUR

WAREHOUSE

Pennsylvania's Lehigh Valley, a region long known for manufacturing, has over the past several years been remade into a center for the shipping and storing of commodities. Increasingly crowded with warehouses and fulfillment centers operated by Amazon and other online retailers, Lehigh Valley is notable simultaneously for its proximity to and distance from New York City, roughly eighty miles away. Its famed industrial decline was once charted in popular songs like Billy Joel's "Allentown," which rhymes the name of the Valley's largest city with "they're closing all the factories down." Today, a local economy once representative of deindustrialization's destructive impact on the livelihoods of countless workers is now an exemplar of American capitalism's reinvention through shipping and logistics. With the rise of warehouses on the peripheries of urban centers, manufacturing has been remade into the circulation and storage of consumer goods.

So goes a narrative common among those who see shipping and logistics as a route to repair the late capitalist dismantling of manufacturing in the United States. Warehouses in Lehigh Valley—and throughout the United States—are representative of increasing American reliance on what anthropologist Anna Tsing terms "supply chain capitalism," an economic structure that is simultaneously "big"—meaning operating at a global, seemingly totalizing scale—but also reliant on linking heterogeneous industries, exploiting conflicts and differences that emerge from the sheer diversity of methods through which local practices are incorporated into the global economy.[1] Globalization does not merely "flatten" the world, as so many once seemed to argue, but produces a range of inequalities and conflicts in managing the entirety of production, a totality that includes mining and manufacturing, as well as shipping and storage. Of course, the uneven exploitation of global diversity in supply chains—which carries over and depends on the material legacies of colonization, as well as the structural determinations of patriarchy and white supremacy—could be argued as central to Ernest Mandel's theorization of late capitalism and its reliance on formal subsumption.[2] For some economic geographers, the tendency of capital to flatten and absorb all is limited by the empirical persistence of practices that remain beyond the boundaries of capitalism, properly speaking, providing hope for alternatives to capital.[3] But for Mandel, the constant creation and subsequent integration of that which is variably beyond the limits of capitalism is a necessary factor that grounds the formal—and eventually, real—subsumptions of capital, all motivated by capital's ability to perpetually save itself from crisis and collapse. In other words, capital produces economic disparity through its withdrawal from regions such as Lehigh Valley, abandoning workers to a life seemingly beyond the limits of capitalist exploitation and then "saving" these same abandoned workers through "new" forms of investment that subsume what capital initially placed beyond its own limits.

Thus, the warehouses of Lehigh Valley reveal two linked but distinct transformations. For one, they represent the centrality of *logistics* in contemporary capitalism, the measurement and tracking of objects as they move across the globe. As the architectural theorist Jesse LeCavalier tells us in his book on the logistics of Walmart, the materiality of production on which contemporary retail relies unites a "territory" that links a range of "depots, warehouses, and distribution centers that enable the movement of material in time and space."[4] These spaces are made up of massive, mostly open, buildings designed for the temporary storage of raw materials for manufacturing and consumer goods. Warehouses are linked with roads, airports, trains, and ports, all designed around the perpetual global circulation of material goods. But additionally, these warehouses demonstrate an essential feature of what Mandel identified—drawing on the arguments of Latin American and African Marxists—as the cultivation of imperialist "dependencies."[5] Through varied extractive logics of exploitation, capital can impoverish particular geographical areas and then pretend to "save" these very same areas with the promise of "development." While Mandel mostly examined how this power relation exemplified imperialist economies of domination between Global North and Global South, he also made it explicit that, through automation, deindustrialization, and the flight of capital, "underdeveloped regions within capitalist countries, just like the 'external colonies,' thus function as *sources of surplus-profits*."[6] In other words, late capitalism relies on the promise of reintegrating geographic regions either decimated or left "undeveloped" by previous waves of capitalist production and extraction. The building of warehouses in Lehigh Valley is not only a result of the centrality of logistics and shipping to contemporary capitalism; it is also because deindustrialization left a surplus population willing to work for lower wages, without meaningful guarantees of rights for workers.

Even though the rise of shipping, logistics, and storage is framed as a way of "saving" regions devastated by deindustrialization, it's not like these warehouses are equivalent to what preceded them. As the *New York Times* reports, warehouse jobs replace industrial manufacturing—along with the hard-fought union contracts that characterized the idealized Fordist factory—with precarious, low-paying, nonunion jobs, jobs that are physically demanding and, in the minds of many employers, are potential targets for future automation.[7] Working in a warehouse is difficult, exhausting, soul-sucking labor. Warehouse labor has a higher injury rate than notoriously dangerous jobs in coal mining, construction, and logging.[8] Horrifically exploitative relations of labor, obvious when a warehouse is used following the assumptions of supply chain capitalism, are, like everything else, documented on YouTube, emphasizing how awful it is to work in a warehouse—primarily focusing on Amazon. This genre of YouTube video isn't particularly popular, at least in comparison to much of what we document in these pages. Yet during the time we spent writing this book, the number of these videos expanded, along with the number of views each has accumulated. These videos are made by people who *aspire* to be popular YouTube influencers, leaving their warehouse jobs behind for the luxury of influence; lamentations about warehouse labor are relayed after we're told to like, comment, and subscribe. Even first-person denunciations of the dehumanizing conditions of contemporary capitalism must be delivered through a means to maintain the commodification of the self.

In these videos, we hear influencer hopefuls tell us about warehouse work and the promise of relatively decent wages—pay that, for a little while, legitimizes constant, mindless repetition, resulting in long-term bodily injury. Most of those who appear in these videos are nonwhite, in stark opposition to the homogeneous class and racial makeup of the most popular YouTubers, a detail that betrays the white supremacy inherent within the platform, social media, America, and the world writ large. We hear of relentless surveillance, of long hours that absorb all leisure time, of infantilizing and unserious "incentives" to maintain morale, like pizza parties and cupcakes,[9] of punitive punishments and rules designed to isolate workers from family members and from each other, of burnout and exhaustion.[10] We hear how the pay, which may be enough to excuse this terrible work for a month or two, conceals the sheer damage warehouse work inflicts on one's entire existence. One creator of this kind of video, Anthony Bender, who posts on YouTube as Ayebender, tells us, "When I started, I was like, 'Oh, man, I'm getting *bank*, I'm making *money*, you know?'" After several months, Bender began to realize just how repetitive and dull the work was, how he was forced to constantly work long hours. He thought he couldn't quit, though, because he was making more money in his warehouse job than he had in any job previously. "It would kill me every day to go in there, like I would dread waking up. . . . It's taxing on your body, it's taxing on your mental health. You're just a robot to them."[11] There are videos that provide tips for how to survive and thrive in a warehouse job, delivered by people who have managed to leave the warehouse life behind.[12] There are videos that aspire to tell us the positives and negatives of working at Amazon, delivered by someone who has been on the job for a few months.[13] There are videos that surreptitiously document a day in the life of someone who packs Amazon boxes for shipping, visualizing the interior of an Amazon warehouse even when the phones and cameras of workers are generally banned.[14] We can watch videos telling us of

constant, excessive hours worked, of a lack of overtime, of how warehouse
work breaks down the body physically and mentally, how it consumes all
of one's time, how it obliterates one's will to live—to such an extent that, in
one video, warehouse work is repeatedly described as "Hell on Earth" and
compared to slavery.[15]

For some of these videos, the message is clear: the warehouse is a space
from which one must *escape*. It should be work that is, at best, temporary,
though comments responding to any one of the videos referenced above
include post after post from people who have been stuck in their warehouse job for decades, affirming the stories relayed in the videos, agreeing
with tales told of the mental and physical exhaustion wreaked by the warehouse. From a simple look at these videos, we know that the warehouse has
little in common with the Fordist factory and even less in common with the
assumed norms of post-Fordist immaterial labor and "creative" forms of
capital. Late capitalism, in a warehouse, presumes that the worker is completely expendable, a body to use up and burn out as quickly as possible.
Those who work in a warehouse are treated as members of a future surplus
population, bodies to leave behind once the potential of exploitation has
been exhausted. The "lucky" can, if these videos are any indication, escape
from the boundaries of the warehouse and enter into a different factory, a
different system of production intertwining late capitalism, one that relies
on the illusion of luxury for a different kind of exhausting and exploitative
labor. Sometimes, we will see, this involves remaking the warehouse itself.

The warehouses in Lehigh Valley have restructured a major part of
the geography and built environment of eastern Pennsylvania according
to the demands of supply chains, the demands of shipping. Roads have
been widened to deal with additional trucks moving in and out of the area.
Land that was formerly used for residential, commercial, and agricultural
purposes is now filled with warehouse after warehouse, crowding out the
people who have lived in the Valley for decades. And the rapid construction of *so many* warehouses has also resulted in a strange contradiction:
although new construction emerges from a shortage of warehouse space,
in which the turn to online shopping (particularly during the COVID pandemic) has shifted retail toward spaces like the warehouse, many of the
new warehouses in Lehigh Valley remain at least partially empty, leading
to fears of a construction bubble.[16] Beyond the Valley, of the 190 million

square feet of North American warehouse space built in 2020 alone, 43 percent was supposedly preleased, and, by some estimates, the United States will need an additional one billion square feet of space by 2025 just to keep up with demand. In places like Lehigh Valley, this has resulted in residents feeling like residential space is increasingly becoming warehouse space, crowding out other possible uses of land.[17] The warehouse, quite literally, subsumes all other forms of activity—economic and noneconomic, capitalist and noncapitalist—in Lehigh Valley. Yet there is an instability in imagining the future of these spaces. Is there too little warehouse space or too much? After people decide that the pandemic is over, returning to their prepandemic daily routines, will the appeal of online shopping decline, resulting in an overabundance of warehouse space? What is lost when warehouses come to dominate acres upon acres of the American landscape?

The warehouse is our final background, one that reveals something particularly contradictory about the rise of supply chain capitalism, logistics, and the centrality of warehouses in contemporary capitalist life. On YouTube, the warehouse exists not only as a space of employment, not only as a physical space to store influencer excess—a place to hold objects, commodities, and things—but also as a rhetorical space not so distinct from the logistical view that understands space as a barrier to the free and rapid movement of physical goods in circulation. To some extent, the glimpses we've seen inside the warehouse thus far rely on inevitable inefficiencies in supply chain capitalism, inevitable moments that a capitalism organized around the global movement of goods breaks down.[18] The videos of HopeScope and Safiya Nygaard, unboxing or testing out Amazon returns, necessarily lead us toward the logistical infrastructures of supply chain capitalism. When these videos begin to visualize supply chains—depicting cargo ships, forklifts, and boxes on pallets, all of which contribute to the excesses of the market—influencers inherently draw out the "accursed share" of the supply chain; their videos focus on the waste that, otherwise, would not be reabsorbed into circulation or production.[19] Allen and Nygaard are, in a sense, parasites of supply chain capitalism, producing content from the inevitable noise and inefficiency in the transmission of a product from one place to another.[20] This is, of course, part of the nihilistic "luxury" of waste described in the previous chapter—ashes to ashes, waste to waste. The *more* of the market needs the supply chains to keep moving.

Yet, at the same time, in influencer culture the warehouse regularly serves a role closer to that of the garage, at least when we described the garage as an "any-space-whatever," a "perfectly singular space, which has merely lost its homogeneity, that is, the principle of its metric relations or the connection of its own parts, so that the linkages can be made in an infinite number of ways. It is a space of virtual conjunction, grasped as pure locus of the possible."[21] As a background of influencer culture, the warehouse shifts from a space of storage and logistical coordination, often on the margins of urban centers of technology, entertainment, and finance, to a space that can become an office, a space of spectacle, a space that replaces the domestic interior of the home. In influencer culture, the warehouse is the point where home, car, and market converge. If warehouses, through an imagined potential of shipping and logistics as organizing features of American capitalism, continue to reshape and dominate the built environment of the United States, their locations chosen due to their simultaneous proximity to and distance from urban centers, then, for influencers, an appropriation of the warehouse makes it into a space for packaging and selling oneself as a commodity. The warehouse is a background that can transform anything into a shippable object to be sold. While the "content" of the warehouse is, in many ways, undetermined, its "form" is necessarily about converting whatever it holds into a commodity in circulation; anything can be content, as long as *content* is a synonym for *product*. We can see this contradiction at play when the workers exploited by supply chain capital document their experiences to become influencers. The warehouse depletes and exhausts, but it also provides a background for content in which one can attempt to package oneself for consumption. More directly, we can see the formal role of the warehouse when various ultrarich influencers intentionally and unintentionally represent the warehouse as a background for their wealth, for their most elaborate and most excessive stunts, and in doing so capture more views than the workers attempting to expose dire information regarding exploitation and unsafe conditions.

The remainder of this chapter examines two influencers who have been mentioned throughout this book but, for the most part, not examined in depth. First is the massively popular and controversial influencer and makeup magnate Jeffree Star; second is the most successful YouTuber of 2021 and 2022, Jimmy Donaldson, better known as MrBeast. We will first discuss a series of videos in which Star revealed many of his Los Angeles–based investments in the manufacturing and distribution of cosmetics and celebrity merchandise and, following his eventual "cancellation," moments that document how Star purchased and fled to a ranch in Wyoming. Star reveals how the warehouse can serve as a space central to supply chain capitalism, as well as a space of content production—a space in which the real commodity is the "self" to be sold, a "self" that is used to mobilize physical commodities held in warehouses. Star is, in many ways, a very traditional capitalist, though his online persona leads one to think that he is merely one influencer among many, many others, immaterially laboring under contemporary capital like anyone else. Star has perpetually worked to differentiate his business of himself—his crafting of an identity for the purpose of attention—from his business of manufacturing and shipping, obscuring his economic activities to maintain his personal economic security. We then turn to a discussion of MrBeast and the elaborate, expensive sets produced within a warehouse he owns. Unlike Star, who sees the warehouse as relatively distinct from the home, who sees his businesses as (somewhat) independent of his brand as an influencer, MrBeast embraces a complete conflation of self, business, home, and warehouse. The warehouse, as an archetypal background of influencer culture, *replaces* the home and garage in videos where individuals renovate and live in warehouses, where warehouses are purchased and remade as locations for excessive videos recreating scenes from film and television, spaces for large-scale stunts that cannot be filmed elsewhere. The turn to the warehouse signifies a complete collapse not of home and office, of public and private, but of person and commodity, person and corporation. The warehouse, in influencer culture, is where a space for the storage of commodities becomes a space for the production of "people" who are, at this point, themselves commodities to be sold, stored, and shipped.

THE INFLUENCER AS MANUFACTURER

The YouTube series "The Secret World of Jeffree Star," from 2018, comprises five separate parts that, in total, amount to around two and a half hours of video.[22] An entire feature-length production on YouTube, "The Secret World" presents itself as a documentary designed to show the intimate personal life of influencer and makeup mogul Jeffree Star.[23] Star first came to prominence in the early 2000s as a somewhat goth, queer MySpace musician and self-made makeup artist from Orange County, with photos and songs posted to the platform, gaining him a large following on early social media. Star's popularity on MySpace placed him in the ranks of similar social media celebrity pioneers who crossed over from their online popularity into deals with record labels and MTV—many of whom are now mostly forgotten, such as Tila Tequila, or are nostalgic remnants of a very specific MySpace style and image, like the band Millionaires. This early period in Star's career culminated in the release of the 2009 studio album *Beauty Killer* through a subsidiary of Warner Music Group, an album that featured a guest spot by Nicki Minaj and made its way onto the *Billboard* 200.[24] After his music career came to an end—which, Star claims, left him essentially bankrupt—he founded his makeup brand, Jeffree Star Cosmetics, in 2014. As MySpace collapsed and platforms such as Facebook, Twitter, and Instagram came to prominence,[25] Star moved to these newer platforms, successfully continuing his role as a popular internet celebrity known not only for videos about makeup and beauty but for bullying, harassing, or otherwise instigating conflict with other influencers, reality stars, and musicians.

The very existence of "The Secret World of Jeffree Star," along with its substantial running length, was motivated by a desire to explain Star's apparently "uncancellable" existence. Even in instances in which Star was heavily criticized for something he said or did—acts overtly racist or sexist, acts intended to belittle or harass—it never seemed as if he had to seriously contend with any consequences, or, at the very least, he never seemed to care about consequences. (These consequences primarily take the form of, for instance, people unsubscribing on YouTube or unfollowing on Twitter, being demonetized by YouTube, consequences addressed with the de rigueur tearful, staged apology videos of an influencer groveling to maintain their livelihood, begging fans to believe that they've learned their lesson, that they've changed, that they've grown. . . . The most significant consequence, though, comes from a loss of brand collaborations, where branded products are simply pulled from shelves.) Star has never seemed concerned with addressing popular outrage or criticism, at best half-heartedly tweeting about "regrets" in response to criticism, using copyright claims to get controversial videos removed from YouTube.[26] But neither has he collaborated with a brand in a way that would cause him to worry about the loss of a deal. As we will soon discuss, Star has always been in control of his own products and merchandise, not beholden to a larger producer to add his name to a line of existing products—a fact he often discusses as vital to his success. One of the few moments in which he did address the many criticisms of his past, the many attempts to "cancel" him, was in a YouTube video from 2017 titled "RACISM."[27] Yet, in this video, Star does not cry and does not apologize for his past actions. Instead, he distances his present self from his past one, suggesting that criticisms for past actions are motivated by people desiring to take him down, wishing him ill. He emphasizes his self-made existence and, in terms of the temporality of the internet, his exceptionally long career.

In his refusal to apologize, his refusal to grovel to his audience, Star consequentially has appeared more "free" than almost any other influencer, as if his brand has been magically immune to market dictates that equate personal value and number of followers, dictates that demand acquiescence from the outrage of the audience. Prior to widespread hysteria around "cancel culture" perpetuated by figures on the political right and "moderate" classical liberals who, with their self-righteous indignation about the "collapse" of liberal ideals, fret about the apparent intolerance of online masses, Star seemed to be unique, completely beyond this entire moral economy and the insincere rituals it produced. Many of those with whom Star regularly associated—other YouTubers such as beauty influencer James Charles and comedy-and-conspiracy-theory YouTuber Shane Dawson—had engaged in the seemingly obligatory, falsely performative influencer apology video, confessing to past misdeeds after endorsement deals were lost, branded products were removed from stores, and the attention of fans dissipated. (Of course, even listing a few of the people here who were "cancelled" at some point indicates the sheer absurdity of this term or, at least, the absurdity of the panic over its imagined effect on "free speech." Charles and Dawson remain, remarkably, in the public spotlight on YouTube and other social media platforms. After brief periods when YouTube demonetized Charles's and Dawson's channels, for sending nude photos to underage boys and for perpetual racism, respectively, both returned to YouTube in 2021.[28] In 2020, after initial allegations against him became public, Charles was host of a YouTube Originals series titled *Instant Influencer*, in which he and guests such as Paris Hilton judged contestants on their ability to market and sell beauty products.[29] Charles's channel has more than twenty-four million subscribers at the time of this writing, and Dawson's has around twenty million.) Even though fears of "cancellation" are vastly overblown, at least for those mentioned here, it is obvious that people like Charles and Dawson are concerned with the maintenance of their audience, essential as it is for maintaining their value as influencers. Star, in contrast, has never really appeared to be concerned in the same way, making him a seeming anomaly of influencer culture who either does not have to—or is merely unwilling to—engage in rituals of public shaming and apology.

Star has also long contended with skepticism from fans and haters that his apparent wealth was a front, that his "luxury" was a ruse, that he was somehow duping us all. Obviously, influencer culture is rife with scammers pretending to be rich. Images of wealth and useless luxury, images of waste, are a means to generate and attract attention. Most of those presenting themselves as rich are, in fact, not rich at all.[30] The belief that Star has merely been scamming us with his seeming opulence is, of course, understandable, when a major assumption of influencer culture is that there is something about *them* that is like *you*, that they are *relatable*, that their lifestyle is not merely desirable, but *obtainable*. Star's story—of emerging from early social media fame through his user-generated content of sound and image—is an archetype of the most extreme Horatio Alger story of influencer culture. Star emerged from poverty and leveraged the early openness of MySpace into fame. Multiple times, Star claims to have started from the bottom—from bankruptcy, from the margins of the Los Angeles entertainment industry[31]—to become the ultrarich, glamorous celebrity he is today. A particularly cynical (but generally accurate) view of social media celebrity and influencer culture is that, for those seeming to be most wealthy, the houses and cars we see are rentals, the likes from audiences are purchased, the subscribers are bots, and the excess we see requires taking on debt. Accepting Star's story relies on the belief that his image is truly self-made, that moving from poverty to extreme wealth through one's own creativity and intelligence is possible today.

"The Secret World of Jeffree Star" was intended to both delve into Star's background and to demonstrate that Star genuinely is as rich as he presents himself as being. And we do get an answer for why Star was, for a while at least, seemingly unable to be cancelled. In the first video of the series, Star says that, by the end of the series as a whole, "You'll see a whole other side of me that people don't really get to see."[32] This series, Star intimates, will be a document of Star not only as an influencer but as a *capitalist*—as a manager, not a worker. It will depict him as someone who speculates on real estate—not just glamorous houses but warehouse space and retail space he rents out to others. It will show him to be an investor—not just in makeup but in at least ten other industries. Star's difference from other influencers, his seeming immunity to criticism, emerges from the material reality of his existence as an investor in business, as someone who does not rely on attention as his primary source of income:

> I love investing, that's my thing, I'm a businessman . . . no one really knows the real tea. I think . . . people don't really understand the full spectrum of what I actually do. I think people just think I make makeup and just do some videos and that's my life . . . I own property, investment properties around the world. I invest in the marijuana business. I own an entire shipment fulfillment center. I mean, I own a merchandise company—I print, manufacture everything myself. I have about ten businesses that I'm currently running besides my brand which is the giant cosmetics company. People don't really know about it because I don't talk about it because I don't think it's exciting, I don't think people are going to want to watch or see it.

There are multiple points in this quote that should be drawn out. First, we've heard much of this logic before, an explanation or deferral which differentiates and legitimizes what is visible to audiences and what remains invisible. When Mia Maples obfuscates her living situation, for example, when she only reluctantly shows us her elaborate production techniques, she suggests that the audience will find it *boring*. Star, similarly, explains that the reality of his life is not truly glamorous, not truly what he depicts over social media. Most of his life, he suggests, is *boring*. The camera captures only what is interesting, that which marks Star as worthy of attention along with his necessary, if minimal, difference from other influencers.[33] The dialectic here, however, is not just about content that may be attention-worthy and that which is not but a difference between the minimal interest of the social media feed and the revelation of details that are, in fact, *fascinating*. In allowing Star's "Secret World" to film his business and corporate strategy, the series revels in this seeming mundane "boringness," showing how it is, in fact, a boringness that is not at all boring. In turning away from "interesting" content, Star shows that he sees himself not as an influencer, properly speaking, but as a manager of a vertically integrated conglomerate, which covers media, real estate, cosmetics, marijuana, clothing, and more. Star's brand is *a* business, but not *the* business; in fact, Star's image should be understood as one product of the broader Jeffree Star media and manufacturing empire. We should imagine Star not in the mold of those with whom he associates—James Charles, Shane Dawson—but of Martha Stewart, of Oprah Winfrey. He is like those people who are owners and CEOs of multinational conglomerates, as well as being the public face of many—but not all—of their operations. Star cannot be cancelled, at least in the way that Charles and Dawson can (temporarily) be (pseudo)cancelled, because he is not a precarious worker laboring under the same conditions as other influencers.

The second point we want to draw from this quote, which is a point we'll return to, is that Star conflates the activities of his businesses with himself. The production of makeup, the manufacturing of products— these are framed as things that Star, personally, does himself. This is a contradiction: Star wants to equate his business with himself but, simultaneously, maintains a distance between the two in which "he" is merely one product sold by his business as a whole. We are seemingly left with a synecdoche in which part and whole continuously oscillate. Is Star (the "brand," the "image") a part that appears, standing in for the whole of Star's business? Or is Star (the person, the capitalist) the "whole" that unifies and effectively *is* all the different corporations and investments for which he takes credit?

Even though Star demurs, suggesting that his role as a corporate CEO and not a beauty influencer is *boring*, a judgment we have already noted as deeply questionable, he nonetheless agrees to take the video's host—and any viewer watching on YouTube—into a space previously undocumented in videos of people we have hitherto believed are like Star himself: we see inside not his house, not his car (though the series is filled with both backgrounds), but his warehouse. We are told that the warehouse is around thirty thousand square feet, occupies multiple buildings, and has roughly 105 employees. We're told of the rapid growth of Star's cosmetics brand, how he's had to expand his warehouse space to keep up with demand. We're shown that his warehouse is not only for his makeup business but for products shipped to other influencers, and even for other media industries, such as shirts and sweatshirts made and marketed through the brand Killer Merch, which Star claims he owns. These other influencers and businesses serviced by Killer Merch are not identified directly in "The Secret World of Jeffree Star" but are often very prominent and today still include some of the most obviously "cancelled" celebrities and influencers around, indicating Star's willingness to underwrite even the most unseemly and disreputable. Killer Merch lists among its clients the massively popular game streamer Ninja, comedian Kevin Hart, and Netflix, manufacturing and distributing branded clothing related to the television show *Stranger Things*.[34] But it also works with the comedian Chris D'Elia, who has been regularly accused of predatory and pedophilic sexual behavior, most prominently the perpetual soliciting of nude photos from underage girls.[35]

It's difficult to know how much we should trust Star's account of what he owns. While he is, certainly, CEO and co-owner of his cosmetics company, early Articles of Organization for Jeffree Star Cosmetics LLC, filed in California, list Star as co-owner, along with two other individuals with whom he shared ownership at the time: Ashely Avildsen, founder of emo and alternative rock label Sumerian Records and, today, film director; and Jeffrey R. Cohen, an intellectual property lawyer, formerly publisher of the music business trade publication *MusicBIZ*, with the law firm Millen, White, Zelano & Branigan, PC, an international firm that specializes in patent, trademark, copyright, and entertainment law.[36] The narrative that Killer Merch, as Star says in "Secret World," came from "a few friends" of his, transforming into a business in which "we ship a lot of people, a lot of people you would recognize," generally rings true, though it obscures how these "friends" include an entertainment industry lawyer. Star's name is not on the documents for Killer Merch LLC,[37] though it is difficult to trace precise ownership of these corporations based on these documents alone. Avildsen, as of 2018, is no longer a part owner of either Jeffree Star Cosmetics, which was incorporated in 2017,[38] or Killer Merch. Recent filings from California list Mark Bubb, the chief revenue officer (CRO) of Jeffree Star Cosmetics, as the co-owner of Killer Merch.[39]

The main point we're making in documenting the ownership of Jeffree Star Cosmetics and Killer Merch is simple: Star is one of several individuals involved in building a significant corporate structure that is intentionally hidden from the view of his audience, a corporate structure that only begins to become evident when Star's warehouse comes into view. Even though, in "Secret World," Star claims that he *is* these businesses, taking some form of public responsibility for all their operations, he is one of a small group of people who maintain ownership and control of a shifting and shadowy group of loosely connected LLCs. Star is distinct from his businesses, though—like we saw in the past with the suturing of image and person, of person and property. Star attempts to both legally and publicly veil his many companies while at the same time rendering them visible as a signifier of excess, of wealth. And this public obscurity is not just in terms of what is visible on YouTube. Through the limitations of oversight on LLCs—not to mention LLCs managed by lawyers—public visibility has consequences for is governmental and legal regulation. The unstable network of ownership, claimed by Star on YouTube but obfuscated beyond the minimal public legal documentation required by the state of California, is the very thing also hidden in the vast majority of Star's videos. We may see the interiors of his gaudy house, of his expensive, luxury cars, but until "The Secret World of Jeffree Star," the network of corporate ownership undergirding Star's financial security had been completely obscured. Star is one product manufactured, sold, and shipped by the warehouse that points toward his vertically integrated existence.

Star reveals the interior of his warehouse in the third video of the "Secret World" series, titled "Switching Lives with Jeffree Star."[40] The video mostly focuses on the series host, Shane Dawson, dressing up like Star. Star ostensibly takes Dawson through the reality of Star's daily routines, a kind of video that Dawson had previously performed with other popular YouTubers. The video opens with Dawson complaining about brand sponsorships falling through, begging the audience for support, letting us know that he needs our views to remain of value to advertisers and sponsors. Given the popularity of his earlier videos in the series, Dawson lets us know he has secured a sponsor and then presents an ad for SeatGeek, an online event-ticketing platform. This opening, in which Dawson grovels for the audience, highlights his role as a broker of attention for brands; it shows him as a potentially precarious influencer, one who must worry about the constant work of valorizing the self—underscoring his apparent difference from the subject of his "documentary," Jeffree Star.

Until about midway through this episode of the series, the real differences between Star and Dawson are not particularly overt. Star, at this point, still seems like a very successful influencer, one who, through his popularity and savvy, has leveraged his ability to attract attention into extravagant wealth. The wealth certainly seems real, as we are given glimpses into Star's house, his cars, his life. After Dawson dresses up in a Gucci tracksuit, a wig, and so on, making him look as much like Star as possible, the two get into Star's custom-made pink Lamborghini (which cost, we are told, $375,000) and drive to Star's warehouse. When Star casually walks through the door to his warehouse, pointing out things like pink details on its structural beams, Dawson is shocked, constantly repeating, over and over and over again, ad nauseum, "What the fuck?" Star points out the various picking stations of his warehouse, the parts dedicated to his cosmetics business as well as the parts reserved for Killer Merch. He says, "Yeah, that's something I don't *ever* talk about or promote, but this is obviously a fulfillment center and a merch company." He opens a door and takes Dawson into the corporate offices, the office kitchen, and a generic meeting room, all of which are spaces like almost any other generic, liminoid office, except for the ubiquity of the color pink. Dawson remains perpetually shocked throughout, as if the everyday banality of Star running a functioning warehouse is completely and utterly mind-blowing. As the warehouse tour goes on, Dawson, serving as viewer surrogate, sees in ever more refined detail just how different he and Star actually are. When asked how much it costs to run the facility per month, Star goes off to ask an employee, who, while staying off camera, refusing to be filmed, reports: "About $75,000 a month without staffing and with staffing it's another $100,000." Star, however, repeatedly takes "responsibility" for his employees, worrying about the growth of the business and future sales. "All these people rely on me, you know," he says. "I mean, this is their full-time job." Star claims that he doesn't intentionally keep the business secret—again, we hear this is all *boring*: "I wouldn't say it's a secret, it's just like, I almost call it 'my day job.' I mean, like to me, and maybe I'm wrong . . . this is almost just like the nine to five. . . . I'm just doing all the paperwork and everything behind the scenes . . . and I just don't think that it would be interesting to people."

Of course, these quotes are filled with contradictions. Were Star *really* "doing all the paperwork and everything behind the scenes," he'd probably know how much the operating costs of his business were. Star must have been aware that revealing the warehouse, revealing his business, wouldn't be boring at all but would amaze the audience just as it amazes Shane Dawson. Yet the illusion under which Star had been operating has been shattered; the warehouse becomes a new way to perform and visualize luxury, wealth, and excess. True luxury, Star suggests, is owning and managing a business. In the process, the fact that this is "interesting" content vanishes completely. If, as Sianne Ngai suggests, the "interesting" is judgment that highlights a minimal distinction in an unending, serial stream of information,[41] Star's warehouse acts as a complete barrier for the movement of future "interesting" content. The idea that Star is at all "like" his audience vanishes absolutely; the belief that Star is just another influencer, if a strangely successful one, disappears. The relation between Star and Dawson is twisted beyond recognition: both are "successful" influencers, and Dawson is, by YouTube standards at least, more successful than Star; his videos regularly have more views and he has long had more subscribers than Star. Star is no longer "like" Dawson; he is no longer "like" other influencers; he is no longer "like" those watching him at home.

Star is a capitalist, not a potentially precarious, struggling influencer groveling to audiences and brands, as Dawson grovels at the beginning of the video. We see that Star the influencer is one part of a broader network of corporate ownership and not even remotely the most significant part. Star seems "free," appearing "uncancellable," because his work as an influencer *is not his work*. Yet Star still pretends, to some degree, that he is "relatable." His appearance onscreen embraces his existence as a product to be sold, a product that must be similar to his audience to be relatable but, simultaneously, distinct and luxurious to be interesting, to be valuable as an object of attention. When asked about his company's income, if that income is in the "hundreds of millions of dollars," Star hesitates for a moment and then responds in the affirmative, following up with "I've never said that out loud before," as if he is surprised by his own wealth. Star, at times, seems to be shocked or embarrassed by the fact that he is a capitalist manager and not an influencer, that he is merely masquerading as an influencer. The warehouse becomes a background against which the varied contradictions in Star's existence become obvious, where he cannot truly be both owner and product, but it is also a necessary location in which the product that is Jeffree Star comes into being, a product needed to sell the makeup that has value because of Star's existence as a YouTuber.

"The Secret World of Jeffree Star" was followed by "The Beautiful World of Jeffree Star,"[42] a seven-part series also narrated and produced by Dawson, this time amounting to more than seven hours of video, all focusing on the creation, manufacturing, and sale of a makeup collaboration between subject and host. Leaning into the representation of corporate practices, "Beautiful World" follows Dawson learning what goes into the design, production, testing, and marketing of Star's brand of cosmetics, with Star now far more willing to embrace his role as corporate manager on camera. In the wake of these two series' popularity, criticisms of the two began to be taken more seriously by many fans and corporate collaborators. Much of this attention seemed to—temporarily, at least—damage Dawson's popularity quite significantly, in part because his many apologies did little to stop his bizarre and racist antics designed to shock for attention. Star, dragged down by Dawson, had to confront accusations yet again. He once more released an apology video of sorts, though one that ends by advertising a new cosmetics line. The video, rather than a sincere apology, was, like almost any influencer video on YouTube, an ad.[43] Fans began to criticize Killer Merch for continuing to manufacture goods for Dawson. Finally, fans were aware of the corporate links maintaining the manufacture of branded merchandise.[44] Star's warehouse was broken into, and some fans accused him of staging the robbery.[45] Makeup lines associated with Star and Dawson were dropped by Morphe, a cosmetics manufacturer and retailer, following perpetual criticisms of Star and Dawson's past and their failure to sufficiently apologize.[46] The aura of Star as uncancellable seemed to have been shattered because "The Secret World" did, in fact, let us in on his secret: the corporate structure hidden in Star's appearance as an influencer, glimpsed finally in the background of the warehouse, a warehouse where Jeffree Star becomes simultaneously one "product" among a range of others and a vertically integrated individual who invests in many different brands, only one of which is his appearance as a product on YouTube.

WAREHOUSES IN WYOMING

In the wake of this controversy, of the shattering of his seemingly "uncancellable" existence, Star retreated from Los Angeles completely, moving during the coronavirus pandemic to Casper, Wyoming. There he bought a ranch for $1.1 million, which he named "Star Ranch"—a yak ranch with more than five hundred acres and forty yaks—along with a nearby ranch for his mother. Star ingratiated the local community through numerous donations, such as a local toy drive and a free Wyoming Symphony Orchestra concert.[47] As we have noted throughout this book, Star's videos in Casper focus on farmer's markets, on heritage brands, on a retreat from his past excess and glamour. Yet Star's Instagram page was regularly filled with examples of filtering this "retreat" through the excesses of influence. In a video from the Casper farmer's market, Star tells us how he "stocked up at the farmer's market. Of course, it's all local businesses . . . made here in Casper, raw honey, so good! Let's do a little haul right here, guys."[48] The market inevitably appears, that constant stream of commodities that, even if it is framed as "socially responsible," as "local," is still about endless excess, endless waste. Star's sponsored events were, as should be expected, exercises in self-branding for his cosmetics business and future ranching career.[49] The concert was accompanied by videos on Instagram announcing that Star would be giving away free eyeshadow palettes, which were all themed around his ranch, along with videos of his after-show meal, a burger made from Star Yak Ranch yak meat, at a local steakhouse. Even though the place appears different, the backgrounds—as a form on which the influencer appears as a commodity—remain the same.

The distinction between city and country once again reappears when Star moves to Wyoming. "The pull of the idea of the country is toward old ways, human ways, natural ways," says Raymond Williams. "The pull of the idea of the city is toward progress, modernisation, development."[50] Conflicts between the imaginary relationship of city to country, the seeming oppositions between the two, reveal negotiations of capitalist crisis in the lived reality of individuals. The retreat to the country in influencer culture is a pessimistic one. The city has become a space of impossibility, in which progress is prevented and belonging has waned. The precarity of influence, rather than an inevitable outcome of late capitalism, becomes a feature of urban excess. The city, Los Angeles, much as it was with Elsie Larson and Emma Chapman of *A Beautiful Mess*, becomes a space of inauthenticity, of failure. For Larson and Chapman, the distinction between city and country is determined by access to homeownership, a financial investment that signifies location in a community. For Star, the separation of city and country is a distinction about the truth of classical liberalism, of "entrepreneurialism." Los Angeles, as "city," is marked as a damaged form of community in which the economic requirements for social embeddedness are impossible, be they access to real estate or, for Star, access to a kind of rugged (pseudo)entrepreneurialism. The entrepreneurial subject is framed as "nature," something only accessible when one moves beyond the decadent space of urbanity:

> I think one of my favorite things of living in Wyoming is how people really support each other. Um, and all the big corporations, yeah, they kind of exist out here, but the fact that everyone is growing their own food, which I'm so excited to be doing soon. Um, making their own honey, barbecue sauce, everything across the board, and there is so much more that I'm going to show when I go back in the next week or two. . . . I love people that just create real entrepreneurship . . . and there are so many amazing ranches and people out here creating stuff, and I love discovering new stuff.[51]

The essence of the country becomes the assumptions of classical liberalism in its Adam Smith variety: that self-interest is also support for others. But this collective self-interest does not undermine competitive entrepreneurialism. Rather, "real entrepreneurship" comes from self-determination on the land, something not antagonistic to "big corporations" but coexistent with them. In his waxing pastoral about the hardworking farmers of Wyoming, Star, yet again, both reveals and conceals the reality of his capitalist interests. Not only does he sound, in this video, like any other neoliberal, imagining the foundational grounding of capitalism as a natural, competitive ability to become an entrepreneur of the self, all supported by the invisible hand of the market, but Star suggests a mimetic desire to become like those at the farmer's market—which, to some extent, both is and is not what he does during his move.

Star's seeming value to those in Wyoming comes from his ability to inject capital into the local economy, to build warehouses that "create jobs." Like other celebrities who were living there at the same time, such as Kanye West and RuPaul, Wyoming is a marginal space to be subsumed by capital, be it through the construction of elaborate buildings (never to be realized, in the case of West),[52] through fracking and the extraction of resources from land (in the case of RuPaul),[53] or, in the case of Star, through the manufacturing of warehouses and shipping fulfillment centers. Star's role in the "country" that is Wyoming is to appropriate lands formerly beyond the space of supply chain capitalism, "developing" them, bringing geographic regions once marginal to late capitalism closer to their centers through their integration into the supply chain. The pastoral imagery of the country speaks to the desirability of social organization outside of the dictates of late capitalism. Yet in expressing this mimetic desire—his desire to be like those people he finds at the farmer's market, these seemingly "natural" capitalists—Star nonetheless acts to decimate this form of social organization, instead privileging Wyoming as an "underdeveloped" state ripe for potentials of exploitation by supply chains. The extractive gas mining activities of celebrities like RuPaul provide a mirror of Star's activities: Wyoming is a region worth attention because capitalism has yet to fully subsume its land, its people, its resources.

Star's move to Wyoming included founding several new businesses and moving previous ones to his new location, not only Jeffree Star Cosmetics but a pet accessory brand named Jeffree Star Pets LLC and another LLC named Scorpio Logistics.[54] Both Jeffree Star Pets and Scorpio Logistics were incorporated in Wyoming in 2020, but both were dissolved about a year later because of Star's failure to file required annual paperwork and pay taxes,[55] even though Jeffree Star Pets still manufactures and sells products on Star's website.[56] Star also filed paperwork in 2021 for another corporation, simply named Jeffree Star LLC, which—as of the time of this writing—is still an active corporation, if delinquent with its paperwork.[57] According to reporting out of Casper, Star's plans included opening a warehouse that would serve as a fulfillment center for "Star Lounge," a brand for Star's branded marijuana paraphernalia and clothing. In August of 2021, Star filed to trademark "Star Yak Ranch" through Jeffree Star LLC, which suggests an intention to brand and sell clothing, pet food, meat, and natural fiber from yaks, along with providing breeding and stud service for yaks.[58]

The point here, yet again, is the uneasy and unsteady relationship between influencer image and the corporate investments hidden behind this image. Wyoming has no personal income tax, and the constantly shifting and reinvented attempts to brand new products and new industries is, in some ways, a synthesis of the precarious influencer's attempts to constantly "hustle" and invent new scams and new business opportunities with a murky corporate logic that obscures the vertical integration of the many diverse aspects of one's life. Star is a vertically integrated individual, in which "he" becomes one part of a vast corporate body, though he refuses the complete conflation of self and corporation, maintaining a distinction between self and business through constantly shifting LLCs over which he claims ownership. In the turn to Wyoming, we begin to see how the image of the influencer, when it comes to vertically integrated individuals like Star, is one product manufactured by a larger conglomeration. The move out of the city, not merely a move to signify "authenticity," to signal one's desire to leave the decadence of the city behind, is a turn toward the inevitable geography of supply chain capitalism, to the dictates of formal subsumptions under late capitalism. Glamour and excess can be represented anywhere. But to be truly profitable requires a warehouse, requires the reduction of labor costs, the reduction of income tax, and the foregrounding of shipping and circulation.

THE SPECTACLE OF THE WAREHOUSE

During the coronavirus pandemic, Jeffree Star Cosmetics and Killer Merch were both recipients of Payment Protection Program loans, or "PPP" loans, federal loans intended to keep workers on payrolls—the former receiving a loan for $413,675, the latter for $649,970, supporting a reported twenty-one and fifty-nine employees respectively.[59] MrBeast also reportedly received a PPP loan to support forty employees.[60] Although some may be shocked to hear about sizable governmental loans for people best known as YouTubers, we know by now that Star and his businesses take in a substantial amount of income, though this income is concealed behind the limited filing requirements of privately held corporations. It may be more surprising to hear not only of MrBeast's PPP loan but that his company, MrBeastYouTube LLC, employs at least forty people. MrBeastYouTube LLC was first incorporated in North Carolina in 2017. In state filing documents, it lists its primary business as, at various points in time, "YouTube Videos" and "Video Productions."[61] It does not appear that Jimmy Donaldson has as diverse a business portfolio as Star, at least from filings for incorporation in North Carolina; the only other MrBeast business venture in Donaldson's name is the now defunct MrBeastCrypto LLC, which was formed a month after Donaldson's video production LLC.[62] Yet, as with tracing the specific ownership of Jeffree Star's business ventures, it is nearly impossible to trace ownership through state filing documents; many of the annual reports for MrBeastYouTube LLC list only the corporation's registered agent and do not list owners or managers beyond the LLC's managing lawyer. Regardless, it is clear that Donaldson considers his production company a small business.[63]

The glimpses we see of MrBeast's warehouse are approached in a completely different manner from those of Star. The warehouse, for Donaldson, is the background against which some of his largest and most elaborate stunts have been staged. In a behind-the-scenes video posted by SoKrispyMedia, a small media effects company (and YouTube channel) hired to produce digital effects for some of MrBeast's videos, we're given a brief, direct glimpse into the "MrBeast Warehouse" somewhere in North Carolina, which appears as a gigantic, empty black space filled with lighting rigs, elevated platforms, and equipment that one would find in a film studio—which is essentially what the MrBeast Warehouse is (fig. 11).[64] SoKrispyMedia was brought in by MrBeast to help develop and execute what would be, at the time, Donaldson's magnum opus: a recreation of Netflix's globally popular South Korean television series *Squid Game*, from 2021, as a video titled "$456,000 Squid Game in Real Life," in which Donaldson invited 456 fans to play (nonlethal) versions of the games, using sets that approximated as closely as possible those of the original show.

FIGURE 11   Warehouse studio: A peek inside Jimmy
Donaldson's filming studio and warehouse space.

Source: SoKrispyMedia, "Making MrBeast's Squid Game in 10 Days," YouTube, Nov. 27, 2021, www.youtube.com/watch?v=VQcO_PYVx30.

The original *Squid Game* is a didactic critique of late capitalism. A group of 456 individuals, all in deep financial debt, are coerced to "freely" play a series of children's games in which losing a game means losing one's life. The winner of the games, the only person left alive at the end, receives a large monetary prize. *Squid Game*, both thematically and stylistically, follows a great deal of South Korean popular culture since 1997, the year of the IMF (International Monetary Fund) Crisis in the Republic of Korea. Since the time of the IMF Crisis, according to Joseph Jonghyun Jeon, South Korean film—and, with *Squid Game*, television—regularly attempts "a systematic diagnosis of how [economic crisis] emerges as a matter of processes, incentives, imbalances and how this economy comes to reproduce itself according to Western models."[65] Most obviously represented by the work of directors such as Park Chan-wook and Bong Joon-ho, a preoccupation with capitalism's contradictions has been a major focus of many examples of contemporary Korean popular culture. *Squid Game*'s creator and director, Hwang Dong-hyuk, was inspired to create his show after a failed, violent seventy-seven-day strike at a factory for Ssangyong Motor Company in 2009,[66] combining popular memories of class conflict with stylistic elements taken from Japanese manga and anime, which were banned in Korea until 1998. The *New York Times* described the Ssangyong factory conflict as a "war zone," with struggles "closely monitored by foreign investors as a test of will both for South Korean unions, known for their militant activism, and for President Lee Myung-bak's government, which has vowed to ensure more 'flexibility' for companies to shed workers at times of economic distress."[67] *Squid Game* makes some of these late capitalist themes overt. The ultimate villains of the show are a masked cadre of representatives of global capital who gleefully consume from a distance the spectacular carnage of debtors killing each other. *Squid Game* thus allegorizes the devastating effects of global capital on daily life when the economies of countries such as South Korea are "developed" through global financial investment—that is, if unions are broken, if workers' wills are brought to heel—with the threat of death implied by the show's "games" paralleling the deaths caused by despair, exhaustion, and burnout experienced by those beyond the boundaries of upward mobility as an economy "develops."

We mentioned Donaldson's recreation of *Squid Game* in the previous chapter. While the Netflix show was the most popular television launch in the streaming service's history at the time, with 142 million households streaming the show during its first four weeks of availability, MrBeast's hit 142 million views after eight days. And, in comparing the productions, minute-to-minute, the recreation cost more to produce than Netflix's show. The original *Squid Game* cost approximately $43,500 per minute of television programming; Donaldson's recreation is estimated to have cost around $134,600 per minute. But what strikes us is how, in MrBeast's video, the anticapitalist allegory of *Squid Game* is deallegorized, made into a simple material reality of capitalist "charity," of capitalist "spectacle," in its recreation. Throughout Donaldson's videos, the warehouse is a space to contain increasingly spectacular stunts, most of which end in a massive giveaway. The parallels between *Squid Game* and MrBeast are shocking, revealing how the warehouse can become an abstract space that permits the control of one over others, in which excess is not merely squandered but directed in manipulating others into "interesting" content, content that relies on perpetuating a constant, churning, cyclical production and destruction of capital.

In his video "How I Gave Away $1,000,000," from December 25, 2018,[68] Donaldson describes how he began making his massively popular videos organized around giving away massive sums of money. He received a branding deal with Quidd, a "digital collectibles marketplace" that specializes in the exchange of rare and limited-edition digital trading cards and stickers,[69] giving the $10,000 he received for the video to a homeless person. Quidd kept paying Donaldson to make similar videos. Increasingly large sums of money would be given away or squandered. MrBeast would eventually eat a "$70,000 Golden Pizza" or donate "$100,000 to Streamers with 0 Viewers."[70] In a number of interviews, however, Donaldson has claimed that although he's figured out how to make videos go viral, in such a way to "practically make unlimited money,"[71] the demand for increasing scale in his videos requires him to put almost all income back into making new videos. "If I make three or four million dollars a month, I just spend it on videos the next month. . . . We literally have, like, razor-thin margins, and just reinvest it all."[72] Donaldson seems to suggest both that he has figured out how to use YouTube and sponsorships to generate endless cash and that the demand for more requires this "endless" cash to be endlessly spent.

The spectacle of excess here gives us a different way to see how the market demands constant and perpetual waste, waste that must increase over time, getting more excessive, more elaborate. But the need to make oneself into a product to be sold, where the self is interchangeable with an increasingly large corporate set of investments and costs, demands that this excess cannot merely be squandered as luxury. In some of his earlier giveaway videos, we can tell that Donaldson is unable to completely control the reactions of people, unable to get people to perform the desired emotional response to create the "best" (meaning most popular, most viral) video. In a video titled "I Gave People $1,000,000 but ONLY 1 Minute to Spend It!," from December 15, 2020,[73] for instance, Donaldson approaches people in an electronics store, but they seem relatively nonplussed, not too excited to be receiving money, not excessively happy to be on YouTube. The video even draws attention to this nonreaction, playing the sound of crickets at moments when the everyday people who "should be" excited and grateful instead provide muted, stunned responses. The quick potential of easy money, it seems, is intended to generate not only excessive waste but excessive emotion. Donaldson wants an emotional response that is over the top, mirroring the face he uses to advertise every single one of his videos, mouth open wide, as if he's screaming, following the tone of voice he employs in most of his videos, yelling, voice cracking, pushed to its limit, like a salesman on a local television ad. The turn to the warehouse, then, appears to be an attempt to use a large, generic, open space to force control through the management of the environment.

In one of the first MrBeast videos that appears to be shot in a warehouse, "Giant Monopoly Game with Real Money," from February 15, 2019, we begin in a large room, the size of which seems industrial because of its very high ceilings, though it's impossible to tell because the walls are lined in cheap black material, and the ceilings are swathed in a canvas-adjacent fabric. The floor is covered, wall-to-wall, with a plastic Monopoly board (fig. 12). The contestants are fans who won a contest to appear in a MrBeast video. With these contests, Donaldson no longer goes out into the world but brings people to him, to his increasingly larger, more elaborate, industrial spaces. The contests implicitly follow a kind of Willy Wonka "Golden Ticket" arrangement.[74] If one buys merch from Donaldson's website, one is automatically entered to win a chance at becoming a MrBeast contestant or, perhaps more accurately, to become MrBeast content. In the video, Donaldson begins by telling all the contestants, none of whom know how to play Monopoly, how the game is played. As the video goes on, Donaldson must constantly keep the game going, reminding everyone of the rules, sometimes physically pushing and moving the players into the correct position. Yet the spectacle is, ultimately, quite boring. At different points MrBeast forces the contestants to call friends or family to cheer them on—attempting to ignite some affective feeling as the game drags. As the game persists, the players clearly become exhausted and ever more bored, caring less about the money at the end. When they lose, they have an exit interview. In one, a contestant says, "It's a lot of money to have lost, but hey, you win some you lose some. I'm just blessed to get to be here." Donaldson is following many of the beats and structures of contemporary reality TV, in which contestants discuss their experience on the show as if it was somehow personally enriching, as if the "point" was not the money or the excess but the "lessons" that were learned from being the object of spectacle.[75]

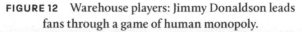

FIGURE 12   Warehouse players: Jimmy Donaldson leads
fans through a game of human monopoly.

Source: Jimmy Donaldson (MrBeast), "Giant Monopoly Game with Real Money," YouTube,
Feb. 15, 2019, www.youtube.com/watch?v=2nd73lyvq4w.

Other videos, such as "Last to Take Hand Off Lamborghini, Keeps
It," from October 23, 2021,[76] appear to be filmed in the same space, this
time outfitted with large vinyl signs, stadium seating, and astroturf. The
warehouse serves as a giant, generic space. Different sets can be cheaply
and quickly constructed, and contingencies can be negated in the name
of corporate control. Donaldson becomes a line manager, surveilling
the content workers who are needed to complete the manufacture of his
videos. Even videos not filmed in the MrBeast Warehouse from around
this time also rely on spatial confinement and enclosure. While some of
this was, perhaps, due to constraints necessitated by the pandemic, videos
such as "Last to Leave $800,000 Island Keeps It," from August 15, 2020,[77]
suggest that Donaldson has purchased an island where he has several
people perform a series of challenges to . . . well, keep the island. "Extreme
$1,000,000 Hide and Seek," a December 18, 2021, video produced with the
assistance of YouTube Originals,[78] sees Donaldson inviting "the ten big-
gest creators on YouTube" into "the largest stadium in the world" to play
hide and seek. Throughout, we watch whispered confession-booth-style
camera interviews, with the participants saying how scared they are, how

they feel they're being hunted for sport. Where many of MrBeast's previous videos—even ones filmed during the coronavirus pandemic—involved
surprising random people with money, attempting to elicit extreme emotional reactions of thanks, these videos signal a turn toward a demand for
control over emotion, control over the bodies and feelings of those who
appear in Donaldson's videos. It's as if Donaldson's warehouse reverses
what was once dubbed the "Fordization of the face," a descriptive phrase
for the extreme emotional control required by managers of Henry Ford's
assembly line. In Ford's factory, "humming, whistling or even smiling on
the job were, in the judgment of Ford Service, evidence of soldiering [delib-
erate resistance to speed-up] or insubordination," with one employee even
being fired for "smiling" and "laughing with the other fellows."[79] Rather
than repressing the emotions, Donaldson's videos, paralleling the transformations of public emotion described by theorists such as Eva Illouz and
Sara Ahmed,[80] demand the proper and constant expression of perpetual
affection, an excess of emotional effluvia that, for Donaldson, is part of the
formula that makes videos go viral.

The structural parallels between Donaldson's videos and *Squid Game*
are, from the outset, striking. Both seem organized around giveaways of
massive sums of money for people who "win" some sort of competition.
These competitions treat individuals as literal game tokens, as manipula-
ble matter to be molded into entertainment. If the Korean series allegorizes
the conflict between national economies and global capital—as late capitalist institutions such as the IMF demand deregulation, "flexibility," and
policies hostile to labor—then MrBeast's location in the American South
should be understood as providing a particularly strange, and particularly
notable, late capitalist background. As Mandel describes in *Late Capitalism*,
the American South, in the global economy prior to the Civil War, was *not*
a region characterized by a capitalist mode of production (even if American
capitalism inherently relied on this region for the totality of its economy).
Slavery in the United States was, instead, a form of "pre-industrial capitalism" embodied in the plantation economy.[81] After the Civil War, the
South had to be "developed" and reintegrated into capitalism, without the
development of manufacturing, realizing itself best in the industries associated with the "New South": finance and banking, tourism, technology

and research, and entertainment. Centers for these industries thus developed in cities such as Charlotte, the Raleigh-Durham-Chapel Hill "Research Triangle," Nashville, Asheville, Savannah, Charleston, Atlanta, and New Orleans, among other urban environments throughout the region.[82] While these cities have become centers of economic activity, many of the more rural communities and towns in the South have remained economically impoverished,[83] with occasional "development" through the building of, for instance, data centers for Facebook and Google in Western North Carolina. MrBeast's physical location, an hour east of Raleigh, positions him in an unusual location specific to late capitalist development in North Carolina—namely, he can maintain a proximity to Raleigh (its tech industries, which include gaming and esports, fields that he could potentially leverage as sponsors) while also maintaining a proximity toward economically depressed areas outside the larger urban centers of the New South. The entertainment of watching people compete for—or just be given— large sums of money is a form that is specific to the political and cultural economy of late capitalism, especially that of the American South, where the city becomes a space of technological, postindustrial "innovation" and the country is left behind. The excessive spending, the large gifts implied by Donaldson's videos, speak to extreme economic imbalances that characterize urban centers and rural margins in late capitalist life, imbalances that are also central to the geographical organization of supply chains described throughout this chapter.

In "$456,000 Squid Game in Real Life!" from November 24, 2021,[84] Donaldson's demand for control is explicit. The contestants even work to repeat the narrative of the original show, understanding their roles as directly repeating the beats of a prestige Netflix drama. Those carrying the numbers of major characters get special treatment, and at one point another player even sacrifices himself for a "main character" of the original television program, deliberately "dying" to preserve the original narrative.

In an article on MrBeast's *Squid Game* reenactment, the *Los Angeles Times* asked reality television editor Katherine Griffin, who has worked on shows such as *The Amazing Race* and *RuPaul's Drag Race All Stars*, to watch the YouTube video and comment on it with her expertise in mind. "Not only is it professionally edited," she said, but look at the production design, the copying of all of these sets. . . . It's made to look like this fun little thing that people can stream on the bus or whatever, but it was a huge expense to make this video, and a lot of professional people are working on it. . . . I have no idea how many editors are on it, because there are no credits. . . . I don't know if YouTube videos do that, but it seems like they ought to, because somebody should get credit for it. If this were a professional reality show on one of the networks, there would be anywhere between two to five editors working on this.[85]

Even though reality TV is notoriously cagey about its own production techniques, veiling them in secrecy,[86] MrBeast's video completely obscures almost all elements of production, leading to a vague sense that the video is, in fact, "amateurish" instead of a professional video production. Obviously, this is incorrect, but this appearance obscures how the warehouse becomes a space for extreme management of human bodies. In SoKrispy-Media's behind-the-scenes video, we see how, for instance, all sets for the MrBeast video were created digitally first, using game engine Unreal (a game engine developed by the Cary, North Carolina, based Epic Games), to "previsualize" the entire video in advance. The contestants of MrBeast's re-enactment were modeled, manipulated, and managed, raw material shaped into a media product, "content" to be delivered over YouTube. While we do not want to conflate the labor of working in an Amazon warehouse with appearing in a MrBeast video, both venues understand the human body as matter to bend, either fitting bodies into the routines and demands of supply chain capitalism or manipulating bodies into the emotional beats needed to generate viral content that seems "real" and "authentic" and "re-latable" but is a product to be sold and exchanged on YouTube.

In MrBeast's "World's Most Dangerous Escape Room!" from January 29, 2022,[87] this tendency in Donaldson's videos, to use the warehouse as a space through which to torture, manipulate, and bend human bodies in the service of "content," surpasses even his *Squid Game* reenactment. In this video, which is only eight minutes long, Donaldson has constructed an elaborate, multiple room set in his warehouse, asking a few contestants to make their way through the maze and escape.[88] The pace of this video is manic, with the pressure and intensity of the situation amplified through-out. The first room of the set has sharp spikes that close in on the video's contestants. Everyone is screaming and seemingly scared, while we see Donaldson watching their fear from a closed-circuit television. Donaldson encourages his contestants with the promise of money, like usual—he has a box of $100,000 for them (fig. 13)—but also hints that the money will be dumped into a fire via conveyer belt if they fail to escape. The excess of destruction, the excess of waste, the excess of affective intensity—the video unites the thrill and pleasure of it all.

Specific rooms of MrBeast's resemble or replicate film and television; part of the escape room is designed to look like the Netflix television show *Floor Is Lava*, a show in which contestants attempt to get money by navigating an obstacle course without touching the floor. Another centerpiece of MrBeast's escape room is a room filled with candy. When his contes-

FIGURE 13 Warehouse spectacle: Jimmy Donaldson threatens to burn money during an escape room challenge.

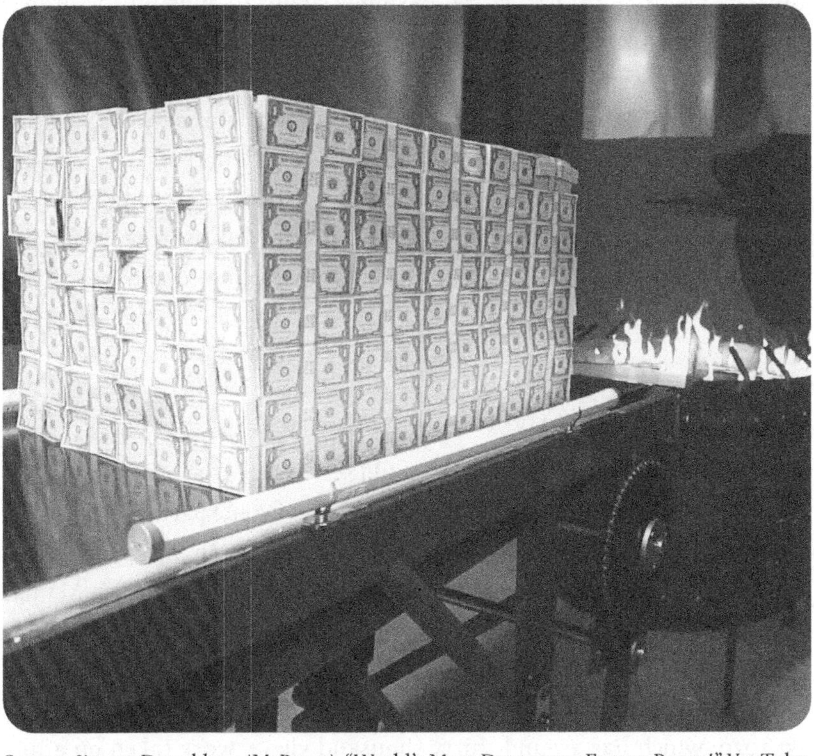

Source: Jimmy Donaldson (MrBeast), "World's Most Dangerous Escape Room!" YouTube, Jan. 29, 2022, www.youtube.com/watch?v=3jS_yEK8qVI.

tants arrive in this room, one hundred bars of chocolate fall from the sky. The contestants must open them all to find a golden ticket to progress. As they unwrap the many bars of chocolate—again taking part in a Willy Wonka-esque situation in which power is asserted through the wonders and delights of mass production—MrBeast takes the moment to introduce us to a new line of chocolate bars, bars that are ostensibly sustainable and healthy, with ethical sourcing of cacao and only five ingredients.[89] The video is an ad, like many of MrBeast's videos are—be they for chocolate, or for a mobile game advertised during his *Squid Game* video, or for his chain of ghost kitchen burger restaurants, MrBeast Burger.[90] While Donaldson may not be as vertically integrated as Jeffree Star, he has used the popularity of his videos to branch out beyond the making of content into the development of branded goods and services. He, too, has used the warehouse to produce himself as a product, an influencer, a lure of attention, as well as the owner of the warehouse. He is a vertically integrated individual who uses the material infrastructures of supply chains to build up and protect his precarity, differentiating himself from other, seemingly similar, influencers by reinventing himself through the logic of late capitalist supply chains. After Donaldson introduces us to his chocolate bar, we're told that if we purchase one, we'll be entered into a contest. Some bars have a golden ticket inside. If we get one of these tickets, then we get to go to his warehouse, an opportunity to become content for the MrBeast content factory, allowing our body to be bent and molded into an emotionally expressive, relatable video.

LIVING IN A WAREHOUSE

Jeffree Star and Jimmy Donaldson would seem to be true exceptions in influencer culture. Yet if we look into the videos of some particularly aspirational YouTubers, we find that even the "normies" are buying up warehouse space in the wake of the current warehouse boom. "The Sensible Mama," an influencer on YouTube and Instagram, among other platforms, who has a PhD and transitioned from research to business after the birth of her child, has around sixteen thousand subscribers. In a video from January 13, 2020, which has around thirty thousand views, we're taken on a tour of The Sensible Mama's warehouse.[91] The Sensible Mama combines social media content creation with a variant on drop-shipping—a method for "order fulfillment," we're told by the online sales platform Shopify, "where a store doesn't keep the product it sells in stock. Instead, the seller purchases inventory as needed from a third party—usually a wholesaler or manufacturer—to fulfill orders." An influencer who engages in drop-shipping may promote specific products on their Instagram or YouTube page and then set up an online store—via a platform like Shopify—to sell these products. Yet, Shopify lets us know, drop-shipping can be subject to inventory issues, supplier mistakes, limited branding, and other shipping complexities, because one is ultimately giving over complete control over the supply chain to online platforms and other, often somewhat anonymous, global wholesalers or manufacturers.[92] The Sensible Mama, in purchasing warehouse space for herself, is still engaging in a kind of drop-shipping, taking slightly more control over the supply chain, advertising products such as blankets, thermoses, diaper bags, art supplies, and children's toys on Instagram and YouTube, selling them on her website, which is itself powered by Shopify.[93] In her warehouse tour, we are told about inventory management, about organizing storage for the most efficient packing of orders, and so on.

Other influencers also have purchased warehouse space to fulfill orders, such as Jeremy Fiedler, an Australian YouTuber who mainly posts videos of scooter riding and tricks, and who has around 120,000 subscribers. In Fiedler's video "I BOUGHT A WAREHOUSE . . ." from April 11, 2019, a video with about ten thousand views, he takes us on a tour of his "warehouse," a storage unit for his branded merch, a space explicitly for managing orders and shipping. Says Fiedler in his video, "Everything in this warehouse is to help make it simple for me to fill out your orders, and all your orders are done by me."[94] Tanner Fox, a YouTuber with more than ten million subscribers, has a video similar to Fiedler's, with more than one million views, titled "I BOUGHT A HUGE WAREHOUSE!!! *OFFICIAL TOUR*," from June 6, 2017.[95] Fox tells us about his branded apparel, about his work in shipping his branded clothing, before we go from his home, into his car, and head to the warehouse—as if following the model of Star's warehouse tour, even though this video precedes Star's.

Fox tells us that his warehouse—like Fiedler's, like The Sensible Mama's—was purchased because of his increasingly large merch shipping business. But in giving his tour, Fox reveals other aspirations, ones that come from owning a large, mostly empty space. "I'm talkin' ramps, I'm talkin' ziplines, I'm talkin' foam pits, I'm talkin' *trampolines*," he says, excitedly. It's going to be his own "Tannasy factory," he states, before breaking down laughing, a reference to the MTV reality television show *Rob Dyrdek's Fantasy Factory*, where Dyrdek, a renowned skateboarding icon, would use a large warehouse in Los Angeles as an indoor skatepark, as well as a space to stage strange stunts. Fox discusses plans for storing his cars and for constructing skateboard ramps. The dream, it would seem, is not just a warehouse as a space to store products to be shipped but to become a space, much like a garage, that can be used to fulfill the dreams of pleasure, excess, and domesticity. The warehouse becomes a dream home, a space to renovate into a "fantasy factory."

A warehouse is, by definition, not a residential space. If we return to the beginning of this chapter, the fear of warehouses in Lehigh Valley comes from their subsumption of all other land, of all residential, commercial, and industrial space. What does it tell us that the "fantasy factory," the "dream house" of influencer culture, is a warehouse? What does it mean that, in these videos, it seems that home, car, and market can all be located within warehouses, a specific kind of building—a generic building—that increasingly covers the planet, remaking geography to connect regions once beyond capital to urban centers through logistics, transportation, and information? What does it mean that this background is the ultimate one of influencer culture, in which individuals see themselves both as products and as owners of a corporate structure that is equivalent to "the self"? Our name for this context—in which corporations are valued more than everyday individuals, and to be worthy of rights, abilities, and "citizenship" today, one must render oneself indistinguishable from a vertically integrated corporation—is the *Corpocene*.

FIVE

CORPOCENE

The home, the car, the market, the warehouse—these backgrounds of influencer culture reveal foundational, if obfuscated, infrastructures of contemporary economic life. Sometimes, these spaces are both obvious and ignored because of their conflation with the "person" we see on screen; the intimacy and closeness of the home merges person and property, fabricating authenticity through private, domestic space. Sometimes, these spaces remain generic, boring, forgettable; the enclosed intimacy of the car requires isolation for authenticity, fungibility a necessity for truth. Sometimes, these spaces point toward a constant churn of more products, more waste, more content; the perpetual *more* of the market requires the influencer to revel in excess to the point of exhaustion to remain "interesting," to remain valuable as a commodity to be exchanged. Sometimes, these spaces draw out the operations of contemporary logistics; the warehouse links supply chains, the home, the car, and the market, and truly "elite" influencers ensure personal control over the production, circulation, and distribution of commodities.

In these spaces, we see how capital demands the production of the self as commodity. But we must go further, beyond the commodification of the self.

As we will explain here, in our concluding chapter, influencer culture conflates person not only with commodity but with *corporation*. Throughout this book, we've seen hints of this conflation—when Jeffree Star discusses his business portfolio and his love of investing, or when Jimmy Donaldson funds start-up after start-up in the name of his YouTube persona. Star and Donaldson serve as exemplars, as ideals, as kinds of people others desire to emulate. Their model of influence is not merely one in which a few otherwise "normal" people happen to be good at getting attention, using social media's capacity to broadcast one's daily life. It is not merely the case that the YouTube elite embrace a platform to amplify their voice—a voice that possesses economic value when leveraged into sponsorships and brand collaborations.[1] Rather, the success of Star and Donaldson comes, in part, *from a combination of person and corporate form*. Beyond usual debates about "corporate personality," beyond the general "corporatization" of everything, this combination of person and corporation, we argue, is foundational for mitigating against the *risk* of life as an influencer. Conflating person and corporation is an act central for the broader context of the present—a context we're terming the *Corpocene*. The Corpocene names the moment when the ideal subject—a model realized in figures like Star and Donaldson—renders equivalent corporeal body and corporate body, where the corporation becomes the model for selfhood, for social relation, for "success." This *inverts* the model of corporate personhood central to countless juridical norms needed for the functioning of modern capital and social life. Not only do corporations appear as "people"—with "personhood" a legal fiction necessary for defining and parceling out the rights and responsibilities of groups and agents that cannot be reduced to single individuals—but *people themselves adopt the structure and function of a corporation*. In the Corpocene, the only thing that truly appears as a "person," as worthy of rights and protections under law, is a corporation.

ANTHROPOCENE, CAPITALOCENE, PLANTATIONOCENE, CORPOCENE

Our use of *Corpocene* to describe a particular articulation of late capitalism is, as may be obvious for almost any neologism that ends with *-cene*, a play on *Anthropocene*. This term was popularized by biologist Eugene Stoermer and chemist Paul Crutzen to describe the planetary, geological age in which the composition of Earth has become irrevocably altered by humanity, in which "nature" has been replaced or forever altered by "culture."[2] The etymological origins of *Anthropocene* can be broken into the prefix *Anthropos-*, which means "human being," and the suffix *-cene*, derived from the Greek *kainos*, which means "recent." In other words, the term should best be interpreted as meaning "a time when geological strata are dominated by remains of *recent human* origin."[3] Yet the massive popularity of *Anthropocene* as a description of our context almost always presumes that this "*recent human* origin" has broad implications. *Anthropocene* becomes shorthand for the numerous crises of the present—climate change, environmental collapse—stressing that these events are not "natural" but are a product of human industry. An implicit argument against a laissez-faire approach to ecology, the popular interpretation of *Anthropocene* rejects a belief that nature will find a way out of ecological collapse on its own (at least, without also annihilating humanity along with vast swathes of other life-forms on Earth). It suggests that we humans must directly address the environmental destruction we have caused (at least, if we hope for human survival beyond a few decades in the future).

Countless writers and theorists on the Left, including many who would otherwise agree with the necessity of actively addressing ecological devastation, have argued that the popular use of *Anthropocene* is riddled with problems—ones that may not inherently be in the term itself but are foundational when *Anthropocene* becomes, as it almost always does, a term to describe more than a geological age. If one presumes *Anthropocene* to indicate how our geological era is solely or mostly determined by human activity, as the term is often understood, then one accepts a strong separation between "man" and "nature," for instance, and sees the current relation between these two entities as slowly leading to doom and destruction. In this interpretation, "man" is essentially hostile to (and outside of) "nature."[4] Calling the present age the Anthropocene, some have argued, equates "humanity" with a set of relations that are more accurately attributed to particular arrangements of *capitalism*, not humanity as such. Rather than an Anthropocene, the environmental destruction we face is brought about by the *Capitalocene*, a term variously employed by writers such as Jason W. Moore, Andreas Malm, David Ruccio, and Donna Haraway. *Capitalo-*

cene, instead of foregrounding the role of humans, describes the relation between ecology and, to use Moore's words, "the historical era shaped by the endless accumulation of capital."[5] Some have argued that *Capitalocene* is too broad—or, conversely, too specific, too narrowly isolated—and it's better to describe our era as the "Plantationocene." It's not industrial capitalism—its reliance on coal-powered factories, the intertwining of factory-based production with a new relationship to nature—that has led to climate change and ecological disaster, because this model mostly characterized Europe. Instead, the culprit should be identified as imperial capital and the plantation, how "large-scale, export-oriented agriculture dependent on forced labor has played a dominant role in structuring modern life since the insertion of European power in the Americas, Asia, and Africa," to use the words of geographer Wendy Wolford.[6]

Perhaps *all* these terms are too large, too totalizing. There has been perpetual intellectual riffing on Crutzen and Stoermer since they popularized *Anthropocene*, with terms like *Anthrobscene, Econocene, Technocene, Misanthropocene*, and *Manthropocene*—all reinventing, rethinking, and reimagining the limits and possibilities of diagnosing our contemporary era, some more serious than others.[7] Yet, as Donna Haraway has argued, "all the thousand names are too big and too small; all the stories are too big and too small. . . . We need stories (and theories) that are just big enough to gather up the complexities and keep the edges open and greedy for surprising new and old connections."[8] Haraway's own neologism improvising on *Anthropocene, Chthulucene*, attempts to move away from the totalizing scale proposed by the varied *cenes*, emphasizing not a singular cause that consequentially determines the totality of the planet but the emergent, collective agencies that together compose the world.[9]

Our proposal of *Corpocene* as a term to supplement the above is to some degree ironic, to some degree serious. Almost all variations on the term *Anthropocene* incorrectly presume that *-cene* means "epoch" or "age" rather than "recent."[10] We acknowledge the interpretation of *-cene* as "age" or "epoch" is a misreading yet still accept it. We generally agree with those who argue that, regardless of the name we give our context, it's not really humans, as such, that have changed the planet but specific modalities of capitalism—industrial and imperial alike. Like Haraway, we agree that most *-cenes* are far too totalizing. But what is Marxist theory without totality?[11] Even though there are countless alternative ways of living, if one cannot sketch a model of the dominant conjuncture how would it be possible to oppose and invent a new way of living?[12]

Unlike almost everyone mentioned above, working to diagnose the dominant structures of the twentieth century guiding our present, we consider the Corpocene to be *emergent* today, not something that names the dominant order of modern social life since around the Industrial Revolution. While the historical precedents of the Corpocene were laid out through both industrial and, especially, imperial capitalism, the Capitalocene and the Plantationocene, we are only now entering the Corpocene, and we see moments of the beginning of this era when we trace the model of subject privileged in influencer culture. The Corpocene is an age in which the corporation and corporal form converge—a convergence even implied by the etymology of *corporation*, from the Latin *corporare*, a word that means "to combine into one body." Our term is intended to foreground the reinvention of the human being, represented by *Anthropos*, through the logic of the corporation. The corporation collapses the differences between distinct "bodies."

THE CORPORATION AND THE "NATURAL" PERSON

A corporation is, traditionally, a joint venture of multiple individuals intended to mitigate the risk of large-scale trade and profit. Tendencies such as monopoly and conglomeration (or horizontal and vertical integration) demonstrate how corporations act as a discrete entity for economic exchange, an entity that greedily and gladly absorbs individuals, bodies, and even other corporations, subsuming them under a singular name. Monopoly and conglomeration can be contrasted with the economic acts of "entrepreneurial" individuals, performed by specific "natural" people who are not insulated against risk and who cannot absorb others and remain entrepreneurs. The entrepreneur, thus, is an inevitably precarious economic actor, at least traditionally.[13]

In the Corpocene, then, the corporation exists as a social form insulated from precarity, from punishment, from risk under conditions in which the state no longer cultivates society but abandons individual citizens to their own resources, letting them slowly die.[14] It mitigates precarity through a multiplication of the self into multiple industries, vertically integrating the self, hiding and revealing particular parts of the self, as if one is no longer an entrepreneurial subject but a distributed self that can act in multiple roles, as if the self is a synergistic business. Any remains of the social contract are replaced not with the privileging of "entrepreneurial" individuals but with massive, conglomerated bodies that appear as individuals, who exist both as corporate brands and as proper names—Jeffree Star, MrBeast, Kim Kardashian, Elon Musk, Jeff Bezos, Bill Gates. Because these corporations appear as singular, "natural" persons, they are mistaken for entrepreneurs, as if they are as precarious as anyone else, as if they are as exposed to the same risk that comes from the collapse of the liberal nation-state as anyone else.

We do not presume a singularity in which the corporate form exists in precisely the same way in each and every instance. Rather, *Corpocene*, for us, names the particular articulation of late capitalism over social media, which spreads far beyond social media into questions of citizenship and state, of subjectivity and relation. It accepts—and foregrounds—how late capitalism itself is a concept that refers to the uneven flexibility of capitalist dependencies and inequalities after the time of imperialist monopoly. Late capitalism, as Ernest Mandel notes, may *appear* to be a heavy rationalized, organized society, a society of total administration in which an individual's "entire life is subordinated to the laws of the market—not only . . . in the sphere of production, but also in the sphere of consumption, recreation, culture, art, education, and personal relations. . . . 'Every-day experience' reinforces and internalizes the neo-fatalist ideology of the immutable nature of the late capitalist social order. All that is left is the dream of escape—through sex and drugs, which in their turn are promptly industrialized."[15] Or, late capitalism appears as an era of a totalized formal—and real—subsumption of daily life through the dictates of capital. Everything that seems to have once been beyond the limits of capital can be subsumed as new sources for "growth," new spaces to extract surplus value. Yet this appearance of total subsumption is at least partially misguided. As Mandel points out, "late capitalism is not a completely organized society at all. It is merely a hybrid and bastardized *combination* of organization and anarchy. . . . The quest for profit and the valorization of capital remain the motor of the whole economic process, with all the unresolved contradictions which they inexorably generate."[16] Even formal subsumption occurs unevenly: capitalism must rely on producing spaces "beyond" capitalism, in outside spaces that may seem "impoverished" because of their abandonment by capital, exteriors that, anarchically, produce new conflicts and possibilities through the essential contradictions of capitalism, such as the inevitable contradiction between use value and exchange value. The formal and real subsumption of "everything" generates, and even requires, people and activities that cannot be subsumed, "abandoned" by capital—a horizon left to rot until capital can "save" (read: exploit) these very spaces once left behind.

When we suggest that influencer culture and social media indicate a real subsumption of selfhood by capital, we do not suggest that there is literally no possibility of selfhood beyond social media. We are arguing that the space of social media requires a particular model of subjectivity to mitigate against precarity—one that looks not toward others for collective action but to the self, which is reinvented as if it were a collective body in the service of economic exchange: a corporation. This is, in practice, an *ideal*, an ideology perpetuated whenever the most successful influencers are viewed on YouTube.[17] As a mode of subjectivity, almost nobody successfully conflates their very identity with a corporate form. Yet the desire to privatize, to conglomerate the self, remains. "Contemporary society is not shaped by multitude so much as *solitude*," claims Byung-Chul Han. "The general collapse of the collective and the communal has engulfed it. Solidarity is vanishing. Privatization now reaches into the depths of the soul itself."[18] Privatization, we suggest, is not merely about being alone but about replacing models of citizenship and public selfhood with an ideal of privatized, secret, concealed corporate interests. The multitude is expressed only as an outgrowth of an individual, who sees in their own individuality the existence of a multiple and distributed corporate form. The inequalities on which late capitalism relies, when it comes to social media, depend on the belief that anyone is equally capable of distributing and privatizing the self. This results in a generalized mass of potential surplus population who attempt to valorize their own identities in the name of achievement, in the name of corporatizing individuality.

When one moves beyond the limits of social media, of influencer culture, one can still find different models of selfhood that remain beyond commodification, "abandoned" by capitalism as "unproductive." The Corpocene, then, is our emerging age or epoch in which the industrialization of the self is central and the self increasingly follows the corporate form. But this industrialization of the self is forever incomplete and chaotic, a constant struggle that is never finished or realized. And, most significant, the dream of escape—from the emotional deadening produced by the capitalist subsumption of social existence—is no longer presented as "industrialized" sex and drugs; rather, through the capitalist subsumption of social existence, it is imagined to produce an "unalienated" selfhood where the influencer, as corporation, is the fulfillment of a truly satisfied existence. Influencer culture, in other words, requires a model that almost archetypally follows what Lauren Berlant described as "cruel optimism." The structural existence of capitalist reality is a barrier for the satisfaction that very same structure promises.[19] This ideal, of fulfillment through subsumption, generates constant contradictions, seen in videos like those we've reviewed throughout these pages, which speak to perpetual exhaustion, burnout, and depression, even when "fulfillment" appears to be within grasp.

PANDEMIC CANCELLATIONS

Why would this industrialization of the self, its cruelly optimistic embrace of corporate form, be something essential for capitalism when mediated by social media? For the truly elite of influencer culture, the precarity of contemporary economic life is mitigated by a distribution of resources that diversifies and fragments the self into a corporate structure that protects against critique, against accusation, against the risk of being in public online. If one's livelihood depends on the value of one's image, then the threat of so-called cancellation, of online public shaming, is a threat that links economic precarity with conditions of spectacle. If the value of one's labor power inherently involves the exchangeability of one's public image, then the main effect of being "cancelled" is the evacuation of economic value from one's commodified self. In structuring the self as a corporation, public accusation is mitigated by a retreat into privatized form. The evacuation of the domestic privacy of daily life through media, technology, and the transformation of the public sphere from the 1960s to the present[20] enables a new privacy to appear—one of corporate contractual arrangements concealed by the potentials of social media to make visible. The inability to see the corporate form that guides these individuals makes it appear as if they are just particularly good at navigating the demands of social life on the internet. Their "success" makes it seem as if there are people who are so savvy, or so popular, that they do not need to worry about "cancellation." But it is the conflation of self and corporation that enables this protection. One protects against criticism, against precarity, against the risk of being visible online, through the diversification and concealment of assets and business ventures—assets and ventures that appear as equivalent to a "self" online. The dialectical counterpart of cancellation, then, is the corporatization of the self.

On social media, we see individuals both willingly and unwillingly making themselves into corporate conglomerations. Not only do we see the elite and the rich on social media—Jeffree Star, Jimmy Donaldson, Emma Chamberlain—diversifying their assets, using corporate structures to avoid "cancellation," but we see other individuals embracing a corporate logic with hesitation given their visibility, their exposure as selves with economic value. One of the most obvious instances of exposure to risk when one had not sufficiently diversified or corporatized selfhood emerged in the immediate wake of March 11, 2020. This was the date the World Health Organization officially declared COVID-19 a pandemic, the date when, in the United States especially, the coronavirus truly came to impact the thoughts and behaviors of many Americans, and, of course, this would include many influencers with global followings based in the United States.

The coronavirus pandemic was, at one point, termed the "great equalizer," as if the vulnerabilities faced by individuals were equivalent, as if the potentials of exposure were the same for all, as if death could affect each and every individual equally.[21] This claim is, of course, laughable. Death never comes for us all in equal measure, on the same footing.[22] Videos made by numerous celebrities and influencers eventually made clear that one could buy their way into early vaccination, into elaborate rituals of testing, into treatment and medication. For those we saw on social media, those once thought of as "microcelebrities,"[23] the ability to use one's money to escape the pandemic, to escape death, began in earnest in those first few months after March, with influencers fleeing their metropolitan locales for more open-air suburban spaces. As the *New York Times* reported at the beginning of April, popular YouTubers and TikTok stars such as Charli D'Amelio and Joe Vulpis documented their attempts at negotiating the pandemic, with D'Amelio, for instance, starting a "distance dance" challenge to advocate for social distancing.[24]

While D'Amelio used the pandemic as a new form of socially "responsible" content, the coronavirus led to more than a few influencers shutting down their accounts temporarily, some permanently, in their documentation of actions that fans and followers saw as morally and politically reprehensible, actions that revealed the separation and otherness of fan and influencer—a violation of the intimate relation we've repeatedly seen throughout this book. Naomi Davis, the writer and star of the popular blog *Love Taza*, posted about her family's renting of an RV so that they could drive from New York City to Arizona. Fashion influencer Arielle Charnas fled to the Hamptons with her family *after* testing positive for COVID-19. Charnas later posted, after significant pushback, "I'm sorry for anyone that I've offended or hurt over the last couple of weeks. We're just trying to navigate through this difficult time, as I'm sure so many people are."[25] Medical experts cried out that this trend of nonessential travel could sway viewer opinions, leading to further disregard toward public health guidelines. At the level of more traditional celebrity, Ellen DeGeneres put another nail in her quickly closing goodwill coffin (hammered even faster after a number of questionable public statements and actions) by writing that staying at home in her multimillion-dollar mansion was "like being in prison," promptly contracting the virus after writing these words.[26] Kim Kardashian celebrated her birthday on a private island, where attendees could pretend the virus never existed. A Twitter post by Kardashian, from October 27, 2020, flaunted photos of her friends and family, maskless and hugging, walking arm in arm along white-sand beaches. In it, Kardashian declared how thankful she was to be able to "pretend things were normal for just a brief moment in time."[27] Countless feeds of various celebrities online were filled with these images of escape, of indulgences only afforded to the rich, documentation of revelry as if death and illness were things that the wealthy could avoid.

Of course, we look to influencers for many reasons. A primary one is, as we have discussed, their displays of excess. The many exhibitions of pecuniary indulgence documented by these videos and images could be another representation of aspirational desire, and it's safe to say that those making these videos, posting these images, assumed that the extravagance performed after the pandemic's onset would have been interpreted similarly as before; despite the pandemic, the ability to waste remained uninterrupted, while the rest of the world locked themselves away, afraid, afflicted, dying. The pleasure of watching many influencers comes, obviously, from this wastefulness; we can consume this waste vicariously, reveling in a luxury inaccessible to most. And, given the moral decadence of true excess, we may desire *both* the pleasures that come from vicarious consumption *and* the pleasures of moral condemnation. We do not want to be responsible for the direct ownership of this excess, of the responsibility that comes from transmuting objects of value into shit. Most likely, many of us do not want the attention one gets from the excess of celebrity and its constant intrusion into one's life.

This duality only intensifies when one's waste becomes something that marks one's exceptionality from a broader economy of death. Kim Kardashian was beloved for her extreme lifestyle (or at least hate-followed for it), so why should this stop because the world is sick? The generation of excessive waste during the pandemic revealed, for many isolated at home, the absolute difference between influencer and influenced; and a relation of aspiration, for some, reversed into a relation of disgust. As writer Bobo Matjila stated in *Teen Vogue*, influencers were "far too removed from the lived experience of the everyday person to have any valuable input" on how to live during the pandemic. But at the same time, their removal from "everyday" life, their wastefulness—the paradox of why we watch them, love them, hate them—could now help to *accelerate* this very distance. Matjila continued: "On one hand influencers position themselves as relatable, but mass relatability only further isolates them from their audience. . . . So actually, we're not all in this together and I'm glad the pandemic has highlighted this."[28]

Or, one of the things the pandemic made visible was how, despite constant attempts to produce intimate closeness through, for instance, the visualization of domestic interiors, through monologues in cars, seeing the excesses of luxury during the pandemic revealed just how distinct some influencers are to those watching on their computers and phones. For some, like *Love Taza*'s Naomi Davis, this led to a complete implosion of her career as an influencer. On March 28, 2020, Davis posted a photo to her Instagram account @taza, showing her family of seven outside a rented RV. Her caption read:

> If you zoom into this photo in front of that big old white thing (which is the top of an RV Camper), you'll see our family of seven as little dots just a few moments before driving out of New York City yesterday (Friday). My heart is breaking for what is happening in New York where I live and around the world right now. And after two full weeks in the apartment, we made the family decision to drive out west so we can have a little more space (namely some outdoor space for the kids) for a little while. While we've been diligent about self-quarantining and social distancing in New York City, we want to make sure we still stay away from others during our trip (even though no one in our family has had any symptoms, you could always be asymptomatic). For this reason, we decided to rent an RV in order to avoid hotels and people and just eat and sleep in the RV on the way. Hopefully a little change of apartment scenery will be just what we need—for everyone's physical health, for my headspace which is spiraling lately—and for our kids' own mental health. This situation is serious everywhere and I am sending my love and prayers to you wherever you are. More on my stories. 💜 (and photo from our friends who caught us packing up on the street outside an apartment window and texted us! Thank you so much for this photo, Weinbergs!)[29]

Like Kardashian, Davis wrote about the safety precautions she and her family had taken to allow them the privilege the post showed. (Of course, this privilege was still unevenly distributed—for Kardashian, a tropical island birthday party, for Davis, an expedition across the country with five children in a cramped RV.) Although there was support for Davis's choice from some of her followers, especially because of her large family and small NYC apartment, many of the comments on the post were negative. Countless mentions of "UNFOLLOW" were braided through angrier messages, including one decrying Davis's "dangerous, reckless behavior. Please don't be so concerned about yourself that you forget you are *more* likely to cause harm to others."[30] And another: "It takes some egregiously insufferable influencer privilege to dramatically flounce from the epicenter during an international health emergency. Wouldn't you say so @lovetaza. Naomi

Davis should have been canceled long ago."[31] Buzzfeed even reached out to a public health expert to comment on Davis's actions, who wrote that she was "highly irresponsible" and "not safe at all."[32]

Davis continued to update her various social media feeds—both her Instagram and blog—for some time after the March 28 post, showing her family celebrating birthdays in their new Arizona home, promoting her upcoming book, *A Coat of Yellow Paint: Moving Through the Noise to Love the Life You Live.*[33] Yet her blog, once populated with new content nearly every day, slowed and finally went quiet after a post on June 7, 2021, describing a birthday celebration in Wyoming for her son.[34] Davis's final Instagram post, from October 1, 2021, was a banal image of one of her small children being kissed by her and her husband. "Beatrice sandwich! And some of the very best pizza we have ever eaten behind us," it read.[35] Comments wondered where she had disappeared, with one commenter stating, "Trolls got on her for moving during the pandemic. They were waiting to pounce after all these years."[36]

Unlike Kardashian, Davis seemed unable to separate her self, her actions, from her branded commodity—the book. The Goodreads page for *A Coat of Yellow Paint* is littered with one- and two-star reviews, all mentioning Davis's privilege and self-indulgence.[37] One reviewer wrote, "I didn't like how she totally skimmed over her COVID debacle, and instead talked about how spring of 2020 ruined her plans. Naomi is continuously tone deaf in her understanding of the world and people who aren't wealthy white women. Meh."[38] Another read:

> Like many, I vaguely knew Davis as a blogger and was mildly fascinated by how different her NYC life was to my own—how she felt comfortable holding up hundreds of people's journeys to twirl on busy crossroads, how she didn't see the rats while encouraging her family to eat on the floor. What really got me interested was the midnight flit 11th-hour escape after lockdown orders were announced. I read this book because it promised honesty, and I assumed that details on that would be included. Sadly not though. Not even any reflection on the huge changes it brought for her, what's good and what's bad. It's just endless platitudes and twee details about haircuts.[39]

Yet another mentions Davis's 2020 move:

> I'm sure Naomi was passionate about this project but it contributes
> nothing of value unless you can relate to the "struggles" of a thin, white,
> affluent woman who doesn't need to work to live. Learning about the
> controversy surrounding her fleeing NYC during the height of the pan-
> demic and seeing how she minimized it by making it seem like her week-
> end plans were cancelled because of rain or something just emphasizes
> how tone-deaf privileged white women are sometimes. Amazon calling
> this a "dancer biography" and "NYC travel guide" is a reach.[40]

Yet another: "Oh gosh just no, I was sent this for free from some giveaway
and actually feel robbed of intellect and time. I spent about 2 hours reading this, and it felt like I was just scrolling on the internet the whole time.
All frosting no flavor. AND didn't she flout pandemic rules and flee NYC
which was her whole image? A little honesty would have gone far."[41] The
reviews mentioning Davis's move from New York in 2020 abound, despite
it not being discussed in the book. (And, as can be seen above, that lack
of discussion is sometimes the reason for a bad review.) Kim Kardashian
does not have to deal with the same kind of accusations, at least not ones
analogous to those that led to Davis's disappearance from social media. As
just one example, it's not like the website for Kardashian's shapewear line,
Skims, is populated with customer reviews decrying Kardashian's wasteful
lifestyle and privilege.

CONFLATIONS OF CORPORATIONS

Despite neoliberalism's seeming requirement of an "entrepreneurial" self,[42]
in which one must constantly struggle, hustle, and be "creative" to avoid
financial ruin,[43] the distinction between, say, Naomi Davis and Kim Kardashian resides in how Kardashian has *transcended* this entrepreneurial
selfhood, sublating it into something larger—to a vertically integrated,
corporate selfhood. While a major symbol of Davis's privilege and lack
of concern for the position of her audience, and thus her "cancellation"
and disappearance from the public stage, was a rented RV, Kardashian
can display photo after photo of her private plane and inevitably remain
center stage. Part of this is, as with Jeffree Star in the previous chapter,

Kardashian's ability to completely intertwine her personal identity and her corporate brand, all while remaining safe and secure through a distributed corporate structure concealed by its appearance as a "self." In a 2022 episode of *The Kardashians*, Kim showed off her newly renovated "Air Kim," her private jet, which included an all-cashmere interior. Kardashian said of the new look, "I wanted it to feel like an extension of me and an extension of my home."[44] The image of the private jet is yet another infrastructural background like those charted in this book, subsuming car and home, endowing them with excessive wastefulness that characterizes true luxury. The background must be "authentic," must be an "extension" of an identity that can claim and absorb countless commodities, countless industries, countless ventures, a void of expenditure that, in the end, only speaks to the demand to generate excessive content.

For Kardashian, one's value comes not only from the ability to attract attention, to be "branded" and sold, but from a distribution of self into a range of multiple industries owned, managed, and controlled by an individual, conflated with that individual, much like naming a private jet after yourself; it is a return, in many ways, to a traditional understanding of industrial capitalism after the rise of immaterial labor in the 1970s, after the perpetuation of an "entrepreneurial" neoliberal selfhood. Davis can only sell herself to an audience—her precarity resides in how the only thing she can sell is her labor power, encapsulated in how her self can attract attention for others. Kardashian has partial ownership of at least twelve businesses and business ventures, almost all of which involve manufacturing and selling physical commodities. Some of Kardashian's businesses have been failures—like the "Kardashian Kard," a prepaid Mastercard from 2010, a venture into the financialized economies of late capitalism. But many—especially those involved in manufacturing consumer goods, like her brands KKW Fragrance, KKW Beauty, her underwear brand Skims,[45] and her skin-care line SKKN—have been massively successful.[46] The conflation of these brands with Kim Kardashian the person is perhaps most overt with KKW Fragrance, the bottle for which was, at one point in time, modeled directly off of Kardashian's torso.[47] While not nearly as lucrative as a number of her other companies, Kardashian's casual, free-to-play game *Kim Kardashian: Hollywood* best demonstrates the integrated synergy between Kardashian's identity and her various businesses. In the mobile game, one attempts to become an A-list star with the help of Kardashian by replicating a (somewhat simplified) narrative of her rise to fame, her personality, and her style. In-app purchases include virtual copies of designer clothes that Kardashian has actually worn, simulated vacations to locations Kardashian has traveled to on the television show *Keeping Up with the Kardashians*, along with digital versions of accessories made visible by either Kardashian's social media, paparazzi imagery, or her television show. For instance, when the family visited Cuba on their television show, they traveled exclusively in a hot pink convertible, which could be purchased within a section of the game set in Havana, effectively integrating television, game, fashion, travel, cars, and more. *Hollywood*, in many ways, is a game that speaks to the total integration of branding, manufacturing, and identity today. Glu Mobile, the company that produced the game, approached Kardashian to collaborate on it because, as spokeswoman Claudia Oropeza stated, she was "the best brand fit in the world."[48] In the sheer distribution of selfhood through all of these industries, along with not only representing the branded goods of others but conflating oneself with one's own brand, a brand that makes numerous material products, is, we want to suggest, a method for corporatizing the self, for insulating against the precarity of life in which self-image appears to be the commodity most of value. Yet, what Kardashian really reveals is how this attention to self, this attention to image, is at least partially a distraction. The self only matters insofar as it conceals a corporate apparatus we mistake for an individual human being.

One might suggest that a major ruse of contemporary capitalism is how we often imagine the individuals we see online—along with billionaires who present themselves as the public face of their corporations, such as Elon Musk, Jeff Bezos, and Mark Zuckerberg—as "entrepreneurs." The "creative" or "intellectual" capital of these individuals, the mythos of the start-up, and the persistence of the "Californian Ideology" all lead to a view that conflates massive conglomerations with the actions of individuals who become metonyms for the corporations they found and head.[49] Additionally, the rise of immaterial labor, the belief that value, today, comes primarily from knowledge, from images, from social relations—beliefs that lead to the mistaken view that the economic valuations of corporations like Tesla, Amazon, and Facebook emerge from the "genius" of their founding individuals—has obscured how the manufacturing and sale of consumer goods still underpins the wealth of today's bourgeoisie. The legacies of industries such as mining and transportation literally provide the capital today's "entrepreneurs" used to start their careers as "creative" capitalists,[50] and few of these businesses can be said to focus on ideas and images rather than the selling or movement of physical consumer goods and raw materials. The Corpocene, we might claim, names the era in which these pseudo-entrepreneurs, these corporations that appear as people, are mistaken for individuals who are "like us," who are "accessible," who are similarly precarious and struggling and hustling. The return to a kind of branded manufacturing detours through an economic order in which "thought" and relationships appear to be the primary commodities sold. But the fragmentation and obfuscation of class in influencer culture reveals how foregrounding ideas, branding, and relationships—and neglecting manufacturing, supply chains, and ownership of physical assets—has distracted us from this emerging conflation of person and corporation.

This conflation will continue and will increase the frustration of those unable to convert oneself into a corporation, who are unable to transcend the boundaries of one's body, distributing the self into a range of concealed contractual and economic relations. In the face of increasingly visible corporate personhood and personal corporate-hood, online mobs will continue to lash out, cancelling precarious individuals like Naomi Davis while expressing baffled futility when those such as Kardashian (or Jeffree Star or MrBeast) seem immune to critique. This frustration will not mean the end of public displays of excessive wealth, only a continued symbiosis between enraged attention and wasteful excess, intertwined in a mutually reinforcing cultural death drive in which total waste, total exhaustion, and death and destruction are the ultimate outcomes—a realization of the complete, luxurious expenditure imagined by Georges Bataille. Even though Bataille, as discussed earlier in this book, saw perpetual waste as that which could drive a kind of communism through total expenditure, an excess that would ensure individual "sovereignty" in a refusal of utility for others, he also saw death as "the most luxurious form of life," because life is that which is the highest value, so the highest luxury would be in squandering life itself.[51]

One example, which shows how these issues begin to play out in the very direct face of climate-catastrophe and bourgeois excess is, yet again, a Kardashian-owned private jet. While it is common knowledge that most of the Kardashian-Jenners own their own private planes, an Instagram post from July 16, 2022, set off yet another backlash toward the waste of the extended Kardashian family. On that day, Kylie Jenner posted a black-and-white image of herself and her longtime partner Travis Scott standing in front of two private jets; the caption read, "you wanna take mine or yours?"[52] This post set off a wide range of negative responses, mostly focusing on the sheer wasteful excess of owning and operating multiple private jets. There were memes about individual responsibility being useless in the face of a celebrity's excess. Flight records of Jenner's plane were posted across the internet, revealing how often Jenner uses her plane for brief trips—a level of wastefulness beyond many commentors' comprehension, Jenner taking consistent weekly flights lasting between three and ten minutes.

This online anger has not and will not lead to Jenner's disappearance. It will not lead to Jenner's name being taken off her branded goods, which will not cease to sell. (Travis Scott will not stop selling concert tickets either, a fact also demonstrated by his album and concert ticket sales only increasing after ten deaths and countless injuries sustained from a preventable stampede at Scott's Astroworld Festival in 2021.)[53] Jenner's excessive display of waste in the face of a burning world produced a huge number of likes alongside any controversy. As anyone who uses social media knows, "likes" are hardly an accurate account of goodwill. They are a representation of any minimal engagement with a public person, and engagement is the lifeblood of social media attention. And perhaps more of a problem: Jenner's display of wealth is yet another reminder that waste is *luxurious*, that climate change is *luxurious*. Creating in one week a carbon footprint larger than most individuals will amass in several lifetimes is the height of luxury. "Life is essentially extravagant, drawing on its forces and its reserves unchecked," says Bataille; "unchecked it annihilates what it has created. The multitude of living beings is passive in this process, yet in the end we resolutely desire that which imperils our life."[54]

THE CORPORATE PERSON

Understanding the specificity of our context—when Kardashian, like the elite influencers we've mostly examined in this book, moves beyond an entrepreneurial selfhood toward a corporate selfhood, distributing risk— requires a brief discussion of the history of "corporate personhood." When elite influencers present themselves and their business activities as fundamentally equivalent, we see how some conflation between "corporation" and "person" occurs. This conflation is new but reliant on tendencies essential to the entirety of modern imperial capitalism. The history of the corporation is linked with the management and mitigation of risk when economic relations expand on a global, international scale. The distinction between a precarious entrepreneur and a massive, distributed corporation has long been central to this understanding of risk. But this distribution of risk can only happen through the creation of an entity that can act as an individual, which cannot be reduced to any one individual; it may be a "person" in the eyes of the law, but it cannot be equated to any "natural" person. In influencer culture, in the Corpocene, the conflation of person and corporation relies on, but in many ways reverses, this long-standing link between corporations and legal personhood. We'll now review a bit of the history of "corporate personhood" to examine how influencer culture performs this reversal.

In Adam Smith's *Wealth of Nations*, the corporate form depends on a legal charter produced and recognized by the state. Through this charter, multiple individuals share ownership and legal liabilities for profits and debts, acting as a singular economic being. One particularly notable kind of corporation, the joint-stock company, an ancestor to almost all publicly held corporations today, Smith holds up as particularly valuable for managing the financial exposure of individuals. For joint-stock companies such as the imperialist behemoth Dutch East India Company, corporate structures are necessary to "establish a new trade with some remote and barbarous nation," with distance and "barbarism," Smith presumes, difficulties implicit in colonial economic exploitation, difficulties that could dissuade global financial expansion and investment.[55] For Smith, the corporation is to be contrasted with the entrepreneur, whose individual acts cannot possibly insulate against risk as a corporation does. In other words, the corporation is an entity produced by law, by the state, to act as an individual. It is a body assembled out of many separate parts, performing as one unified being, a being that necessarily appears to exceed the material existence of any singular actor. The corporation is essential for the move beyond industrial to imperial capital, in which exploration and exploitation of geographical regions beyond Europe were necessary for economic growth, spatially "fixing" problems of overproduction.[56] Yet the real benefit of creating a corporation is to distribute debt, risk, and liability to ensure that the individual human beings who make up the corporation are, at least somewhat, insulated from the acts of the corporation as a whole, insulated from the uncertainty of global imperialism.[57]

An entrepreneur, as a single individual, is a "natural person." The entrepreneur, as an individual, is legally responsible for all investments and debts occurring in daily economic activities. Of course, many of the rights and responsibilities given to an entrepreneur have nothing to do with the individual's economic existence as an entrepreneur. But, when it comes to legal, economic culpability for their business dealings, law can, usually without question, understand the entrepreneur as a person. A corporation, given that it is a singular "individual" made up of many other individuals, cannot be said to be a "person" in the same way as an entrepreneur. Yet the corporation is, legally, fictionally, a "person" in the eyes of the state for reasons of legal culpability—a conflation that descends from not only basic definitions of the corporation advanced by Smith but from questions about the rights and abilities of ecclesiastic bodies in the thirteenth century.[58] Almost any modern definition of a corporation presumes it to be legally equivalent to a person, though the discourse of corporate personhood was only popularized in the United States and other Anglophone countries around 1900, through the writings of English legal historian Frederic William Maitland and his summarizing of corporate personhood as accepted in common law. "The corporation is (forgive this compound adjective) a right-and-duty-bearing unit," Maitland wrote, noting that the rights afforded this corporate "person" were not precisely the same as other "persons." A corporation could not be married, for instance. Yet, Maitland claimed, when it comes to questions of law and state, "in a vast number of cases you can make a legal statement about x and y which will hold good whether these symbols stand for two men or for two corporations, or for a corporation and a man."[59]

Debates about corporate personhood, descending from Maitland, have almost always been about whether corporations should be considered, for the sake of law, the equivalent of a "natural" person, a human being, and in some contexts, a "citizen." In 1911, Baltimore lawyer Arthur W. Machen Jr. published the article "Corporate Personality" in the *Harvard Law Review*, drawing on and extending the work of legal scholars like Maitland. "From the earliest period of our judicial history, lawyers and judges have reiterated the doctrine that a corporation is an intangible legal entity, without body and without soul," wrote Machen.[60] In taking up the problem of "corporate personality," Machen sought to review arguments from European sources, juridical and philosophical alike, attempting to determine, first, whether a corporation was a "real and natural entity, recognized but not created by law," and second, if that real and natural entity was "a person," thus subject to guaranteed rights and abilities under law.[61]

In European debates, Machen claimed, some scholars, like Maitland and Smith, saw a corporation as a legal fiction created by the state, while others saw the corporation as a pure fiction, "merely an abbreviated way of writing the names of several members."[62] Still others drew on vitalist claims to argue that a corporation should be understood as an "organism," an "animal," which even "possesses organs like a human being. It is endowed with a will and with senses. It even possesses sex: some corporate organisms, like the church, are feminine, while others, such as the state, are masculine."[63] Like other vitalisms common throughout the 1800s, derived in part from scientific discoveries related to blood circulation, the corporation became a literal body in which the movement of some "substance," such as capital, would act like a vital fluid that maintained the body's health.[64]

Machen saw these debates as a question of ontology, about a distinction between an idealism—which would see a corporation as an object or entity that possessed an equivalent reality to any other object or entity—and a materialism—which denied the existence of a corporation beyond the individuals who, together, made up the corporation itself. But through logical, metaphorical arguments, comparing the corporation to other "real" entities that could be broken down into parts (such as a river, broken down into atoms of oxygen and hydrogen, or "the Church," the "Republican Party," or "any other aggregation of men for good or evil"), Machen concluded that a corporation must be *real*, even if it cannot be said to be either ideal or material.[65] Machen differs from Maitland in arguing that the corporation is not inherently a legal fiction; he does not believe that the state, essentially, produces the corporation for the sake of legal regulation. The same, however, cannot be said for the corporation as a *person*. Or, for Machen, corporations exist as real things, but there is nothing to say that corporations have rights, have abilities, have obligations, until the state claims it to be a "person."

What does it mean for something to be, from the perspective of law, a "person"? Machen begins by following Maitland, suggesting that, legally, personhood is "not a rational, living creature similar to a man, but a mere 'subject of rights,'"[66] not something inherently equivalent to a human being. If a corporation is a "subject of rights," then under the law, it could be considered a person. But Machen complicates this simple understanding of personhood: in practice, personhood is not about rights but *liabilities*, which are found in an ability to understand *punishment* for violation of law. For Machen, morality and rationality are central for understanding one's legal position. A person, for Machen, must be something the state can punish and something that acts in a way that grasps the potential of punishment.[67] Thus, Machen concludes, "the proposition 'A corporation is a person' is either a mere metaphor or is a fiction of law."[68] Although corporations, Machen argues, are real, they cannot be considered persons because of the absence of morality and rationality. A corporation cannot, in and of itself, understand particular actions as punishable by law, because it lacks the moral faculty of judgment.[69]

More than a decade after Machen's arguments about corporate personality, the pragmatist philosopher John Dewey, in a 1926 article in the *Yale Law Journal*, pushed some of the implications of prior writings on corporate personhood further, concluding that "for the purposes of law the conception of 'person' is a legal conception; put roughly, 'person' signifies what law makes it signify."[70] Instead of the ontological claims of Machen, Dewey accepts an appropriately pragmatist view of personhood: what matters is not that something can be classified as a person while something else cannot but the "social consequences" of ascribing rights and duties to something. "There are some things, bodies singular and corporate, which clearly act differently, or have different consequences, depending upon whether or not they possess rights and duties, and according to what specific rights they possess and what obligations are placed upon them."[71] If placed in a historical context beyond that acknowledged by jurists such as Machen, providing a corporation with personhood is something that can both expand and limit corporate power beyond punishment alone. "In an 'individualistic' period," Dewey argues, which he defines as "an era chiefly concerned with the rights of private property and contract," the identification of a corporation as a legal person "might even enlarge its rights, privileges and immunities."[72] Regardless, when it comes to arguing between the existence of corporations as persons against the belief they are not, "each theory has been used to serve the same ends, and each has been used to serve opposing ends."[73] Corporate personhood, for Dewey, is ultimately an incoherent idea without ontological grounding, an idea that can only be grasped through the specific ends that equating corporation and person performs. The corporation—as a legal entity—is always, to some extent, a "person," because it is only through legal understandings of personhood that a corporation can be given legal rights and responsibilities but also be punished for violating these rights and responsibilities. It is a necessary fiction: a corporation is not literally a "person," but it is a person in the same way that other fictional legal entities are. Is the legal fiction of corporate personhood there to regulate the "rights" of a corporation? Or is it put in service of *expanding* these "rights"? Is it there to mete out punishment? Or is it there to expand potentials of action?

In recent years, the legal understanding of the corporation as a subject of rights has greatly increased in significance once again, especially in American public life. In the wake of a series of Supreme Court decisions, beginning with the 2010 ruling in *Citizens United v. Federal Election Commission*,[74] which found that corporations possess a right to free speech in the form of unlimited corporate spending on election campaigns,[75] American public life has seemingly privileged corporate rights and abilities over those of so-called "natural" persons.[76] In the *Citizens United* ruling, there is an explicit acknowledgment that corporate entities possess the same rights as "natural" persons, though these rights may be expressed differently and at different scales. Or, in the pragmatist terms of Dewey, the problem with the *Citizens United* decisions is not in the inherent ascription of "personhood" to a corporation. Although this link cannot be justified through the "originalist" arguments popular among some members of the Supreme Court,[77] corporations have long been "persons" in the eyes of the law, and, as Dewey shows, this "personhood" can both restrict and privilege the actions of a corporation. The problem is that *Citizens United*, by equating corporate spending with the exercise of speech, created a "right" to be enjoyed by corporate persons but not by "natural" persons. Where for Maitland, Machen, Dewey, and almost all other theorists of corporate personhood, the corporation is a legal person that *cannot* perform many of the acts given to "natural" persons—getting married, voting in elections, running for office, and so on—the *Citizens United* ruling effectively created a right given to corporate persons that cannot be enjoyed by individuals beyond the ultrarich: unlimited spending to influence elections.

In influencer culture, the conflation of person and corporation occurs not precisely in the sense of "corporate personhood" or "corporate personality," though it relies on the transformation of "personhood" sketched above. In legal debates, the problem of considering a corporation a "person" emerges from, initially, questions about the regulation of rights and abilities of a body that cannot be reduced to a single human being. It turns toward problems of punishment and culpability but is ultimately a category that can be used to both expand and limit the power of corporate entities. In recent years, the conflation of corporation and person—and the move to place the rights of a corporation *above* those of an individual human—ends up provoking questions about scale and financial exposure. In the *Citizens United* case, one of the main "ends" that emerged from the Supreme Court's ruling was a conflation of the right to free speech—the right codified in the First Amendment—with spending on advertising.[78] Because a corporation cannot "speak" as such, if it is to be given the rights of a "person," then its ability to buy ads, to distribute media content, must be considered the medium through which the corporation can participate in public discourse. Justice John Paul Stevens's dissent to *Citizens United* makes it obvious that this provokes problems of access: everyday citizens do not have the financial access to multimillion-dollar ad buys that well-funded corporate entities have; the conflation of money with speech limits the potential of individuals from participating in public debate. But the argument in favor of the ruling presents one simple reason why this concern over money no longer matters in the eyes of those on the Supreme Court—the *internet* permits equal access to a new public sphere, accessible to all regardless of funding.[79] This argument is obviously flawed. As everyone except for those deluded idealists still enrapt with the mythos of Silicon Valley knows, not everyone has an equal voice on the internet. And turning to influencer culture and its reinvention of corporate personhood shows just how absurd the *Citizens United* case ruling was in presuming some equivalence between equal access and the rights of personhood.

Influencer culture inverts the historical articulation between corporation and person after a ruling like *Citizens United*, embracing contradictions that simultaneously link and differentiate person and corporation. If a corporation is a body of multiple individuals linked together by law for purposes of distributing risk and liability, in influencer culture we find individuals, seemingly "natural" persons, *passing themselves off as a corporation*. Corporations may be seen as people from a legal perspective, but today, it seems, "people" themselves also follow the structure of the corporation—though the reasoning behind corporatization is similar. The logic of *Citizens United*—deferral to internet access notwithstanding—is that to be worthy of full rights and abilities under law one *must be a corporation*. In today's hierarchy of value between citizens and persons, a corporation ranks higher than so-called "natural" persons. The mirroring of the corporate form by influencers is to mitigate and distribute risk, risk that comes from, on one hand, the evacuation of rights and abilities from "natural persons" who increasingly find their existence diminished, impoverished, and precarious, and, on the other, living as if one is a commodity in which one's value comes from being seen and exchanged.

CORPORATE CITIZENS

The Corpocene begins when corporations become full citizens, worthy of rights and abilities under the rule of law—a realization and intensification of traditional notions of corporate personhood. In this realization and tacit acceptance of corporate personhood, the corporation is given privileges and responsibilities of citizenship that *exceed* those of "natural" persons; they are provided a voice in the court of public life, with laws and policy framed in the "public" interest targeted toward the well-being of conglomerated and monopolistic industries. Moving beyond the simple acceptance of a corporation as a person, as a legal fiction necessary for reasons of punishment and culpability, a fiction that enables, for instance, the juridical meting out of fines, in the Corpocene the corporation is privileged as the *ideal* "citizen," with the rights of individuals impoverished in relation. Since corporations are privileged as citizens and social actors in contemporary public life, what were formerly known as "people" and "citizens," "natural" persons afforded rights and abilities based on the requirements of the state and the happenstance of birth, become a mass of surplus population to be used and discarded—that is, unless a "person" can pass themselves off as a corporation. The Corpocene is the dialectical sublation of the opposition between corporation and person, a synthesis of the two that privileges and maintains the corporate form.

In the Corpocene we see, on one hand, the collapse of labor power and identity and, on the other, the collapse of subjectivity and the vertically integrated conglomerate. These two conflations, in which self and business are confused and intertwined, should be understood as both a grounding of the possibilities of class on the internet and an obstacle preventing many possible directions for class struggle and organization. When we see Jeffree Star and Jimmy Donaldson organize themselves through LLCs in which they serve as representatives of a corporation but also act as if they *are* the corporation, we can see the logic of the Corpocene at work. These are not "businesses" following a "sole proprietorship" model, in which Star or Donaldson is, as an individual, legally culpable for all risk, debts, and liabilities that exist under their names. Jeffree Star LLC, simultaneously *is* Star and completely *exceeds* him, a corporate "person" that both is and is not reducible to Star as a "natural" person. All of Kim Kardashian's business dealings follow a similar logic. Skims both *is* Kardashian (even including her name—Kim—in its name) and yet cannot be reduced to her. The corporation is the person, yet the corporation exceeds the person, mitigating risk, insulating the person that the corporation comes to represent.

The Corpocene describes the moment in which capital is anthropomorphized, as the individual aspires to act as the equivalent of vertically integrated capital—an aspiration designed to move the protections afforded the corporation onto individuals in reaction to the "risk" of living one's life in public view. To protect against cancellation, the "public" front of the corporation—meaning the persona of the influencer as presented online—conceals the business arrangements still equated with the "self," arrangements hidden behind what is visible over social media. If one cannot manage this corporate divide between public image and private investment, like *Love Taza*'s Naomi Davis, then one slowly vanishes from the internet, from social media, from a career of luxury and influence, all as one's livelihood dries up.

We live in an era in which billionaire CEOs have become celebrities. Elon Musk and Jeff Bezos take in record paychecks, with Musk, in particular, leading the way in redefining how chief executives are paid, vastly increasing wealth disparities between the upper echelons of management and workers on assembly lines.[80] Musk hosts *Saturday Night Live*; his tweets seem to manipulate financial markets while he distributes his businesses across many different industries, businesses of which he presents himself as equivalent. While we may know that Tesla and Musk are not the same thing—legally or materially—countless fanboys of the celebrity billionaire presume that Musk's public persona indicates a level of equivalence between the two. Musk's purchase of Twitter seems motivated by a desire to forcibly broadcast his own voice, controlling a media outlet through widely erratic whims and desires. Through their excessive wealth, both Musk and Bezos—along with several other billionaire CEOs—are working to literally colonize space, finding a way to reach resources on other planets or even discover a way off this one, as the global temperature increases to the point where Earth will become uninhabitable. While space is being colonized, we may laugh at what should be a futuristic horror; we laugh at those doing the colonizing, as they wear stupid hats and fly into the sky on dick-shaped rockets. This is our paradox, our world, our Corpocene. Taken alongside the logic of influencer culture, the fetish for billionaires is yet another fact revealing our desire for excess and expenditure—luxury—to the point of complete annihilation.

These same billionaires aren't stopping with space but are interested in appropriating time, as well, putting clocks in mountains. Jeff Bezos has put more than $42 million into constructing "The Clock of the Long Now," a project originally conceived by computer scientist and entrepreneur

Danny Hillis, within a mountain Bezos owns in Texas. It will tick once a year for at least ten thousand years, with a cuckoo coming out every millennium. The purpose of this clock, according to founding board member and futurist Stewart Brand (*of course* our conception of slow time has to have a corporate board today, in the Corpocene), will be to "embody deep time for people" and "be charismatic to visit," as well as "be famous enough to become iconic in the public discourse."[81] Billionaires will own space and time—or at least this seems to be the goal—while they conflate their personhood with the corporations they manage. Space and time will have corporate boards, becoming "people" under law, with monuments that are themselves "famous." Meanwhile "natural persons" are rendered powerless, beyond legal regulation, stripped of rights and privileges, abandoned by capital and left to wither unless one can make oneself exchangeable, valuable—unless one can make oneself a corporation.

In Lacanian psychoanalysis, the moment of intervention is inherently traumatic. One must rupture the fantasy, confronted with what Lacanians often refer to as a "traumatic encounter with the Real," an encounter with something that escapes language, escapes sense, escapes meaning—a horrific confrontation that shatters fantasy, requiring one to rethink and reframe one's very conception of reality. So many things today seem like they should induce this traumatic encounter but are met instead with a slow shrug that indicates that the truth has been known all along, and nothing can be done. Call it "enlightened false consciousness" or a "decline of symbolic efficiency."[82] It's not like we do not *know* the reality of the world, the horror of the corporate appropriation of everything, of how this appropriation will increasingly render more and more as surplus population to be discarded, forgotten, beyond the boundaries of capital. Instead, if I cannot go back to unknowing, if I cannot will myself into ignorance, I will know very well about the awfulness of the present and simply *not care* about it or, perhaps slightly better, convince myself that there is no alternative to the present.[83] And I will revel in the luxury, excess, and waste my passivity requires. This creates a generation, an entire audience of anyone consuming social media, of incredibly educated, knowledgeable, but ultimately passive participants. Knowledge is power, but knowledge is horror. We have learned, with help from our influencer friends, to make palatable the unpalatable, to walk hand in hand with our own destruction, to learn more about it in order to push it further away.

CAPITAL, COMMUNITY, CORPOCENE

The Corpocene, then, is a name for a moment in which corporate logic replaces and remakes the possibility of community, self, and relation, contained within an individual body that appears as both a "natural" person and a corporate structure. All forms of struggle and conflict must begin from a position that understands "community" and "individuality," as performed over social media, as social relations produced by late capitalism, offering few direct routes of resistance. The Corpocene did not begin entirely with social media but is an outgrowth of the imperial era, in which the self becomes a new frontier. This turn inward renders the possibility of class struggle almost impossible. In an age of the real subsumption of community by capital, says Jacques Camatte, "capital had to absorb the movement that negates it, the proletariat, and establish a unity in which the proletariat is merely an object of capital. . . . It follows that all forms of working-class political organizations have disappeared."[84] Camatte is lamenting forms of social organization that cannot be truly considered unities of workers—organizations that take the form of a "racket" or "gang," which rely on hierarchies and financial investments, "firms" that follow a corporate structure and may appear to oppose "legitimate" forms of capitalist organization but nonetheless mirror capitalism rather than oppose it. If the proletariat is supposed to be that which negates capital, the racket and the gang absorb the proletariat, rendering class struggle impossible. "Class conflicts," Camatte says, "are replaced by struggles between the gangs-organizations which are the varied modes of being of capital. . . . All organizations that want to oppose capital are engulfed by it."[85] Camatte's solution to the problem of the racket and the gang is a somewhat libertarian form of communism, where the "revolutionary must not identify himself with a group but recognize himself in a theory that does not depend on a group or on a review, because it is the expression of an existing class struggle."[86] Class struggle, for Camatte, should exist without hierarchy, with the "expression" of class conflict not through particular, unified groups making specific, contingent demands but through a broader, almost universal conflict without organization.

In the Corpocene, we see a deepening of the tendency described by Camatte: not only do collective forms of social organization repeat the logic of the corporation, but *individuals* now mirror the corporate form. The individual cannot be grasped as an entity that could possibly withstand the real subsumption of community by capital. What we have seen, over the course of this book, is how influencers should be grasped as a synthesis of an individual with the material reality of contemporary capitalism, with real estate, with markets, with supply chains. The appearance of an influencer as an individual distinct from these capitalist infrastructures only happens through a phenomenological apprehension that differentiates figure and ground, a differentiation that forever articulates influencer and infrastructure while rendering infrastructure obscure. Attending to these grounds reintroduces the influencer as a new kind of corporate person, revealing how the real subsumption of capital has pushed even beyond the pessimistic diagnosis of Camatte to constituting the very being of a "person" today.

What does it mean that, from looking at the videos of influencers, it is almost impossible to formally distinguish between precarious influencers and influencers who should be understood as vertically integrating their own identities, investing in means of production of the self? Today, the subject of social media follows a corporate form. Class struggle, when it comes to the internet, must first reject the view that internalizes corporate logic at the level of subjectivity. Influencer culture itself will not permit the abandoning of this model of subjectivity. The resistance to capital today must abandon "influence" as a model of social relation.

FURTHER VIEWING

Some of the videos that were essential to our analysis are listed here. For readers inclined to delve into our primary sources, we encourage you to watch these with our arguments in mind, along with other videos created by those listed here and elsewhere in this book.

Introduction
Kara Del Toro reveals the secret of the no-mirror mirror selfie.

Kara Del Toro (@karajewel). "Secrets Bloggers Don't Want You to Know Part 1." TikTok, Feb. 1, 2021, www.tiktok.com/@karajewel/video/6924442856014761222.

Chapter 1: Home
Elsie Larson gives a tour of the home *A Beautiful Mess* purchased and renovated to donate to Habitat for Humanity.

A Beautiful Mess. "ABM Habitat House Tour (Before + After)." July 31, 2015, www.youtube.com/watch?v=b3ktNmJmxQM.

Elsie Larson shows off the renovations of her Nashville home.

A Beautiful Mess. "Elsie's Home Video Tour." Nov. 6, 2019, www.youtube.com/watch?v=jNRj5EO_iKw.

Gamer and YouTube star PewDiePie reacts to a home tour video of Emma Chamberlain's new home.

AnyHome. "PewDiePie Reacts to Emma Chamberlain's $3.9 Million Dollar Home." June 23, 2021, www.youtube.com/watch?v=fM8SJtOD2_0.

Jeffree Star shows off his lavish home in Hidden Hills, CA.

Jeffree Star (jeffreestar). "Official Jeffree Star DREAM House Tour!" YouTube, Jan. 1, 2020, www.youtube.com/watch?v=XHn5H9YdFWw.

Mia Maples diagrams her home ownership and living situations while answering viewer questions.

Mia Maples. "Relationship Status? Living Situation? New Dog? Answering Your Questions FINALLY!" YouTube, August 14, 2020, www.youtube.com/watch?v=h5vad7uQvw4.

Mia Maples shows her recording rooms to viewers.

Mia Maples. "STUDIO TOUR !! *House Transform ed into a Complete YouTube Studio*." YouTube, June 11, 2021, www.youtube.com/watch?v=ZxLXiTgivig.

Chapter 2: Car

Emma Chamberlain monologues while driving.

Emma Chamberlain (emma chamberlain). "I Literally Lost My Car." YouTube, Jan. 2, 2018, www.youtube.com/watch?v=BUjslatDPzl.

Nikita Crump explains the day-to-day experience of living in her car.

Nikita Crump. "LIVING IN A CAR: Day 366—How I Stay Warm/Cool at Night." YouTube, Nov. 1, 2020, www.youtube.com/watch?v=5wRcxxA4HOY.

Alyssa Vanilla, who lives in her car, describes the perks of travel.

Alyssa Vanilla. "How I Travel the Country Alone Even Though I Have Anxiety." YouTube, June 2, 2021, www.youtube.com/watch?v=Ono6ECFSJYw.

Chapter 3: Market

Emma Chamberlain visits her childhood bedroom and discusses selling various mementos.
    Emma Chamberlain (emma chamberlain). "My Childhood Bedroom." YouTube, Nov. 8, 2021, www.youtube.com/watch?v=oK27MiJZrRo.

Jimmy Donaldson's recreation of *Squid Game*, which cost more per-minute than the original Netflix series.
    Jimmy Donaldson (MrBeast). "$456,000 Squid Game in Real Life!" You-Tube, Nov. 24, 2021, www.youtube.com/watch?v=oe3GPea1Tyg.

Ryan Kaji pulls a seemingly endless number of toys from a Papier-mâché egg in one of his most popular videos of all time.
    Ryan Kaji (Ryan's World). "GIANT Lightning McQueen Egg Surprise with 100+ Disney Cars Toys." YouTube, July 1, 2015, www.youtube.com/watch?v=T1dlt2RhrDw&t=136s.

Jimmy Donaldson buys and trashes a storage unit.
    Jimmy Donaldson (MrBeast). "I Bought an Abandoned Storage Unit and Found This . . ." YouTube, Dec. 1, 2017, www.youtube.com/watch?v=yUXlx2l8kko (video no longer available).

Hope Allen buys and sifts through an enormous box of Amazon returns.
    Hope Allen (HopeScope). "I Bought Amazon RETURNS for CHEAP! *Disaster*." YouTube, March 9, 2021, www.youtube.com/watch?v=H_U29oAqsiw.

Hope Allen discusses the logistics of how she was able to buy a box of Amazon returns.
    Hope Allen (HopeScope). "I Bought LOST Cargo Packages for CHEAP." YouTube, Dec. 23, 2021, www.youtube.com/watch?v=AXv4Y87oCLY.

Safiya Nygaard visits an Amazon returns store.
    Safiya Nygaard, "I Went to an Amazon Returns Store." YouTube, Oct. 14, 2021, www.youtube.com/watch?v=D6V85qfsu3g.

Jenna Phipps documents a thrift store shopping trip.

Jenna Phipps. "Thrift with Me for Some Trendy Y2k Clothes \\ Thrifting Value Village in Vancouver, Canada." YouTube, Jan. 17, 2021, www.youtube.com/watch?v=I6VoPXcJsxM.

Jenna Phipps cleans out her closet to make room for more clothes.

Jenna Phipps. "MASSIVE CLOSET CLEAN OUT + CLOSET TOUR... I Got Rid of Half of My Clothes," YouTube, May 12, 2021, www.youtube.com/watch?v=g5knduCqndE.

Safiya Nygaard and Tyler Williams try out many cooking tools, including one that peels a sausage.

Safiya Nygaard and Tyler Williams (Safiya & Tyler). "Testing Out More Bizarre Kitchen Gadgets from the Internet." YouTube, August 10, 2021, www.youtube.com/watch?v=k6YDStI9veI.

Chapter 4: Warehouse

Anthony Bender provides tips for "surviving" a job at Amazon.

Anthony Bender (Ayebender). "The Truth about Warehouse Work." YouTube, May 4, 2020, www.youtube.com/watch?v=wznjpoQnUio.

Ciara Jenae secretly films her last day working for Amazon.

Ciara Jenae. "Day in the Life of an Amazon Packer Vlog | My Last Day at Amazon." YouTube, August 24, 2022, www.youtube.com/watch?v=IfEE8YoySz4.

A peek inside Jimmy Donaldson's filming studio and warehouse space via a behind-the-scenes video by the effects team hired to help him recreate *Squid Game*.

SoKrispyMedia. "Making MrBeast's Squid Game in 10 Days." YouTube, Nov. 27, 2021, www.youtube.com/watch?v=VQcO_PYVx3o.

Jimmy Donaldson challenges his friends and one viewer to an escape room challenge in which he will burn their prize money if they fail.

Jimmy Donaldson (MrBeast). "World's Most Dangerous Escape Room!" YouTube, Jan. 29, 2022, www.youtube.com/watch?v=3jS_yEK8qVI.

The "Sensible Mama" shows off her newly purchased warehouse where she will expand her business.

The Sensible Mama. "I BOUGHT A WAREHOUSE // TOUR." YouTube, Jan. 13, 2020, www.youtube.com/watch?v=orsn7DRZJ_A.

Tanner Fox introduces viewers to his future warehouse and game room.

Tanner Fox. "I BOUGHT A HUGE WAREHOUSE!!! *OFFICIAL TOUR*." YouTube, June 6, 2017, www.youtube.com/watch?v=8XqaCYK5BDk.

NOTES

Introduction

1. Horkheimer and Adorno, *Dialectic of Enlightenment*, 124.
2. Dobson, Carah, and Robards, "Digital Intimate Publics."
3. See, e.g., Lury, *Brands*.
4. David Marchese, "YouTube Made Emma Chamberlain a Star. Now She's Leaving It Behind," *New York Times Magazine*, Feb. 17, 2023, www.nytimes.com/interactive/2023/02/20/magazine/emma-chamberlain-interview.html.
5. Taylor Lorenz, "Instagram's Wannabe-Stars Are Driving Luxury Hotels Crazy," *The Atlantic*, June 13, 2018, www.theatlantic.com/technology/archive/2018/06/instagram-influencers-are-driving-luxury-hotels-crazy/562679.
6. See, among others, Duffy, *(Not) Getting Paid*; Pham, *Asians Wear Clothes*; and Harris, *Kids These Days*.
7. Quoted in Lorenz, "Instagram's Wannabe-Stars."
8. Marwick, "Instafame."
9. Andrea Park, "Caroline Calloway's 'Creativity Workshop' Taught Me Nothing about Creativity but a Lot about Scamming," *W Magazine*, Jan. 2019, www.wmagazine.com/story/caroline-calloway-creativity-workshop.
10. US Securities and Exchange Commission, "SEC Charges Kim Kardashian for Unlawfully Touting Crypto Security," press release, Oct. 3, 2022, www.sec.gov/news/press-release/2022-183.
11. Marchese, "YouTube Made Emma Chamberlain a Star."
12. See, e.g., Hund, *The Influencer Industry*, 12–35.
13. Katz and Lazarsfeld, *Personal Influence*.
14. Weimann, *The Influentials*.
15. Tarde, "Origins and Functions of Elites," 245–51.

16. Veblen, *Theory of the Leisure Class*, 32–33.

17. Veblen, 35–101.

18. Lazzarato, "Immaterial Labor."

19. See *Endnotes*, "Misery and Debt."

20. Mattie Kahn, "Is There Life after Influencing?" *New York Times*, April 14, 2023, www.nytimes.com/2023/04/11/style/lee-tilghman-influencer.html.

21. See, e.g., Horkheimer and Adorno, *Dialectic of Enlightenment*, 125.

22. Horkheimer and Adorno, 24.

23. See Klein, *No Logo*, 30.

24. The YouTube video series "The Secret World of Jeffree Star," discussed in chapter 4, exists in large part because of skepticism about the actual wealth of its subject. Also see Marwick, "Instafame."

25. See, e.g., Kuehn and Corrigan, "Hope Labor"; Abidin, "Visibility Labour"; Pham, *Asians Wear Clothes*; Duffy, *(Not) Getting Paid*; and Precarity Lab, *Technoprecarious*.

26. For a small selection of a broad field, with arguments that differ about the essential function of race and racism in determining contemporary culture, see Bonilla-Silva, *Racism without Racists*; Alexander, *The New Jim Crow*; Wilderson, *Afropessimism*; Sharpe, *In the Wake*; and Towns, *On Black Media Philosophy*.

27. Orgad and Gill, *Confidence Culture*, 45.

28. An anonymous marketer quoted in Christin and Lu, "The Influencer Pay Gap," 11.

29. Wanna Thompson, "How White Women on Instagram Are Profiting Off Black Women," *Paper*, Nov. 14, 2018, www.papermag.com/white-women-blackfishing-instagram-2619714094.html.

30. hooks, *Black Looks*, 21–39.

31. Noble, *Algorithms of Oppression*, 1.

32. Benjamin, *Race after Technology*, 5–6 (emphasis in the original).

33. McIlwain, *Black Software*, 7.

34. Chun, *Discriminating Data*, 49.

35. Cf. Ngai, *Our Aesthetic Categories*.

36. Benjamin, *Race after Technology*, 4.

37. Angela Johnson, "Tarte Cosmetics Just Hosted a Lavish Influencer Trip to Dubai, Should We Care?" *The Root*, Jan. 21, 2023, www.theroot.com/tarte-cosmetics-just-hosted-a-lavish-influencer-trip-to-1850015287.

38. CT Jones, "How a Makeup Brand Melted Down TikTok," *Rolling Stone*, May 11, 2023, www.rollingstone.com/culture/culture-features/tarte-drama-makeup-brand-tiktok-1234733560.

39. Njathi, "The Glitz and Glamour Platform Economy," 42.

40. Njathi, 43–44.

41. Benjamin, *Race after Technology*, 36.

42. Benjamin, *Viral Justice*, 176–78.

43. Cf. Towns, *On Black Media Philosophy*.

44. Benjamin, *Viral Justice*, 52.

45. See Taylor, *Race for Profit*.

46. See Hund, *The Influencer Industry*.

47. Kaitlyn Tiffany, "The Influencer Industry Is Having an Existential Crisis," *The Atlantic*, March 31, 2023, www.theatlantic.com/technology/archive/2023/03/tiktok-instagram-influencers-algorithm-labor-union/673584.

48. Tiffany.

49. Taylor Lorenz and Laura Zornosa, "Are Black Creators Really on 'Strike' from TikTok?" *New York Times*, Sept. 3, 2021, www.nytimes.com/2021/06/25/style/black-tiktok-strike.html.

50. Tiffany, "The Influencer Industry."

51. Camatte, *This World We Must Leave*, 91–92.

52. Mandel, *Late Capitalism*.

53. Marx, *Capital*, 1:1054–55.

54. See Srnicek and Williams, *Inventing the Future*; Bastani, *Fully Automated Luxury Communism*; and Wendling, *Karl Marx on Technology and Alienation*.

55. Dean, "Communism or Neo-Feudalism?"; Wark, *Capital Is Dead*.

56. Fisher, *Capitalist Realism*.

57. Williams, *The Long Revolution*, 68.

58. Srnicek, *Platform Capitalism*.

59. Joshua Holmes (@joshomz), "Reply to @karamelioness What being a content creator & influencer is like vs working a 9–5 job, if you don't already have rich parents," TikTok, Jan. 27, 2022, www.tiktok.com/@joshomz/video/7057988600645913902.

60. Silvia Killingsworth, "And the Word of the Year Is . . ." *New Yorker*, Nov. 19, 2013, www.newyorker.com/culture/culture-desk/and-the-word-of-the-year-is.

61. "Robert Cornelius' Self-Portrait: The First Ever 'Selfie,'" *Public Domain Review*, Nov. 19, 2013, https://publicdomainreview.org/collection/robert-cornelius-self-portrait-the-first-ever-selfie-1839.

62. Jenny Howard, "The Brief (and Bizarre) History of Selfies in Space," *National Geographic*, June 21, 2019, www.nationalgeographic.com/science/article/space-selfies-brief-and-bizarre-history-national-selfie-day.

63. Hannah Williams, "Portraits Are a Fine Art, so Let's Embrace the Selfie," *The Conversation*, June 26, 2014, https://theconversation.com/portraits-are-a-fine-art-so-lets-embrace-the-selfie-28375.

64. Marx and Engels, *The German Ideology*, 36; Jameson, *Marxism and Form*, 326; Williams, "Base and Superstructure," 31–32.

65. Alex Williams, "Here I Am Taking My Own Picture," *New York Times*, Feb. 19, 2006, www.nytimes.com/2006/02/19/fashion/sundaystyles/here-i-am-taking-my-own-picture.html.

66. Guinness, "Self-Portraiture and Self-Performance," 40.

67. See Bollmer and Guinness, "Phenomenology for the Selfie," 165.

68. Artemisa Clark (@bustilacaca), Instagram, accessed April 11, 2022, www.instagram.com/bustilacaca (private account).

69. Guadamuz, "The Monkey Selfie."

70. See Bollmer and Guinness, "Phenomenology for the Selfie."

71. How we describe the self-portrait, then, would seemingly relate to the very idea of naturalism and its economic logic as described by Walter Benn Michaels: "being oneself depends on owning oneself, and owning oneself depends on producing oneself" (Michaels, *The Gold Standard*, 13).

72. Quoted in Annelisa Stephan, "What's the Difference between a Selfie and a Self-Portrait?," *Getty Iris Blog*, Jan. 21, 2015, https://blogs.getty.edu/iris/whats-the-difference-between-a-selfie-and-a-self-portrait (emphasis in the original).

73. Stephan, "What's the Difference."

74. Stephan.

75. Eichhorn, *The End of Forgetting*.

76. Chun, *Programmed Visions*, 167–73.

77. Jurgenson, "Digital Dualism and the Fallacy of Web Objectivity," *Society Pages*, Sept. 13, 2011, https://thesocietypages.org/cyborgology/2011/09/13/digital-dualism-and-the-fallacy-of-web-objectivity/.

78. Stephan, "What's the Difference."

79. This means we reject Michael Fried's distinction between theatricality and absorption and similar claims about the autonomy of the artwork. See Fried, *Absorption and Theatricality*.

80. Kara Del Toro (@karajewel), "Secrets Bloggers Don't Want You to Know Part 1," TikTok, Feb. 1, 2021, www.tiktok.com/@karajewel/video/6924442856014761222.

81. Ngai, *Theory of the Gimmick*, 3.

82. Léa-Elisabeth (@lea.elisabeth.a), Instagram, accessed April 11, 2022, www.instagram.com/lea.elisabeth.a (no longer available).

83. Ngai, *Theory of the Gimmick*, 101.

84. Thom Waite, "Influencers are Scamming Us with This Selfie Mirror Trick," *Dazed*, March 17, 2021, www.dazeddigital.com/life-culture/article/52228/1/influencers-are-scamming-us-with-this-selfie-mirror-trick-instagram-tiktok.

85. Emilia Patrarca, "This Influencer Conspiracy Will Make You Question Everything," *The Cut* (*New York Magazine*), March 19, 2021, www.thecut.com/2021/03/influencer-mirror-selfie-picture-fakes.html.

86. Ellie Violet Bramley, "'The Fakery Is All Part of the Fun': The Hoax of the Mirror Selfie," *The Guardian*, March 22, 2021, www.theguardian.com/fashion/2021/mar/22/the-fakery-is-all-part-of-the-fun-the-hoax-of-the-mirror-selfie.

87. See Azoulay, *Civil Imagination*.

88. Foucault, *The Order of Things*, 4–5.

89. Foucault, 11.

90. Foucault, 16.

91. Han, *The Transparency Society*, 1–2.

92. Cassandra Green, "Turns Out Influencers Are Hoodwinking Us All with Their False 'Mirror' Selfies," *Body and Soul*, April 1, 2021, www.bodyandsoul.com.au /health/turns-out-influencers-are-hoodwinking-us-all-with-their-false-mirror -selfies/news-story/4d4bbb3e5e76ed2aaccbb96ef666aace.

93. Han, *Disappearance of Rituals*, 12.

94. Carey, *Communication as Culture*, 11–28.

95. Han, *Disappearance of Rituals*, 13.

96. Derrida, *Specters of Marx*.

97. Mandel, *Late Capitalism*, 43.

98. Mandel, 44.

99. Much of Shoshanna Zuboff's *Age of Surveillance Capitalism* could be read as an outline of how technology has formally subsumed most aspects of human sociality.

100. Camatte, *This World We Must Leave*, 182.

101. Camatte, *Capital and Community*, 108–9.

102. Veblen, *Theory of the Leisure Class*.

103. Cf. Camatte, *This World We Must Leave*, 64–65.

104. Guinness, *Schizogenesis*.

105. Williams, "Here I Am Taking My Own Picture."

106. Dan Brooks, "How Far Can You Go to Resist Being the Subject of a Viral Video?" *New York Times Magazine*, Sept. 1, 2021, www.nytimes.com/2021/09/01/ magazine/tiktok-pranks.html.

107. Brooks.

108. Hund, *The Influencer Industry*; Duffy, *(Not) Getting Paid*.

109. Jameson, *Marxism and Form*, 322.

Chapter 1

1. See Guinness, "Self-Portraiture and Self-Performance."

2. Debord, *Society of the Spectacle*.

3. Baudrillard, *Simulacra and Simulation*, 21.

4. Meyerowitz, *No Sense of Place*; Berlant, *Queen of America*; Warner, *Publics and Counterpublics*.

5. Federici, "Social Reproduction Theory," 55.

6. Scholz, "Patriarchy and Commodity Society," 127.

7. Taylor, *Race for Profit*.

8. Mia Maples, "Mia Maples," YouTube, www.youtube.com/c/MiaMaples. Maples's account on YouTube was originally named Ivorygirl42.

9. Mia Maples, "About," YouTube, www.youtube.com/c/MiaMaples/about.

10. Mia Maples, "Mia Ma-Plays," YouTube, accessed August 1, 2022, www.you tube.com/channel/UCvRhblKpR8SH7VHhooKnTog. This channel has, since our initial writing, been subsumed into the "second channel" YouTube trend in which

influencers create a second channel in which they offer extra content, host lives-treams, hold giveaways, and upload content they deem unfit for their primary channel. Mia Maples's second channel is named "More Mia Maples."

11. Mia Maples, "Relationship Status? Living Situation? New Dog? Answering your questions FINALLY!" YouTube, August 14, 2020, www.youtube.com/watch?v=h5vad7uQvw4.

12. Mia Maples, "MOVING OUT Ep#4 Let's Tackle The BASEMENT !! FINALLY another episode !!" YouTube, August 7, 2020, www.youtube.com/watch?v=OjeWN l7f-u0.

13. For Maples, this seems to be accurate. In later videos, we learn that there is an editing basement in which she and her mother sit and work on the production side of things while her father brings them snacks. She continues to utilize her family and place them in starring roles. The limits of this seem to extend only to her husband, who appeared in a handful of videos before their marriage. After up-loading an official wedding video, he has not appeared in either the foreground or background of Maples's videos. Maples is a rarity: while many YouTubers include their family and friends in their content, few take part in the actual process of pro-duction. More often than not, influencers hire a producer to help out. Increasingly, we hear the voices of these producers as the influencer speaks to them instead of, or in addition to, an assumed online audience. These producers often become stars in their own right, inspiring the adoration of fans.

14. Horkheimer and Adorno, *Dialectic of Enlightenment*, 111.

15. Dyer, *Stars*.

16. Fortmueller, *Below the Stars*, 17–49.

17. Mia Maples, "MOVING OUT . . . Let the Renovations Begin!! EP#1," You-Tube, Sept. 28, 2018, www.youtube.com/watch?v=ZusxNOwREel&t=212s.

18. Dyer, *Heavenly Bodies*, 6.

19. A Beautiful Mess, "A Beautiful Mess Photo App," *A Beautiful Mess*, May 9, 2013, https://web.archive.org/web/20200811004322/https://abeautifulmess.com/a-beautiful-mess-photo-app; Elsie Larson, "Announcing Our New App—A Color Story!" *A Beautiful Mess*, Jan. 12, 2016, https://abeautifulmess.com/announcing-our-new-app-a-color-story/.

20. Emma Chapman, "Emma's House Buying Story," *A Beautiful Mess*, August 14, 2012, https://web.archive.org/web/20200804114415/https://abeautifulmess.com/emmas-house-buying-story.

21. Bollmer, *Inhuman Networks*, 78.

22. Hester and Srnicek, "Shelter against Communism."

23. See, e.g., Adorno, "Free Time."

24. Williams, *The Country and the City*, 7.

25. See Davis, *City of Quartz*.

26. See Justin Fox, "Are Millennials Finally Ready to Binge on Housing?" *Bloomberg*, April 15, 2021, www.bloomberg.com/opinion/articles/2021-04-15/home-ownership-for-millennials-may-finally-be-within-reach; Nigel Wilson, "U.S.

Millennials: Home Ownership and the Growing Chasm between Aspiration and Reality," *Forbes*, August 18, 2021, www.forbes.com/sites/nigelwilson/2021/08/18/us -millennials-home-ownership-and-the-growing-chasm-between-aspiration-and -reality. Also see Yana Davidovich, Cecilia Herrick Reynolds, Ning Kang, and KT Thomas, *Millennials and Housing: Homeownership Demographic Research* (Freddie Mac Single Family Marketing Analytics, 2021), https://sf.freddiemac.com/content /_assets/resources/pdf/fact-sheet/millennial-playbook_millennials-and-housing .pdf

27. Hillary Hoffower, "Millennial Homeownership Is Causing the US to Run Out of Houses," *Business Insider*, April 13, 2021, www.businessinsider.com/millen nial-homeownership-driving-housing-shortage-prices-new-builds-2021-4.

28. Elsie Larson, "Elsie's Home Buying Story," *A Beautiful Mess*, Feb. 21, 2013, https://abeautifulmess.com/elsies-home-buying-story.

29. Elsie Larson, "The Story of Our Local Boutique," *A Beautiful Mess*, May 8, 2013, https://abeautifulmess.com/the-story-of-our-local-boutique.

30. Elsie Larson, "Episode #42: Oops, I'm Moving Again," *A Beautiful Mess*, July 6, 2020, https://abeautifulmess.com/episode-42-oops-im-moving-again.

31. Elsie Larson, "New Adventure: We're Giving Away a House!!!" *A Beautiful Mess*, Oct. 20, 2014, https://abeautifulmess.com/new-adventure-were-giving-away -a-house.

32. Elsie Larson, "Elsie's Forever Home Q+A," *A Beautiful Mess*, Jan. 8, 2020, https://abeautifulmess.com/elsies-forever-home-qa.

33. Anna Lee, comment on Elsie Larson, "Elsie's Forever Home Q+A," *A Beautiful Mess*, Nov. 2, 2020, https://abeautifulmess.com/elsies-forever-home-qa/#com ment-1275859.

34. Larson, "Elsie's Forever Home Q+A."

35. Angie, comment on Elsie Larson, "Elsie's Forever Home Q+A," *A Beautiful Mess*, Jan. 9, 2020, https://abeautifulmess.com/elsies-forever-home-qa/#comment -973661.

36. Janet W, comment on Elsie Larson, "Elsie's Forever Home Q+A," *A Beautiful Mess*, Jan. 8, 2020, https://abeautifulmess.com/elsies-forever-home-qa/#comment -972730; Katelin, comment on Elsie Larson, "Elsie's Forever Home Q+A," *A Beautiful Mess*, Jan. 8, 2020, https://abeautifulmess.com/elsies-forever-home-qa/#com ment-972922; Laura, comment on Elsie Larson, "Elsie's Forever Home Q+A," *A Beautiful Mess*, Jan. 8, 2020, https://abeautifulmess.com/elsies-forever-home-qa/ #comment-972943.

37. Larson, "New Adventure: We're Giving Away a House!!!"

38. Elsie Larson, "Episode #110, One Year in Our Home with Jeremy Larson," *A Beautiful Mess*, August 23, 2021, https://abeautifulmess.com/episode-110-one-year -in-our-home-with-jeremy-larson.

39. See Han, *The Transparency Society*; and Han, *The Burnout Society*.

40. Despite Larson's 2021 discussion of home-purchasing and renovation-based burnout, she announced in the spring of 2023 that she would be selling her

latest Nashville home—deemed the "forever home"—to move back to Springfield. *A Beautiful Mess* has already, as of April 2023, begun uploading renovation-based content of this home.

41. See, among others, Jones, "Media-Bodies and Screen-Births"; Heyes, "Cosmetic Surgery and the Televisual Makeover"; and Zylinska, "Of Swans and Ugly Ducklings."

42. Yet, the more recent rejection of some of these discourses in the form of "body positivity" often carry similar, if not identical directives, about becoming a "real" or "true" self, if not through surgery, then through a range of consumer products. See Orgad and Gill, *Confidence Culture*, 29–55.

43. Marx, *Capital*, 1:272.

44. McCarthy, "Reality Television," 17.

45. Ian Parker, "HGTV Is Getting a Renovation," *New Yorker*, March 22, 2021, www.newyorker.com/magazine/2021/03/29/hgtv-is-getting-a-renovation.

46. Larson, "Elsie's Forever Home Q+A."

47. Elsie Larson, "Episode #99: How to Bond with Your Home (When It Doesn't Come Instantly)," *A Beautiful Mess*, July 5, 2021, https://abeautifulmess.com/episode-99-how-to-bond-with-your-home-when-it-doesnt-come-instantly.

48. Elsie Larson, "Episode #86: The Best Business and Life Advice We've Ever Received," *A Beautiful Mess*, April 19, 2021, https://abeautifulmess.com/episode-86-the-best-business-and-life-advice-weve-ever-received.

49. Elsie Larson, "Episode #16: Business Advice for Our Younger Selves," *A Beautiful Mess*, Feb. 3, 2020, https://abeautifulmess.com/episode-16-business-advice-for-our-younger-selves.

50. Elsie Larson, "Episode #63: Listener AMA Biz + Money," *A Beautiful Mess*, Nov. 23, 2020, https://abeautifulmess.com/episode-63-listener-ama-biz-money.

51. Interestingly, this video is hosted on the AnyHome channel, not PewDiePie's own channel. AnyHome, "PewDiePie Reacts to Emma Chamberlain's $3.9 Million Dollar Home," YouTube, June 23, 2021, www.youtube.com/watch?v=fM8SJtOD2_0.

52. Emma Chamberlain, "I MOVED . . ." YouTube, June 15, 2021, www.youtube.com/watch?v=lUhM1zRW324&t=243s.

53. AnyHome, "INSIDE OF EMMA CHAMBERLAIN'S NEW $4.3 MILLION DOLLAR HOME," YouTube, June 21, 2021, https://www.youtube.com/watch?v=8dTpCgFbt98.

54. James Leggate, "YouTuber Emma Chamberlain, 20, Leases Los Angeles Home for $35,000 Per Month," *Fox Business*, July 16, 2021, www.foxbusiness.com/real-estate/youtuber-emma-chamberlain-leases-home-35k-month.

55. Gladys Lai, "Emma Chamberlain's New, Light-Filled Los Angeles Estate Is the Epitome of Zen," *Vogue Australia*, June 20, 2021, www.vogue.com.au/vogue-living/design/emma-chamberlains-new-lightfilled-los-angeles-estate-is-the-epitome-of-zen/image-gallery/ce17521ca8dfd276451322265adbe283; Gladys Lai, "Emma Chamberlain's Newly-Listed $5.26 Million West Hollywood Mansion Is an Archi-

tectural Showstopper," *Vogue Australia*, April 7, 2021, www.vogue.com.au/culture/
features/emma-chamberlains-newlylisted-526-million-west-hollywood-mansion
-is-an-architectural-showstopper/image-gallery/47dbb9e1b3977bdebfaaa7e0b11cb
b61.

56. This line was originally spoken by Star in an Instagram story. For documentation, see Daniella Scott, "A Detailed Timeline of Jeffree Star and Nathan
Schwandt's Relationship," *Cosmopolitan*, Jan. 9, 2020, www.cosmopolitan.com/uk
/entertainment/a30451994/jeffree-star-nathan-schwandt-relationship-timeline
-history/.

Chapter 2

1. Emma Chamberlain (emma chamberlain), "GROCERY SHOPPING CURES
BOREDOM," YouTube, March 7, 2021, www.youtube.com/watch?v=cTvQ8inelRU.

2. Emma Chamberlain (emma chamberlain), "ugg season," YouTube, Oct. 31,
2021, www.youtube.com/watch?v=vLlreLOw2nM.

3. Emma Chamberlain (emma chamberlain), "haunted," YouTube, August 22,
2021, www.youtube.com/watch?v=UNRCO3rNugs.

4. Emma Chamberlain (emma chamberlain), "i lowkey crashed into someones
car (plz don't tell my mom)," YouTube, Oct. 17, 2017, www.youtube.com/watch?v=
DkDy1R5l8vY.

5. Jerry Seinfeld, *Comedians in Cars Getting Coffee*, Netflix, accessed August 1,
2022, https://www.netflix.com/title/80171362.

6. Zoli Honig (@zolihonig), Twitter, Jan. 22, 2020, https://twitter.com/zoliho
nig/status/1220138926116982785.

7. Katherine Schaffstall, "James Corden Responds to Viral Clip Showing He's
Not Driving during 'Carpool Karaoke,'" *Hollywood Reporter,* Jan. 30, 2020, www
.hollywoodreporter.com/news/general-news/james-corden-responds-carpool
-karaoke-clip-him-not-driving-1274919.

8. Hamilton and Hoyle, "Moving Cities," 29.

9. Shawn Cooke, "Why Do So Many Dudes Film Themselves Talking in
Their Cars?" *Mic*, March 9, 2020, www.mic.com/p/why-do-so-many-dudes-film
-themselves-talking-in-their-cars-22601289.

10. Cooke.

11. See, e.g., Bruns, *Blogs, Wikipedia, Second Life, and Beyond*; and Shirky, *Here
Comes Everybody*.

12. Cooke, "Why Do So Many Dudes?"

13. See Bollmer, *Inhuman Networks*; and Dean, *Democracy and Other Neoliberal
Fantasies*.

14. Preciado, *Pornotopia*.

15. See Michaels, *The Gold Standard*.

16. Meyerowitz, *No Sense of Place*.

17. Kellner, *Media Spectacle*, 4–8.

18. Berlant, *Queen of America*; Warner, *Publics and Counterpublics*.

19. Debord, *Society of the Spectacle*, 7.

20. Jimmy Donaldson (MrBeast), "I Uber'd People and Let Them Keep the Car," YouTube, Oct. 24, 2020, www.youtube.com/watch?v=loZri9hq7z4.

21. Jimmy Donaldson (MrBeast), "I Opened a Free Car Dealership," YouTube, August 29, 2019, www.youtube.com/watch?v=3LLnjRLrvLU.

22. Julian de Medeiros, "Full Class: Surplus Enjoyment/Zizek + Squid Game/James Bond," YouTube, Oct. 18, 2021, www.youtube.com/watch?v=argZWvaSK-0.

23. Graham and Marvin, *Splintering Urbanism*, 117; Southworth and Ben-Joseph, *Streets and the Shaping of Towns and Cities*, 5.

24. Ellen Dunham-Jones, cited in Graham and Marvin, *Splintering Urbanism*, 118.

25. Graham and Marvin, *Splintering Urbanism*, 118.

26. Auge, *Non-Places*, 34.

27. Pope, *Ladders*, 5.

28. Pope, 114.

29. Packer, *Mobility without Mayhem*.

30. Williams, *Television*.

31. Melania Juntti, "Why Cars Are the Best Place to Have Tough Conversations with Kids," Fatherly, Oct. 2, 2020, www.fatherly.com/parenting/why-cars-are-the -best-place-to-have-tough-conversations.

32. See DeCerteau, *Practice of Everyday Life*, 93.

33. Juntti, "Why Cars Are the Best Place."

34. Fred Peipman, "Kids in the Car: Talking to Teens," *Psychology Today*, Feb. 29, 2016, www.psychologytoday.com/us/blog/parenting-across-the-gap/201602/ kids-in-the-car-talking-teens.

35. Kelly Wallace, "OMG! Your Teen Actually Talks to You?" CNN, Feb. 27, 2014, www.cnn.com/2014/02/19/living/talking-to-teens-communication-parents.

36. Graham and Marvin, *Splintering Urbanism*, 230.

37. Inkoo Kang, "My Car Is My YouTube Studio," *Slate*, Feb. 1, 2018, https://slate .com/technology/2018/02/why-so-many-youtube-videos-take-place-inside-cars .html.

38. Erlanger and Ortega Govela, *Garage*, 3–4.

39. Quoted in Erlanger and Ortega Govela, 25.

40. Erlanger and Ortega Govela, 33–34.

41. Erlanger and Ortega Govela, 37.

42. Erlanger and Ortega Govela, 63, 66.

43. Erlanger and Ortega Govela, 107, 110.

44. Deleuze, *Cinema 1*, 109.

45. Foucault, *The Birth of Biopolitics*, 226.

46. Boltanski and Chiapello, *New Spirit of Capitalism*; Lazzarato, "Immaterial Labor."

47. Preciado, *Pornotopia*, 17–19.

48. Gamini Connect, "How to Vlog in the Car—Best GoPro and Microphone

Setup with Sample Footage (and Vlogging Fails)," YouTube, June 4, 2020, www.you
tube.com/watch?v=5CaqjtYiqYQ.

49. Mark Dsouza, "Why Do a Lot of Vloggers Film in Their Cars?" Quora, accessed August 1, 2022, www.quora.com/Why-do-a-lot-of-vloggers-film-in-their
-cars/answer/Mark-Dsouza-13.

50. Nikita Crump, "LIVING IN A CAR: Day 366—How I Stay Warm/Cool at
Night," YouTube, Nov. 1, 2020, www.youtube.com/watch?v=5wRcxxA4HOY.

51. Alyssa Vanilla, "Why I Live in My Car," YouTube, Nov. 9, 2020, www.youtube
.com/watch?v=fbGJDs94eSg.

52. Alyssa Vanilla (@alyssavanilla), Instagram, accessed August 1, 2022, www.in
stagram.com/alyssavanilla.

53. Nikita Crump (@nikitacrump), Instagram, accessed August 1, 2022, www.in
stagram.com/nikitacrump.

Chapter 3

1. Mirowski and Nik-Khah, *The Knowledge We Have Lost*.

2. Baudrillard, *The Consumer Society*, 65.

3. Benjamin, *Selected Writings*, 3:101–35.

4. Bollmer and Guinness, "'Do You Really Want to Live Forever?'" 82; also see
Bollmer, *Materialist Media Theory*, 51–78.

5. Barthes, *Camera Lucida*; Peters, *Speaking into the Air*; Kittler, *Gramophone,
Film, Typewriter*.

6. Emma Chamberlain (emma chamberlain), "My Childhood Bedroom," You-
Tube, Nov. 8, 2021, www.youtube.com/watch?v=oK27MiJZrRo.

7. Marx, *Capital*, 1:125–77; Simmel, *The Philosophy of Money*.

8. Simmel, *The Philosophy of Money*, 89.

9. Simmel, 346–54.

10. See Brinkema, *Life-Destroying Diagrams*, 22.

11. Smythe, "Communications," 3.

12. Richard Serra and Carlota Fay Schoolman, *Television Delivers People*, You-
Tube, March 30, 1973, www.youtube.com/watch?v=LvZYwaQlJsg.

13. Fuchs, *Culture and Economy*, 228–30.

14. See Zuboff, *Age of Surveillance Capitalism*.

15. Crary, *24/7*; Sharma, *In the Meantime*.

16. Andrejevic, *Infoglut*; Bollmer, *Inhuman Networks*.

17. Ngai, *Our Aesthetic Categories*, 1.

18. Bateson, *Steps to an Ecology of Mind*, 272.

19. Steffan Powell, "YouTube Rich List: MrBeast Was the Highest-Paid Star of
2021," *BBC News*, Jan. 14, 2022, www.bbc.com/news/entertainment-arts-59987711.

20. "With Less High-Demand Content Available, Total TV Usage Drops in February; Streaming Stays Strong," *Nielsen Insights*, March 2023, www.nielsen.com/
insights/2023/with-less-high-demand-content-available-total-tv-usage-drops-in
-february-streaming-stays-strong/.

21. L. Cesi, "Highest-Earning YouTube Stars 2021," *Statistia*, Nov. 15, 2022, https://www.statista.com/statistics/373772/youtubers-monetization-earnings-celebrity/.

22. Jimmy Donaldson (MrBeast), "Beast Philanthropy," YouTube, accessed July 4, 2023, www.youtube.com/channel/UCAiLfjNXkNv24uhpzUgPa6A.

23. As our argument about MrBeast's need to create increasingly excessive content proves, the *Squid Game* video was soon surpassed by controversy around a 2023 video in which Donaldson paid for the surgeries of one thousand glaucoma patients. Jimmy Donaldson (MrBeast), "1,000 Blind People See for the First Time," YouTube, Jan. 28, 2023, www.youtube.com/watch?v=TJ2ifmkGGus.

24. Amanda Silberling, "MrBeast's 'Real Life Squid Game' and the Price of Viral Stunts," *TechCrunch*, Dec. 3, 2021, https://techcrunch.com/2021/12/03/mrbeast-squid-game-creator-economy-viral.

25. Mauss, *The Gift*.

26. Powell, "YouTube Rich List."

27. Katz and Lazarsfeld, *Personal Influence*; Weimann, *The Influentials*.

28. Jay Caspian Kang, "The Boy King of YouTube," *New York Times Magazine*, Jan. 8, 2022, www.nytimes.com/2022/01/05/magazine/ryan-kaji-youtube.html.

29. Kang.

30. Kang.

31. Althusser, *Lenin and Philosophy*, 115–20.

32. See, e.g., Žižek, *Plague of Fantasies*, 53, though there are many discussions of how the failure of Lacan's *objet petit a* to satisfy is the very point of desire, ensuring one can continue to desire, as what one truly desires is the continual possibility of *more*.

33. Ryan Kaji (Ryan's World), "GIANT Lightning McQueen Egg Surprise with 100+ Disney Cars Toys," YouTube, July 1, 2015, www.youtube.com/watch?v=Tldlt2RhrDw.

34. See Eichhorn, *The End of Forgetting*.

35. Ryan Kaji (Ryan's World), "HUGE EGGS Suprise Toys Challenge with Inflatable Water Slide," YouTube, April 13, 2016, www.youtube.com/watch?v=jjd-BeTX6Uo.

36. Kang, "The Boy King of YouTube."

37. Kang, "The Boy King of YouTube."

38. Jeffree Star (jeffreestar), "Buying Myself a NEW $700,000 McLaren!" YouTube, Feb. 5, 2022, www.youtube.com/watch?v=OiDXZlvjiio.

39. Jeffree Star (jeffreestar), "Trying the World's MOST Beautiful Makeup . . . Is It Jeffree Star Approved?!" YouTube, Jan. 21, 2022, www.youtube.com/watch?v=kLfBAIsZaMU.

40. Jeffree Star (jeffreestar), "Getting Rid of $1,000,000 of Makeup," YouTube, March 8, 2019, www.youtube.com/watch?v=MbtesOrC5t4.

41. Veblen, *Theory of the Leisure Class*, 17.

42. Veblen, 75.

43. Bataille, *The Accursed Share*, 1:25.

44. Bataille, *The Accursed Share*, 2-3:237-75.

45. Marwick, "Instafame," 155.

46. Armitage and Roberts, "The Spirit of Luxury," 3.

47. Armitage and Roberts, 11-14.

48. Jimmy Donaldson (MrBeast), "I Bought an Abandoned Storage Unit and Found This . . ." YouTube, Dec. 1, 2017, www.youtube.com/watch?v=yUXIx2l8kko (video no longer available).

49. Baudrillard, *Consumer Society*, 62.

50. Baudrillard, 65.

51. Hope Allen (HopeScope), "I Bought Amazon RETURNS for CHEAP! *disaster*," YouTube, March 9, 2021, www.youtube.com/watch?v=H_U290Aqsiw.

52. Cf. Coley, "'Destabilized Perception.'"

53. Hope Allen (HopeScope), "I Spent $7,000 on LOST CARGO Packages," YouTube, Jan. 13, 2022, www.youtube.com/watch?v=KDdfv56T16s.

54. Hope Allen (HopeScope), "I Bought LOST Cargo Packages for CHEAP," YouTube, Dec. 23, 2021, www.youtube.com/watch?v=AXv4Y87ocLY.

55. Bataille, *The Accursed Share*, vol. 1.

56. See, e.g., Hu, *A Prehistory of the Cloud*; and Parks and Starosielski, *Signal Traffic*.

57. Rossiter, *Software, Infrastructure, Labor*, 3.

58. Hope Allen (HopeScope), "I Bought Target RETURNS for CHEAP *everything is brand new!?*," YouTube, May 21, 2021, www.youtube.com/watch?v=Dweo SucZoqY.

59. Safiya Nygaard, "I Went to an Amazon Returns Store," YouTube, Oct. 14, 2021, www.youtube.com/watch?v=D6V85qfsu3g.

60. Allen has her own collaboration video with Nygaard, showing the same day's activities through her own lens, in which she returns lost luggage she purchased to its original owner. Hope Allen (HopeScope), "I Bought LOST LUGGAGE and RETURNED IT to the Owner + ft Safiya Nygaard," YouTube, June 25, 2022, www.youtube.com/watch?v=v5aHcu19wio.

61. Safiya Nygaard, "I Went to a Lost Luggage Store," YouTube, June 25, 2022, www.youtube.com/watch?v=h31p4OLbqSc.

62. Nygaard, "I Went to an Amazon Returns Store."

63. Ruth Maclean, "'Everyone's Looking for Plastic': As Waste Rises, so Does Recycling," *New York Times*, Jan. 31, 2022, www.nytimes.com/2022/01/31/world/africa/senegal-plastic-waste-recycling.html.

64. Iheka, *African Ecomedia*, 3.

65. Parks and Starosielski, introduction, 5; Andrejevic, "Estranged Free Labor," 162.

66. Iheka, *African Ecomedia*, 81-83.

67. Cf. Mayer, *Below the Line*, 31-65.

68. Savannah Sicurella, "When Second Hand Becomes Vintage: Gen Z Has

Made Thrifting a Big Business," *NPR*, June 18, 2021, www.npr.org/2021/06/18/ 1006207991/when-second-hand-becomes-vintage-gen-z-has-made-thrifting-a -big-business.

69. Ghost Soda Clothing, Instagram, accessed April 8, 2022, www.instagram .com/shopghostsoda.

70. Eliza Huber, "For Gen Z, Thrifting Isn't Just a Way to Shop, It's a Lifestyle," Refinery29, Oct. 29, 2020, www.refinery29.com/en-us/2020/10/10014753/thrifting -gen-z-thrift-shopping-trend.

71. Huber.

72. The Learning Network, "What Students Are Saying about Gen Z's Values, Thrift-Shopping, and Beloved Family Members," *New York Times*, Nov. 11, 2021, www.nytimes.com/2021/11/11/learning/what-students-are-saying-about-gen-zs -values-thrift-shopping-and-beloved-family-members.html.

73. Much like the Amazon return haul, the "Thrift with Me" video is a genre on YouTube with hundreds (if not thousands) of video examples. Phipps provides many exemplars of this genre.

74. Ana Luisa runs its own influencer program. See Ana Luisa, "Ana Luisa In- fluencers," www.analuisa.com/pages/become-an-influencer.

75. Jenna Phipps, "Thrift with Me for Mystery Boxes! We Also Do Some Thrift Flips," YouTube, Sept. 30, 2020, www.youtube.com/watch?v=MkqxxiZaX8k.

76. Jenna Phipps, "Closet Clean Out + Closet Tour \\ Getting Rid of Half My Clothes & Buy Them For $5," YouTube, Dec. 6, 2020, www.youtube.com/watch? v=WT8pDuOOl34; Jenna Phipps, "MASSIVE CLOSET CLEAN OUT + CLOSET TOUR . . . I Got Rid of Half of My Clothes," YouTube, May 12, 2021, www.youtube .com/watch?v=g5knduCqndE.

77. Phipps, "MASSIVE CLOSET CLEAN OUT."

78. Drew Scott (Lone Fox), "THRIFT WITH ME for Home Decor + HUGE HAUL ✴ *I Found My Dream Vintage Chair!*," YouTube, July 15, 2021, www.you tube.com/watch?v=ikFz0pUxvAE.

79. Kim Ebrahimi, "THRIFTING the Fall Wardrobe of Our Dreams 👜 🛍 // THRIFT WITH ME 2021 (Try-on Haul at End)," YouTube, Sept. 26, 2021, www.you tube.com/watch?v=Z3dBCLP2ZlA.

80. Alexa Sunshine (Alexa Sunshin83), "COME THRIFT WITH ME $1 JET RAG SALE ✴ My BEST + Most INSANE Thrift Trip! $1 Try on Thrift Store Haul," You- Tube, Sept. 19, 2021, www.youtube.com/watch?v=G_f-4F9xtTo.

81. Jeffree Star (jeffreestar), "My SECRET Black VAULT Closet Tour," YouTube, Oct. 30, 2021, www.youtube.com/watch?v=LnoEaI6Y2ec.

82. As will be discussed later, Star's disavowal of designer wear is not a dis- avowal of wealth or excess but likely a move up the ladder of wealth. Star's turn to heritage brands and a "simpler" style speaks to the rising trend of "quiet luxury," in which the truly elite and wealthy embrace more banal and more expensive clothes and accessories. This "trend" has roots in the practices of nineteenth-century American industrialists, as well as seventeenth-century French nobility.

83. Caplan and Gillespie, "Tiered Governance and Demonetization," 2.

84. Nygaard, "I Went To An Amazon Returns Store."

85. Safiya Nygaard and Tyler Williams (Safiya & Tyler), "Testing Out More Bizarre Kitchen Gadgets from the Internet," YouTube, August 10, 2021, www.youtube.com/watch?v=k6YDStI9veI.

86. See Sampson, *A Sleepwalker's Guide to Social Media.*

Chapter Four

1. Tsing, "Supply Chains and the Human Condition."

2. See Mandel, *Late Capitalism*, 44–74.

3. Gibson-Graham, *The End of Capitalism.*

4. LeCavalier, *The Rule of Logistics*, 35.

5. See, e.g., Rodney, *How Europe Underdeveloped Africa*; Amin, *Unequal Development*; and Frank, *Capitalism and Underdevelopment in Latin America.*

6. Mandel, *Late Capitalism*, 90.

7. Michael Corkery, "A New Crop in Pennsylvania: Warehouses," *New York Times*, May 27, 2021, www.nytimes.com/2021/05/26/business/lehigh-valley-warehouses-ecommerce.html.

8. Corkery, "A New Crop." Also see US Bureau of Labor Statistics, "Injuries, Illnesses, and Fatalities," www.bls.gov/iif/home.htm. This claim is based on the data from 2017.

9. Anthony Bender (Ayebender), "The Truth about Warehouse Work," YouTube, May 4, 2020, www.youtube.com/watch?v=wznjpoQnUio.

10. jimmah winnah, "The Truth about Warehouse Jobs," YouTube, June 10, 2019, www.youtube.com/watch?v=DYpLIOjnznU.

11. Bender, "The Truth about Warehouse Work."

12. Human Encoded, "SURVIVE Working Any Warehouse (No BS) TIPS," YouTube, Dec. 30, 2020, www.youtube.com/watch?v=yHMkUCIlxUA.

13. See, e.g., Kaelle Robillo (kaelle), "ONE MONTH WORKING AT AMAZON WAREHOUSE: PROS & CONS," YouTube, Oct. 6, 2021, www.youtube.com/watch?v=MQjVIJkvNPY.

14. Kaelle Robillo (kaelle), "A Day in the Life of an AMAZON WAREHOUSE PACKER in 60 secs #shorts," YouTube, Nov. 9, 2021, www.youtube.com/watch?v=iHmzpzER4Us.

15. DarrylsWorld, "The Truth about Warehouse Jobs | My Experience," YouTube, July 29, 2021, www.youtube.com/watch?v=ma4Pxih9OYA.

16. Corkery, "A New Crop."

17. CNBC, "Why Warehouses Are Taking Over the U.S.," YouTube, Nov. 29, 2021, www.youtube.com/watch?v=-KfodFAw8EQ.

18. Neilson and Mezzadra, *Border as Method*; Rossiter, *Software, Infrastructure, Labor.*

19. Cf. Bataille, *The Accursed Share*, vol. 1.

20. See Serres, *The Parasite.*

21. Deleuze, *Cinema 1*, 109.

22. The five parts of this series are all by Shane Dawson (shane), and are, in order, "The Secret World of Jeffree Star," YouTube, August 1, 2018, www.youtube.com/watch?v=xUf2-sjGqQw; "Becoming Jeffree Star for a Day," YouTube, August 2, 2018, www.youtube.com/watch?v=uxtT_6d0DWQ; "Switching Lives with Jeffree Star," YouTube, August 3, 2018, www.youtube.com/watch?v=MLvb3pWk-rU; "The Secret Life of Jeffree Star," YouTube, August 8, 2018, www.youtube.com/watch?v=9q2PgfYbppY; and "The Truth about Jeffree Star," YouTube, August 9, 2018, www.youtube.com/watch?v=MhTw1SUxWTA.

23. Part of this "uncancellable" reputation emerged from a 2017 event termed "Dramageddon," in which Star had a public falling out with several other fashion and beauty YouTubers, Manny Gutierrez (better known as Manny MUA), Laura Lee, Nikita Dragun, and Gabriel Zamora. Through a series of perceived slights between Star and these other beauty influencers, the careers of everyone involved, aside from Star, were severely damaged. A similar thing happened again in 2019, with "Dramageddon 2.0," in which Star and beauty YouTuber Tati Westbrook publicly criticized James Charles for sexually predatory behavior, attacks that, a year later, seemed to *increase* the popularity of both Star and Charles while damaging the popularity of Westbrook. See Lindsay Dodgson, "How YouTube's Beauty Community Fell Apart with an Explosive Feud Called 'Dramageddon,'" *Insider*, August 28, 2021, www.insider.com/dramageddon-youtube-jeffree-star-manny-mua-laura-lee-gabriel-zamora-2021-8; and Kat Tenbarge, "One Year after the Beauty YouTuber War Burned Their Community to the Ground, New Battle Lines Have Been Drawn between the Growing Stars That Started It All," *Insider*, May 20, 2020; www.insider.com/jeffree-star-james-charles-dramageddon-2-tati-westbrook-2020-5. For an academic discussion of Dramageddon 2.0, albeit one that comes to different conclusions than we do here, see Lewis and Christin, "Platform Drama."

24. Billboard, "Chart History: Jeffree Star," www.billboard.com/artist/jeffree-star/chart-history/billboard-200.

25. Gehl, "Real (Software) Abstractions."

26. Zoe Haylock, "The Complete Timeline of the Many Attempts to 'Cancel' Shane Dawson and Jeffree Star," *Vulture*, Sept. 2, 2020, www.vulture.com/2020/09/shane-dawson-jeffree-star-youtube-drama-explained.html.

27. Jeffree Star (jeffreestar), "RACISM." YouTube, June 20, 2017, www.youtube.com/watch?v=Su6Fel7lHVg.

28. Taylor Lorenz, "The Problem with Shane Dawson and Jeffree Star: What Happened to These YouTube Stars?" *New York Times*, July 11, 2020, www.nytimes.com/2020/06/29/style/shane-dawson-jeffree-star-youtube-taylor-lorenz.html; Zoe Haylock, "James Charles Denies Accusation of Grooming an Underage Fan," *Vulture*, Feb. 26, 2021, www.vulture.com/2021/02/james-charles-accusation-grooming-underage-fan.html.

29. James Charles, "The Competition Begins—Instant Influencer," YouTube, April 24, 2020, www.youtube.com/watch?v=sSC2q1Q-7KM.

30. Taylor Lorenz, "On the Internet, No One Knows You're Not Rich. Except This Account," *New York Times*, Nov. 12, 2019, www.nytimes.com/2019/11/11/style/baller-busters-online-scams.html.

31. For instance, Star claims he got his start lying about his age and doing makeup for pornographic photo shoots. See "LAist Interview: Jeffree Star," *LAist*, March 10, 2008, Internet Archive, https://web.archive.org/web/20080314011437/http://laist.com/2008/03/10/jeffree_star_interview.php.

32. Dawson, "The Secret World of Jeffree Star."

33. See Ngai, *Our Aesthetic Categories*, 110–73.

34. Killer Merch, "Killer Merch," accessed June 8, 2022, www.killermerch.com.

35. Joe Otterson, "Chris D'Elia Denies Allegations of Sexually Harassing Teenagers," *Variety*, June 17, 2020, variety.com/2020/tv/news/chris-delia-sexual-harassment-denial-1234640625.

36. State of California Secretary of State, "Articles of Organization of a Limited Liability Company (LLC): Jeffree Star Cosmetics LLC," June 25, 2014, 201417710278; State of California Secretary of State, "Statement of Information (Limited Liability Company): Jeffree Star Cosmetics LLC," Sept. 19, 2016, 16-331137.

37. State of California Secretary of State, "Articles of Organization of a Limited Liability Company (LLC): Killer Merch, LLC," May 8, 2014, 201413210194; State of California Secretary of State, "Statement of Information (Limited Liability Company): Killer Merch, LLC," Dec. 31, 2018, 18-E26028.

38. State of California Secretary of State, "Statement of Information: Jeffree Star Cosmetics, Inc." Dec. 8, 2017, FS78747.

39. Avildsen's name does not appear on the Statement of Information incorporating Jeffree Star Cosmetics, so it appears that around 2017 he had left Jeffree Star Cosmetics and Killer Merch, possibly to focus on his screenwriting and directing career.

40. Dawson, "Switching Lives with Jeffree Star."

41. Ngai, *Our Aesthetic Categories*, 5.

42. Dawson, "The Beautiful World of Jeffree Star."

43. Jeffree Star (jeffreestar), "Doing What's Right," YouTube, July 18, 2020, www.youtube.com/watch?v=hOuwNiCa-zU.

44. Kat Tenbarge, "Shane Dawson Quietly Launched New Merchandise While Staying Silent on His Controversies," *Insider*, August 14, 2020, www.insider.com/shane-dawson-launches-new-pig-merchandise-killer-merch-silent-controversies-2020-8.

45. Sandra Song, "Jeffree Star Responds to Fake Robbery Accusations," *Paper Magazine*, August 10, 2020, www.papermag.com/jeffree-star-robbery-acccusations-2646943216.html.

46. Haylock, "The Complete Timeline."

47. Kat Tenbarge, "Jeffree Star's New Neighbors in Wyoming Say His Money Made a Good Impression on the Community, Despite the Beauty Mogul's Stained Image," *Insider*, August 24, 2021, www.insider.com/jeffree-star-casper-wyoming -move-controversies-donations-money-lounge-yaks-2021-8.

48. Jeffree Star, Instagram Stories, August 21, 2021, www.instagram.com/ jeffreestar (no longer available).

49. This transformation is documented in a recent three-part Shane Dawson series on Star, beginning with the video "The Cancelled World of Jeffree Star and Shane Dawson," YouTube, Nov. 1, 2022, www.youtube.com/watch?v=5rJyBAkQ UTA.

50. Williams, *The City and The Country*, 297.

51. Star, Instagram Stories.

52. "Kanye West Approved to Build Mega-mansion in WY," *TMZ*, July 7, 2020, www.tmz.com/2020/07/07/kanye-west-approved-build-massive-home-mansion -permit-wyoming-ranch/; Matt Sullivan and Cheyenne Roundtree, "Kanye West Used Porn, Bullying, 'Mind Games' to Control Staff," *Rolling Stone*, Nov. 24, 2022, www.rollingstone.com/music/music-features/kanye-west-yeezy-porn-bullying -kim-kardashian-1234635221.

53. Cassidy Randall, "Rumors of RuPaul's Fracking Ranch May Be Surprising to Some—but Not His Wyoming Neighbors," *The Guardian*, August 28, 2020, www .theguardian.com/environment/2020/aug/28/fracking-wyoming-ranchers-ru paul.

54. Dan Cepeda, "Jeffree Star: 'We Do Have a Lot of New Businesses' in Casper, 'Employing All Local People,'" *Oil City News*, April 9, 2021, oilcity.news/communi ty/2021/04/09/jeffree-star-we-do-have-a-lot-of-new-businesses-in-casper-employ ing-all-local-people.

55. As of May 2021, both of these LLCs were reinstated through the filing of necessary paperwork and payment of taxes. For more details, see State of Wyo-ming Secretary of State, "Limited Liability Company Articles of Organization: Jeffree Star Pets, LLC," Sept. 4, 2020, 2020-000942297, wyobiz.wyo.gov/Business /FilingDetails.aspx?eFNum=10211313522012701012424812607007201310606817 7 090; and State of Wyoming Secretary of State, "Limited Liability Company Articles of Organization: Scorpio Logistics, LLC," Sept. 4, 2020, 2020-000942287, wyobiz .wyo.gov/Business/FilingDetails.aspx?eFNum=255184109182183078101221169000 0 80098079047169026.

56. Jeffree Star Cosmetics, "Jeffree Star Pets," accessed June 8, 2022, https://jef freestarcosmetics.com/pages/jeffree-star-pets.

57. State of Wyoming Secretary of State, "Limited Liability Company Articles of Organization: Jeffree Star LLC," March 8, 2021, 2021-000986717, wyobiz.wyo .gov/Business/FilingDetails.aspx?eFNum=2240841250670371680380360330860 89 253151112156130.

58. Justia Trademarks, "Star Yak Ranch—Trademark Details," Sept. 29, 2021, https://trademarks.justia.com/908/65/star-yak-90865972.html. Also see Kat Ten-

barge, "Jeffree Star moved from an LA mansion to a ranch in Wyoming where he raises yaks. Here's how his journey unfolded," *Insider*, August 31, 2021, www.insider .com/jeffree-star-wyoming-from-la-mansion-yak-ranch-timeline-2021-8.

59. ProPublica, "Jeffree Star Cosmetics, Inc." *Tracking PPP*, accessed June 8, 2022, https://projects.propublica.org/coronavirus/bailouts/loans/jeffree-star-cos metics-inc-5057397707; ProPublica, "Killer Merch LLC," *Tracking PPP*, accessed June 8, 2022, https://projects.propublica.org/coronavirus/bailouts/loans/killer -merch-llc-5041437701.

60. Palmer Haasch, "Companies Owned by YouTubers MrBeast and Jeffree Star Got Hundreds of Thousands of Dollars in Coronavirus Relief Loans," *Insider*, Sept. 9, 2020, www.insider.com/mrbeast-faze-clan-jeffree-star-cosmetics-ppp -loans-coronavirus-relief-2020-9.

61. State of North Carolina Department of the Secretary of State, "Limited Liability Company Articles of Organization: MrBeastYoutube, LLC," Oct. 6, 2017, C2017 278 0026; State of North Carolina Department of the Secretary of State, "Business Corporation Annual Report: MrBeastYoutube, LLC," July 24, 2018," C2018 130 02345.

62. "MrBeastCrypto, LLC," *OpenCorporates*, accessed June 8, 2022, https://open corporates.com/companies/us_nc/1636681.

63. This is evidenced not only by the PPP loan but also because Donaldson's businesses are primarily operated through lawyers and, today, the CT Corporation, a major North Carolina Registered Agent service that has managed paperwork for more than three hundred thousand businesses in North Carolina since its founding in 1892. See Wolters Kluwer, www.wolterskluwer.com/en/solutions/ct -corporation/north-carolina-registered-agent, accessed June 8, 2022.

64. SoKrispyMedia, "Making MrBeast's Squid Game in 10 Days," YouTube, Nov. 27, 2021, www.youtube.com/watch?v=VQcO_PYVx30.

65. Jeon, *Vicious Circuits*, 4.

66. "*Squid Game* Director Says People Deeply Relate to Theme of Economic Inequality," *Channel24*, Oct. 28, 2021, www.news24.com/channel/tv/news/squid -game-director-says-people-deeply-relate-to-theme-of-economic-inequality-202 11028-2.

67. Choe Sang-Hun, "Workers End Standoff at South Korean Auto Plant," *New York Times*, August 6, 2009, www.nytimes.com/2009/08/07/world/asia/07seoul .html.

68. Jimmy Donaldson (MrBeast), "How I Gave Away $1,000,000," YouTube, Dec. 25, 2018, www.youtube.com/watch?v=9-HphHIJS9c.

69. Quidd, "Quidd Market," https://market.onquidd.com, accessed June 8, 2022.

70. Jimmy Donaldson (MrBeast), "I Ate A $70,000 Golden Pizza," YouTube, Feb. 29, 2020, www.youtube.com/watch?v=F4Y3Pkn95Gl; Jimmy Donaldson (MrBeast), "Donating $100,000 to Streamers with 0 Viewers," YouTube, March 24, 2019, www .youtube.com/watch?v=Y6jC6VaO3jo.

71. Lucas Shaw and Mark Bergen, "The North Carolina Kid Who Cracked You-Tube's Secret Code," *Bloomberg*, Dec. 22, 2020, www.bloomberg.com/news/articles /2020-12-22/who-is-mrbeast-meet-youtube-s-top-creator-of-2020#xj4y7vzkg.

72. Amanda Silberling, "MrBeast's 'Real Life Squid Game' and the Price of Viral Stunts," *TechCruch*, Dec. 3, 2021, https://techcrunch.com/2021/12/03/mrbeast -squid-game-creator-economy-viral.

73. Jimmy Donaldson (MrBeast), "I Gave People $1,000,000 but ONLY 1 Minute to Spend It!" YouTube, Dec. 15, 2020, www.youtube.com/watch?v=LeYsRMZFUqo.

74. Donaldson would eventually literalize this in his video "I Built Willy Won-ka's Chocolate Factory!" YouTube, June 4, 2022, www.youtube.com/watch?v=Hwy bp38GnZw.

75. Ouellete and Hay, *Better Living through Reality TV*; Andrejevic, *Reality TV*.

76. Jimmy Donaldson (MrBeast), "Last to Take Hand Off Lamborghini, Keeps It," YouTube, Oct. 23, 2021, www.youtube.com/watch?v=qlsgdOVGAo4.

77. Jimmy Donaldson (MrBeast), "Last to Leave $800,000 Island Keeps It," You-Tube, August 15, 2020, www.youtube.com/watch?v=NkEoAMGzpJY.

78. Jimmy Donaldson (MrBeast), "Extreme $1,000,000 Hide and Seek," You-Tube, Dec. 18, 2021, www.youtube.com/watch?v=ooNgUctWoLQ.

79. Cited in Liu, *The Laws of Cool*, 94.

80. See Illouz, *Cold Intimacies*; and Ahmed, *The Promise of Happiness*.

81. Mandel, *Late Capitalism*, 58–59.

82. See Mayer, *Almost Hollywood, Nearly New Orleans*, for a specific case study of how these economic models have invested in New Orleans as a space of enter-tainment production and tourism.

83. See Wood, *Southern Capitalism*.

84. Jimmy Donaldson (MrBeast), "$456,000 Squid Game in Real Life!" You-Tube, Nov. 24, 2021, www.youtube.com/watch?v=oe3GPea1Tyg.

85. Matt Pearce, "How Much Did MrBeast's 'Squid Game' Remake on You-Tube Cost? We Did the Math," *Los Angeles Times*, Dec. 9, 2021, www.latimes.com /entertainment-arts/story/2021-12-09/mr-beast-youtube-squid-game-video-hit.

86. See Fox, "You Are Not Allowed to Talk about Production."

87. Jimmy Donaldson (MrBeast), "World's Most Dangerous Escape Room!" YouTube, Jan. 29, 2022, www.youtube.com/watch?v=3jS_yEK8qVI.

88. In this specific video, all the "contestants" are Donaldson's friends and col-laborators. Sometimes, however, these friends are competing with "real" individ-uals and fans. The relation between these "friends" and "fans" is beyond the scope of this chapter.

89. Feastables, https://feastables.com, accessed June 8, 2022.

90. MrBeast is not the first or only celebrity to utilize chocolate bars as mer-chandise. RuPaul, as well as several former *RuPaul's Drag Race* contestants sell their own branded chocolate through the company Chocolab. ChocoLab, https:// chocolab.com, accessed April 19, 2023.

91. The Sensible Mama, "I BOUGHT A WAREHOUSE // TOUR," YouTube, Jan. 13, 2020, www.youtube.com/watch?v=orsn7DRZJ_A.

92. Corey Ferreira, "What Is Dropshipping?" *Shopify Blog*, Jan. 12, 2022, www.shopify.com/blog/what-is-dropshipping.

93. The Sensible Mama, https://thesensiblemama.com, accessed June 8, 2022.

94. Jeremy Fiedler, "I BOUGHT A WAREHOUSE . . ." YouTube, April 11, 2019, www.youtube.com/watch?v=opG4aj1a_To.

95. Tanner Fox, "I BOUGHT A HUGE WAREHOUSE!!! *OFFICIAL TOUR*" YouTube, June 6, 2017, www.youtube.com/watch?v=8XqaCYK5BDk.

Chapter 5

1. See Gillespie, "The Politics of 'Platforms.'"

2. Crutzen and Stoermer, "The 'Anthropocene,'" 17–18.

3. Ian Angus, "Anthropocene: What's in a Name?" *Climate & Capitalism*, Nov. 9, 2015, https://climateandcapitalism.com/2015/11/09/anthropocene-whats-in-a-name./

4. See Haraway et al., "Anthropologists Are Talking—About the Anthropocene."

5. Moore, "The Capitalocene, Part 1," 3. Also see Haraway, "Anthropocene, Capitalocene, Plantationocene, Chthulucene"; and Moore, "Anthropocene or Capitalocene?"

6. Wolford, "The Plantationocene," 1622.

7. Moore, "Anthropocene or Capitalocene?," 6.

8. Haraway, "Anthropocene, Capitalocene, Plantationocene, Chthulucene," 160.

9. Haraway, *Staying with the Trouble*.

10. Angus, "Anthropocene."

11. Cf. Jay, *Marxism and Totality*.

12. Williams, *Marxism and Literature*, 114.

13. While many believe our era to be foundationally "entrepreneurial," we find it interesting that there is a neglected strain of Keynesian economic theory that argued information technology would undermine and do away with the notion of the "entrepreneurial" corporation—corporations run by sole proprietors, who fill a concrete role as "boss." While Keynesian theory saw the entrepreneurial corporation ending because of the distribution of information and knowledge throughout the corporation, we see, instead, the movement in which bosses come to see their identity as encompassing the totality of their business ventures. For more on this Keynesian argument, see Galbraith, *The New Industrial State*.

14. This could also be considered a hallmark of neoliberalism. See, e.g., Foucault, *The Birth of Biopolitics*; and Berlant, *Cruel Optimism*.

15. Mandel, *Late Capitalism*, 502.

16. Mandel, 502.

17. This is implied by more general processes to "distribute" subjectivity and "appropriate" the identities of others as expressions of the self. See Guinness, "The Coloniser and Corpus Nullius."

18. Han, *In the Swarm*, 14.

19. Berlant, *Cruel Optimism*.

20. See Berlant, *Queen of America*; Illouz, *Cold Intimacies*; and Meyerowitz, *No Sense of Place*, among others.

21. See Mein, "COVID-19 and Health Disparities."

22. Cf. Mbembe, *Necropolitics*.

23. Senft, *Camgirls*.

24. Taylor Lorenz, "Flight of the Influencers," *New York Times*, April 2, 2020, www.nytimes.com/2020/04/02/style/influencers-leave-new-york-coronavirus .html.

25. Charnas later deleted this post from her Instagram grid, along with all of her content from March 30, 2020 through April 24, 2020. See Laura Pitcher, "Is the Influencer Era Coming to an End?, *Teen Vogue*, Dec. 30, 2020, www.teenvogue.com /story/is-the-influencer-era-coming-to-an-end.

26. Pitcher, "Is the Influencer Era Coming to an End?"

27. Kim Kardashian (@KimKardashian), Twitter, Oct. 27, 2020, https://twitter .com/KimKardashian/status/1321151217482014726.

28. Quoted in Pitcher, "Is the Influencer Era Coming to an End?"

29. Naomi Davis (@taza), Instagram, March 28, 2020, www.instagram.com/p/ B-SjTReD-ml (no longer available).

30. Davis.

31. Davis.

32. Stephanie McNeal, "An Influencer Is Getting Tons of Hate Online for Fleeing NYC with Her 5 Kids for a Cross-Country Road Trip amid the Coronavirus Pandemic," *Buzzfeed*, March 30, 2020, www.buzzfeednews.com/article/ stephaniemcneal/an-influencer-is-getting-tons-of-hate-online-for-fleeing.

33. Naomi Davis, *A Coat of Yellow Paint: Moving Through the Noise to Love the Life You Live* (New York: Harper Horizon, 2021).

34. Naomi Davis (@taza), Instagram, July 7, 2021, www.instagram.com/p/CRA -RMfjzAI (no longer available).

35. Naomi Davis (@taza), Instagram, Oct. 1, 2021, www.instagram.com/p/CU gnlzrFwTV (no longer available).

36. Davis.

37. "*A Coat of Yellow Paint: Moving Through the Noise to Love the Life You Live* by Naomi Davis," *Goodreads*, www.goodreads.com/en/book/show/54287725-a-coat -of-yellow-paint.

38. Melissa, review of "*A Coat of Yellow Paint: Moving Through the Noise to Love the Life You Live* by Naomi Davis," *Goodreads*, Feb. 7, 2021, www.goodreads.com/ review/show/3824197490?book_show_action=true&from_review_page=1.

39. Emily, review of "*A Coat of Yellow Paint: Moving Through the Noise to Love*

the Life You Live by Naomi Davis," *Goodreads*, April 9, 2021, www.goodreads.com/re
view/show/3934504612?book_show_action=true&from_review_page=1.

40. Stephanie, review of "*A Coat of Yellow Paint: Moving Through the Noise to
Love the Life You Live* by Naomi Davis," *Goodreads*, April 8, 2021, www.goodreads
.com/review/show/3933546134?book_show_action=true&from_review_page=1.

41. Samantha, review of "*A Coat of Yellow Paint: Moving Through the Noise to
Love the Life You Live* by Naomi Davis," *Goodreads*, April 17, 2021, www.goodreads
.com/review/show/3950938189?book_show_action=true&from_review_page=1.

42. Foucault, *The Birth of Biopolitics*.

43. McRobbie, *Be Creative*.

44. "Never Go Against the Family," *The Kardashians*, season 1, episode 8, June
2, 2020.

45. The massive success of Skims has overshadowed yet another controversy
and space of potential "cancellation" for Kardashian. The brand of shapewear was
originally called "Kimono," and Kardashian went so far as to begin the process of
trademarking the name of the Japanese garment. Of course, upset abounded over
this cultural appropriation, but Kardashian insisted she would not be changing the
name. Eventually she recanted. The name was then changed to Skims, and this controversy has been all but forgotten. See Kim Kardashian (@KimKardashian), Twitter, July 1, 2019, https://twitter.com/KimKardashian/status/1145691430100205570
and https://twitter.com/KimKardashian/status/1145691518025388035.

46. Lottie Winter, "Every Single One of Kim Kardashian's Businesses—From
Dash to Skims—Ranked," *Glamour UK*, Jan. 28, 2022, www.glamourmagazine.co
.uk/gallery/kim-kardashian-businesses.

47. Zarah Ching, "Kim Kardashian's Infamous KKW Fragrance Has Re-
stocked," *hypebae*, May 22, 2018, https://hypebae.com/2018/5/kim-kardashian-kkw
-fragrance-perfume-restock.

48. Quoted in Jenna Wortham, "Kim Kardashian, an Unlikely Mobile Video
Game Hit," *New York Times*, July 30, 2014, https://archive.nytimes.com/bits.blogs
.nytimes.com/2014/07/30/kim-kardashian-an-unlikely-mobile-video-game-hit.

49. Barbrook and Cameron, "The Californian Ideology"; Moulier-Boutang,
Cognitive Capitalism.

50. Elon Musk's father, for instance, owned an emerald mine in Zambia, which
supplied Musk with his initial capital. See Adam Smith, "Elon Musk's 50th: Taking
a Look into the Billionaire's Wealth—From Emeralds to SpaceX and Tesla," *The Independent*, June 28, 2021, www.independent.co.uk/space/elon-musk-birthday-ceo
-tesla-b1874017.html.

51. Bataille, *Accursed Share*, 2–3:84–86.

52. Kylie Jenner (@kyliejenner), Instagram, July 15, 2020, www.instagram.com/
p/CgDCvEDvUJz (no longer available).

53. Gary Mcwilliams and Erwin Seba, "Deaths at Travis Scott Concert Due to
Accidental Suffocation, Medical Examiner Says," *Reuters*, Dec. 16, 2021, www.reu
ters.com/world/us/houston-medical-examiner-rules-deaths-travis-scott-concert

-were-accidental-2021-12-16; Yuyiy Andriyashchuk, "Travis Scott's Astroworld Album Sees Increase in Sales amid Festival Tragedies," *The Blast*, Nov. 15, 2021, https://theblast.com/123260/travis-scotts-astroworld-album-surprisingly-sees-in creases-in-sales-amid-festival-tragedies.

    54. Bataille, *Erotism*, 86.

    55. Smith, *The Wealth of Nations*, 1007.

    56. Harvey, "Globalization and the 'Spatial Fix.'"

    57. Tyler Halloran, "A Brief History of Corporate Form and Why It Matters," *Fordham Journal of Corporate and Financial Law*, Nov. 18, 2018, https://news.law .fordham.edu/jcfl/2018/11/18/a-brief-history-of-the-corporate-form-and-why-it -matters.

    58. Dewey, "The Historic Background," 665–66.

    59. Cited in Dewey, 656.

    60. Machen, "Corporate Personality," 253.

    61. Machen, 262.

    62. Machen, 257.

    63. Machen, 256.

    64. See Bollmer, *Inhuman Networks*, 27–45; and Sennett, *Flesh and Stone*.

    65. Machen, "Corporate Personality," 261.

    66. Machen, 262.

    67. Cf. Foucault, *Discipline and Punish*.

    68. Machen, "Corporate Personality," 266.

    69. Machen, 267. The law has regularly regarded fictions as persons, persons who go by names such as John Doe and Richard Roe, even though these "fictions" are often anonymous substitutions for actual people, people who can understand the potential for punishment. Machen's definition denies personhood to infants and children, the insane, and anyone else considered to lack moral judgment and reasoning. From a pragmatic perspective, this is why children and the insane are not punished in the same way as those judged to be full persons under law.

    70. Dewey, "The Historic Background," 655.

    71. Dewey, 661.

    72. Dewey, 668.

    73. Dewey, 669.

    74. Citizens United v. Federal Election Commission, 558 U.S. 310 (2010).

    75. Cf. Greene, "Rhetorical Capital."

    76. See Ripkin, *Corporate Personhood*.

    77. See the arguments outlined in Justice Stevens's dissenting opinion and Justice Scalia's concurring opinion to Citizens United v. Federal Election Commission, 558 U.S. 310 (2010).

    78. Greene, "Rhetorical Capital."

    79. Citizens United v. Federal Election Commission, 558 U.S. 310 (2010), 55.

    80. Andrew Ross Sorkin et al, "Elon Musk Fuels Record C.E.O Paydays," *New*

York Times, June 27, 2022, www.nytimes.com/2022/06/27/business/dealbook/elon
-musk-tesla-ceo-pay.html.

81. The Long Now Foundation, "About Long Now," http://longnow.org/about.

82. Žižek, *The Sublime Object of Ideology*; Sloterdijk, *Critique of Cynical Reason*; Andrejevic, *Infoglut*.

83. Fisher, *Capitalist Realism*.

84. Camatte, *This World We Must Leave*, 26.

85. Camatte, 42.

86. Camatte, 32–33.

BIBLIOGRAPHY

This bibliography contains secondary and academic sources referred to throughout this book. Primary, popular, and journalistic sources are referenced in the notes of each chapter.

Abidin, Crystal. "Visibility Labour: Engaging with Influencers' Fashion Brands and #OOTD Advertorial Campaigns on Instagram." *Media International Australia* 161, no. 1 (2016): 86–100.

Adorno, Theodor W. "Free Time." In *The Culture Industry: Selected Essays on Mass Culture*, edited by J. M. Bernstein, 187–97. London: Routledge, 1991.

Ahmed, Sara. *The Promise of Happiness*. Durham, NC: Duke University Press, 2010.

Alexander, Michelle. *The New Jim Crow: Mass Incarceration in the Age of Colorblindness*. Rev. ed. New York: New Press, 2012.

Althusser, Louis. *Lenin and Philosophy, and Other Essays*. Translated by Ben Brewster. New York: Monthly Review Press, 1971.

Amin, Samir. *Unequal Development: An Essay on the Social Formations of Peripheral Capitalism*. Translated by Brian Pearce. New York: Monthly Review Press, 1976.

Andrejevic, Mark. "Estranged Free Labor." In *Digital Labor: The Internet as Playground and Factory*, edited by Trebor Scholz, 149–64. New York: Routledge, 2013.

———. *Infoglut: How Too Much Information Is Changing the Way We Think and Know.* New York: Routledge, 2013.

———. *Reality TV: The Work of Being Watched*. Lanham, MD: Rowman & Littlefield, 2004.

Armitage, John, and Joanne Roberts. "The Spirit of Luxury." *Cultural Politics* 12, no. 1 (2016): 1–22.

Augé, Marc. *Non-places: Introduction to an Anthropology of Supermodernity*. Translated by John Howe. New York: Verso, 1995.

Azoulay, Ariella Aïsha. *Civil Imagination: A Political Ontology of Photography*. New York: Verso, 2012.

Barbrook, Richard, and Andy Cameron. "The Californian Ideology." *Science as Culture* 6, no. 1 (1996): 44–72.

Barthes, Roland. *Camera Lucida: Reflections on Photography*. Translated by Richard Howard. New York: Hill and Wang, 1982.

Bastani, Aaron. *Fully Automated Luxury Communism: A Manifesto*. London: Verso, 2019.

Bataille, Georges. *The Accursed Share: An Essay on General Economy*. Vol. 1. Translated by Robert Hurley. New York: Zone, 1988.

———. *The Accursed Share: An Essay on General Economy*. Vols. 2 and 3. Translated by Robert Hurley. New York: Zone, 1991.

———. *Erotism: Death and Sensuality*. Translated by Mary Dalwood. San Francisco: City Lights, 1962.

Bateson, Gregory. *Steps to an Ecology of Mind*. Chicago: University of Chicago Press, 2000.

Baudrillard, Jean. *The Consumer Society: Myths and Structures*. London: Sage, 1998.

———. *Simulacra and Simulation*. Translated by Sheila Glaser. Ann Arbor: University of Michigan Press, 1995.

Beller, Jonathan. *The Cinematic Mode of Production: Attention Economy and the Society of the Spectacle*. Hanover, NH: Dartmouth College Press, 2006.

Benjamin, Ruha. *Race after Technology: Abolitionist Tools for the New Jim Code*. Cambridge: Polity, 2019.

———. *Viral Justice: How We Grow the World We Want*. Princeton, NJ: Princeton University Press, 2022.

Benjamin, Walter. *Selected Writings*. Vol. 3, *1935–1938*. Edited by Howard Eiland and Michael W. Jennings. Translated by Edmund Jephcott, Howard Eiland, and Others. Cambridge, MA: Harvard University Press, 2002.

Berlant, Lauren. *Cruel Optimism*. Durham, NC: Duke University Press, 2011.

———. *The Queen of America Goes to Washington City: Essays on Sex and Citizenship*. Durham, NC: Duke University Press, 1997.

Bollmer, Grant. *Inhuman Networks: Social Media and the Archaeology of Connection*. New York: Bloomsbury Academic, 2016.

———. *Materialist Media Theory: An Introduction*. New York: Bloomsbury Academic, 2019.

Bollmer, Grant, and Katherine Guinness. "'Do You Really Want to Live Forever?' Animism, Death, and Digital Images." *Cultural Studies Review* 24 (2018): 79–96.

———. "Phenomenology for the Selfie." *Cultural Politics* 13, no. 2 (2017): 156–76.

Boltanski, Luc, and Ève Chiapello. *The New Spirit of Capitalism*. Translated by Gregory Elliott. London: Verso, 2005.

Bonilla-Silva, Eduardo. *Racism without Racists: Color-Blind Racism and the Persistence of Racial Inequality in America*. 5th ed. Lanham, MD: Rowman & Littlefield, 2018.

Brinkema, Eugenie. *Life-Destroying Diagrams*. Durham, NC: Duke University Press, 2021.

Bruns, Axel. *Blogs, Wikipedia, Second Life, and Beyond: From Production to Produsage*. New York: Peter Lang, 2008.

Camatte, Jacques. *Capital and Community*. Translated by David Brown. New York: Prism Key Press, 2011.

———. *This World We Must Leave and Other Essays*. Edited by Alex Trotter. New York: Autonomedia, 1995.

Caplan, Robyn, and Tarleton Gillespie. "Tiered Governance and Demonetization: The Shifting Terms of Labor and Compensation in the Platform Economy." *Social Media + Society* 6, no. 2 (April–June 2020): 1–13.

Carey, James W. *Communication as Culture: Essays on Media and Society*. Boston: Unwin Hyman, 1989.

Certeau, Michel de. *The Practice of Everyday Life*. Translated by Steven Rendall. Berkeley: University of California Press, 1984.

Christin, Angèle, and Yingdan Lu. "The Influencer Pay Gap: Platform Labor Meets Racial Capitalism." *New Media & Society* (2023): 1–24.

Chun, Wendy Hui Kyong. *Discriminating Data: Correlation, Neighborhoods, and the New Politics of Recognition*. Cambridge, MA: MIT Press, 2021.

———. *Programmed Visions: Software and Memory*. Cambridge, MA: MIT Press, 2011.

Coley, Rob. "'Destabilized Perception': Infrastructural Aesthetics in the Films of Adam Curtis." *Cultural Politics* 14, no. 3 (2018): 304–26.

Couldry, Nick, and Ulises A. Mejias. *The Costs of Connection: How Data Is Colonizing Human Life and Appropriating It for Capitalism*. Stanford, CA: Stanford University Press, 2019.

Crary, Jonathan. *24/7: Late Capitalism and the Ends of Sleep*. London: Verso, 2013.

Crutzen, Paul J., and Eugene F. Stoermer. "The 'Anthropocene.'" *IGBP Newsletter* 41 (2000): 17–18.

Davis, Mike. *City of Quartz: Excavating the Future in Los Angeles*. London: Verso, 2006.

Dean, Jodi. "Communism or Neo-Feudalism?" *New Political Science* 42, no. 1 (2020): 1–17.

———. *Democracy and Other Neoliberal Fantasies: Communicative Capitalism and Left Politics*. Durham, NC: Duke University Press, 2009.

Debord, Guy. *Society of the Spectacle*. Translated by Ken Knabb. London: Rebel Press, 2005.

Deleuze, Gilles. *Cinema 1: The Movement-Image*. Translated by Hugh Tomlinson and Barbara Habberjam. Minneapolis: University of Minnesota Press, 1986.

Derrida, Jacques. *Specters of Marx: The State of the Debt, the Work of Mourning, and the New International*. Translated by Peggy Kamuf. New York: Routledge, 1994.

Dewey, John. "The Historic Background of Corporate Legal Personality." *Yale Law Journal* 35, no. 6 (1926): 655–73.

Dobson, Amy Shields, Nicholas Carah, and Brady Robards. "Digital Intimate Publics and Social Media: Toward Theorising Public Lives on Private Platforms." In *Digital Intimate Publics and Social Media*, edited by Amy Shields Dobson, Brady Robards, and Nicholas Carah, 3–27. Cham, Switzerland: Palgrave, 2018.

Duffy, Brooke Erin. *(Not) Getting Paid to Do What You Love: Gender, Social Media, and Aspirational Work*. New Haven, CT: Yale University Press, 2017.

Dyer, Richard. *Heavenly Bodies: Film Stars and Society*. 2nd ed. London: Routledge, 2004.

———. *Stars*. New ed. London: BFI, 1998.

Eichhorn, Kate. *The End of Forgetting: Growing Up with Social Media*. Cambridge, MA: Harvard University Press, 2019.

Endnotes. "Misery and Debt." *Endnotes* 2 (2010): 20–51, https://files.libcom.org/files /Endnotes 2.pdf.

Erlanger, Olivia, and Luis Ortega Govela. *Garage*. Cambridge, MA: MIT Press, 2018.

Federici, Silvia. "Social Reproduction Theory: History, Issues and Present Challenges." *Radical Philosophy* 2, no. 4 (2019): 55–57.

Fisher, Mark. *Capitalist Realism: Is There No Alternative?* Winchester: Zero Books, 2009.

Fortmueller, Kate. *Below the Stars: How the Labor of Working Actors and Extras Shapes Media Production*. Austin: University of Texas Press, 2021.

Foucault, Michel. *The Birth of Biopolitics: Lectures at the Collège de France, 1978–1979*. Edited by Michel Senellart. Translated by Graham Burchell. Basingstoke: Palgrave Macmillan, 2008.

———. *Discipline and Punish: The Birth of the Prison*. Translated by Alan Sheridan. New York: Vintage, 1977.

———. *The Order of Things: An Archaeology of the Human Sciences*. New York: Vintage, 1970.

Fox, Ragan. "'You Are Not Allowed to Talk about Production': Narratization on (and off) the Set of CBS's *Big Brother*." *Critical Studies in Media Communication* 30, no. 3 (2013): 189–208.

Frank, Andre Gunder. *Capitalism and Underdevelopment in Latin America: Historical Studies of Chile and Brazil*. New York: Monthly Review Press, 1969.

Fried, Michael. *Absorption and Theatricality: Painting and Beholder in the Age of Diderot*. Berkeley: University of California Press, 1980.

Fuchs, Christian. *Culture and Economy in the Age of Social Media*. New York: Routledge, 2015.

Galbraith, John Kenneth. *The New Industrial State*. Princeton, NJ: Princeton University Press, 2007.

Gehl, Robert W. "Real (Software) Abstractions." *Social Text* 30, no. 2 (2012): 99–119.

Gibson-Graham, J. K. *The End of Capitalism (As We Knew It): A Feminist Critique of Political Economy*. Minneapolis: University of Minnesota Press, 2006.

Gillespie, Tarleton. "The Politics of 'Platforms.'" *New Media & Society* 12, no. 3 (2010): 347–64.

Graham, Stephen, and Simon Marvin. *Splintering Urbanism: Networked Infrastructures, Technological Mobilities, and the Urban Condition*. London: Routledge, 2001.

Greene, Ronald Walter. "Rhetorical Capital: Communicative Labor, Money/Speech, and Neo-liberal Governance." *Communication and Critical/Cultural Studies* 4, no. 3 (2007): 327–31.

Guadamuz, Andrés. "The Monkey Selfie: Copyright Lessons for Originality in Photographs and Internet Jurisdiction." *Internet Policy Review* 5, no. 1 (2016): https://doi.org/10.14763/2016.1.398.

Guinness, Katherine. "The Coloniser and Corpus Nullius." *Parallax* 26, no. 1 (2020): 76–88.

———. *Schizogenesis: The Art of Rosemarie Trockel*. Minneapolis: University of Minnesota Press, 2019.

———. "Self-Portraiture and Self-Performance." In *Visual Culture Approaches to the Selfie*, edited by Derek Conrad Murray, 40–59. New York: Routledge, 2022.

Hamilton, Kerry, and Susan Hoyle. "Moving Cities: Transport Connections." In *Unsettling Cities: Movement/Settlement*, edited by John Allen, Doreen Massey, and Michael Pryke, 54–100. London: Routledge, 1999.

Han, Byung-Chul. *The Burnout Society*. Translated by Erik Butler. Stanford, CA: Stanford University Press, 2015.

———. *The Disappearance of Rituals: A Topology of the Present*. Translated by Daniel Steuer. Cambridge: Polity, 2020.

———. *In the Swarm: Digital Prospects*. Translated by Erik Butler. Cambridge, MA: MIT Press, 2017.

———. *The Transparency Society*. Translated by Erik Butler. Stanford, CA: Stanford University Press, 2015.

Haraway, Donna J. "Anthropocene, Capitalocene, Plantationocene, Chthulucene: Making Kin." *Environmental Humanities* 6 (2015): 159–65.

———. *Staying with the Trouble: Making Kin in the Chthulucene*. Durham, NC: Duke University Press, 2016.

Haraway, Donna J., Noboru Ishikawa, Scott F. Gilbert, Kenneth Olwig, Anna L. Tsing, and Nils Bubandt. "Anthropologists Are Talking—About the Anthropocene." *Ethnos* 81, no. 3 (2016): 535–64.

Harris, Malcolm. *Kids These Days: Human Capital and the Making of Millennials*. New York: Back Bay, 2018.

Harvey, David. "Globalization and the 'Spatial Fix.'" *Geographische Revue* 2 (2001): 23–30.

Hester, Helen, and Nick Srnicek. "Shelter against Communism." *E-flux Architecture* (2021): www.e-flux.com/architecture/workplace/430312/shelter-against-communism.

Heyes, Cressida J. "Cosmetic Surgery and the Televisual Makeover." *Feminist Media Studies* 7, no. 1 (2007): 17–32.

hooks, bell. *Black Looks: Race and Representation*. Boston: South End Press, 1992.

Horkheimer, Max, and Theodor W. Adorno. *Dialectic of Enlightenment: Philosophical Fragments*. Edited by Gunzelin Schmid Noerr. Translated by Edmund Jephcott. Stanford, CA: Stanford University Press, 2002.

Hu, Tung-Hui. *A Prehistory of the Cloud*. Cambridge, MA: MIT Press, 2016.

Hund, Emily. *The Influencer Industry: The Quest for Authenticity on Social Media*. Princeton, NJ: Princeton University Press, 2023.

Iheka, Cajetan. *African Ecomedia: Network Forms, Planetary Politics*. Durham, NC: Duke University Press, 2021.

Illouz, Eva. *Cold Intimacies: The Making of Emotional Capitalism*. Cambridge: Polity, 2007.

Jameson, Fredric. *Marxism and Form: Twentieth-Century Dialectical Theories of Literature*. Princeton, NJ: Princeton University Press, 1971.

Jay, Martin. *Marxism and Totality: The Adventures of a Concept from Lukács to Habermas*. Berkeley: University of California Press, 1984.

Jeon, Joseph Jonghyun. *Vicious Circuits: Korea's IMF Cinema and the End of the American Century*. Stanford, CA: Stanford University Press, 2019.

Jones, Meredith. "Media-Bodies and Screen-Births: Cosmetic Surgery Reality Television." *Continuum* 22, no. 4 (2008): 515–24.

Katz, Elihu, and Paul F. Lazarsfeld. *Personal Influence: The Part Played by People in the Flow of Mass Communications*. London: Routledge, 2006.

Kellner, Douglas. *Media Spectacle*. London: Routledge, 2003.

Kittler, Friedrich A. *Gramophone, Film, Typewriter*. Translated by Geoffrey Winthrop-Young and Michael Wutz. Stanford, CA: Stanford University Press, 1999.

Klein, Naomi. *No Logo: Taking Aim at the Brand Bullies*. New York: Picador, 2000.

Kuehn, Kathleen, and Thomas F. Corrigan. "Hope Labor: The Role of Employment Prospects in Online Social Production." *Political Economy of Communication* 1, no. 1 (2013): 9–25.

Lazzarato, Maurizio. "Immaterial Labor." In *Radical Thought in Italy: A Potential Politics*, edited by Paolo Virno and Michael Hardt, translated by Paul Colilli and Ed Emory, 132–47. Minneapolis: University of Minnesota Press, 1996.

LeCavalier, Jesse. *The Rule of Logistics: Walmart and the Architecture of Fulfillment*. Minneapolis: University of Minnesota Press, 2017.

Lewis, Rebecca, and Angèle Christin. "Platform Drama: 'Cancel Culture,' Celebrity, and the Struggle for Accountability on YouTube." *New Media & Society* 24, no. 7 (2022): 1632–56.

Liu, Alan. *The Laws of Cool: Knowledge Work and the Culture of Information*. Chicago: University of Chicago Press, 2004.

Lury, Celia. *Brands: The Logos of the Global Economy*. London: Routledge, 2004.

Machen, Arthur W. "Corporate Personality." *Harvard Law Review* 24, no. 4 (1911): 253–67.

Mandel, Ernest. *Late Capitalism*. Translated by Joris De Bres. London: Verso, 1975.

Marwick, Alice W. "Instafame: Luxury Selfies in the Attention Economy." *Public Culture* 27, no. 1 (2015): 137–60.

Marx, Karl. *Capital*. Vol. 1. Translated by Ben Fowkes. New York: Penguin, 1976.

Marx, Karl, and Frederick Engels. *The German Ideology: Karl Marx and Frederick Engels Collected Works*. Vol. 5. Translated by Clemens Dutt, W. Lough, and C. P. Magill. New York: International Publishers, 1976.

Mauss, Marcel. *The Gift: Forms and Functions of Exchange in Archaic Societies*. Translated by Ian Cunnison. London: Cohen & West, 1966.

Mayer, Vicki. *Almost Hollywood, Nearly New Orleans: The Lure of the Local Film Economy*. Berkeley: University of California Press, 2017.

———. *Below the Line: Producers and Production Studies in the New Television Economy*. Durham, NC: Duke University Press, 2011.

Mbembe, Achille. *Necropolitics*. Translated by Steven Corcoran. Durham, NC: Duke University Press, 2019.

McCarthy, Anna. "Reality Television: A Neoliberal Theater of Suffering." *Social Text* 25, no. 4 (2007): 17–41.

McIlwain, Charlton D. *Black Software: The Internet and Racial Justice, from the AfroNet to Black Lives Matter*. New York: Oxford University Press, 2020.

McRobbie, Angela. *Be Creative: Making a Living in the New Culture Industries*. Cambridge: Polity, 2016.

Mein, Stephen A. "COVID-19 and Health Disparities: The Reality of 'The Great Equalizer.'" *Journal of General Internal Medicine* 35, no. 8 (2020): 2439–40.

Meyrowitz, Joshua. *No Sense of Place: The Impact of Electronic Media on Social Behavior*. New York: Oxford University Press, 1985.

Michaels, Walter Benn. *The Gold Standard and the Logic of Naturalism: American Literature at the Turn of the Century*. Berkeley: University of California Press, 1987.

Mirowski, Philip, and Edward Nik-Khah. *The Knowledge We Have Lost in Information: The History of Information in Modern Economics*. New York: Oxford University Press, 2017.

Monea, Alexander. *The Digital Closet: How the Internet Became Straight*. Cambridge, MA: MIT Press, 2023.

Moore, Jason W. "Anthropocene or Capitalocene? Nature, History, and the Crisis of Capitalism." In *Anthropocene or Capitalocene? Nature, History, and the Crisis of Capitalism*, edited by Jason W. Moore, 1–11. Oakland, CA: PM Press, 2016.

———. "The Capitalocene, Part I: On the Nature and Origins of Our Ecological Crisis." *Journal of Peasant Studies* 44, no. 3 (2017): 594–630.

Moulier-Boutang, Yann. *Cognitive Capitalism*. Translated by Ed Emery. Cambridge: Polity, 2011.

Mezzadra, Sandro, and Brett Neilson. *Border as Method, or, the Multiplication of Labor*. Durham, NC: Duke University Press, 2013.

Ngai, Sianne. *Our Aesthetic Categories: Zany, Cute, Interesting*. Cambridge, MA: Harvard University Press, 2012.

———. *Theory of the Gimmick: Aesthetic Judgement and Capitalist Form*. Cambridge, MA: Harvard University Press, 2020.

Njathi, Anne Wangari. "The Glitz and Glamour Platform Economy: Issues for Instagram Monetization for Influencers in Nairobi, Kenya." PhD diss., NC State University, 2023.

Noble, Safiya Umoja. *Algorithms of Oppression: How Search Engines Reinforce Racism.* New York: New York University Press, 2018.

Orgad, Shani, and Rosalind Gill. *Confidence Culture.* Durham, NC: Duke University Press, 2022.

Ouellette, Laurie, and James Hay. *Better Living through Reality TV: Television and Post-Welfare Citizenship.* Malden, MA: Blackwell, 2008.

Packer, Jeremy. *Mobility without Mayhem: Safety, Cars, and Citizenship.* Durham, NC: Duke University Press, 2008.

Parks, Lisa, and Nicole Starosielski. Introduction to *Signal Traffic: Critical Studies of Media Infrastructures*, edited by Lisa Parks and Nicole Starosielski, 1–27. Urbana: University of Illinois Press, 2015.

——, eds. *Signal Traffic: Critical Studies of Media Infrastructures.* Urbana: University of Illinois Press, 2015.

Peters, John Durham. *Speaking into the Air: A History of the Idea of Communication.* Chicago: University of Chicago Press, 1999.

Pham, Minh-Ha T. *Asians Wear Clothes on the Internet: Race, Gender, and the Work of Personal Style Blogging.* Durham, NC: Duke University Press, 2015.

Pope, Albert. *Ladders.* 2nd ed. New York: Princeton Architectural Press, 2014.

Precarity Lab. *Technoprecarious.* London: Goldsmiths University Press, 2020.

Preciado, Paul B. *Pornotopia: An Essay on* Playboy's *Architecture and Biopolitics.* New York: Zone, 2014.

Ripken, Susanna. *Corporate Personhood.* Cambridge: Cambridge University Press, 2019.

Rodney, Walter. *How Europe Underdeveloped Africa.* Washington, DC: Howard University Press, 1981.

Rossiter, Ned. *Software, Infrastructure, Labor: A Media Theory of Logistical Nightmares.* New York: Routledge, 2016.

Sampson, Tony D. *A Sleepwalker's Guide to Social Media.* Cambridge: Polity, 2020.

Scholz, Roswitha. "Patriarchy and Commodity Society: Gender without the Body." In *Marxism and the Critique of Value*, edited by Neil Larsen, Mathias Nilges, Josh Robinson, and Nicholas Brown, 123–42. Chicago: MCM, 2014.

Senft, Theresa M. *Camgirls: Celebrity and Community in the Age of Social Networks.* New York: Peter Lang, 2008.

Sennett, Richard. *Flesh and Stone: The Body and the City in Western Civilization.* New York: Norton, 1994.

Serres, Michel. *The Parasite.* Translated by Lawrence R. Schehr. Minneapolis: University of Minnesota Press, 2007.

Sharma, Sarah. *In the Meantime: Temporality and Cultural Politics.* Durham, NC: Duke University Press, 2014.

Sharpe, Christina. *In the Wake: On Blackness and Being*. Durham, NC: Duke University Press, 2016.

Shirky, Clay. *Here Comes Everybody: The Power of Organizing without Organizations*. New York: Penguin, 2009.

Simmel, Georg. *The Philosophy of Money*. New York: Routledge, 2011.

Sloterdijk, Peter. *Critique of Cynical Reason*. Translated by Michael Eldred. Minneapolis: University of Minnesota Press, 1987.

Smith, Adam. *The Wealth of Nations*. Edited by Edwin Cannan. London: Electric Book Co., 1998.

Smythe, Dallas W. "Communications: Blindspot of Western Marxism." *Canadian Journal of Political and Social Theory* 1, no. 3 (1977): 1–27.

Southworth, Michael, and Eran Ben-Joseph. *Streets and the Shaping of Towns and Cities*. New York: McGraw-Hill, 1997.

Srnicek, Nick. *Platform Capitalism*. Cambridge: Polity, 2017.

Srnicek, Nick, and Alex Williams. *Inventing the Future: Postcapitalism and a World without Work*. London: Verso, 2015.

Tarde, Gabriel. "The Origins and Functions of Elites." In *Gabriel Tarde: On Communication and Social Influence*, edited by Terry N. Clark, 245–51. Chicago: University of Chicago Press, 1969.

Taylor, Keeanga-Yamahtta. *Race for Profit: How Banks and the Real Estate Industry Undermined Black Homeownership*. Chapel Hill: University of North Carolina Press, 2019.

Towns, Armond R. *On Black Media Philosophy*. Berkeley: University of California Press, 2022.

Tsing, Anna. "Supply Chains and the Human Condition." *Rethinking Marxism* 21, no. 2 (2009): 148–76.

Veblen, Thorstein. *Theory of the Leisure Class*. New York: Penguin, 1979.

Wark, McKenzie. *Capital Is Dead*. London: Verso, 2019.

———. *A Hacker Manifesto*. Cambridge, MA: Harvard University Press, 2004.

Warner, Michael. *Publics and Counterpublics*. New York: Zone, 2002.

Weimann, Gabriel. *The Influentials: People Who Influence People*. Albany: State University of New York Press, 1994.

Wendling, Amy E. *Karl Marx on Technology and Alienation*. Basingstoke: Palgrave Macmillan, 2009.

Wilderson, Frank B. *Afropessimism*. New York: Liveright, 2020.

Williams, Raymond. "Base and Superstructure in Marxist Cultural Theory." In *Problems in Materialism and Culture: Selected Essays*, 31–49. London: Verso, 1980.

———. *The Country and the City*. Oxford: Oxford University Press, 1975.

———. *The Long Revolution*. New York: Harper & Row, 1961.

———. *Marxism and Literature*. Oxford: Oxford University Press, 1977.

———. *Television: Technology and Cultural Form*. Edited by Ederyn Williams. London: Routledge, 2003.

Wolford, Wendy. "The Plantationocene: A Lusotropical Contribution to the Theory." *Annals of the American Association of Geographers* 111, no. 6 (2021): 1622–39.

Wood, Phillip J. *Southern Capitalism: The Political Economy of North Carolina, 1880–1980.* Durham, NC: Duke University Press.

Žižek, Slavoj. *The Plague of Fantasies.* London: Verso, 1997.

———. *The Sublime Object of Ideology.* London: Verso, 1989.

Zuboff, Shoshana. *The Age of Surveillance Capitalism: The Fight for a Human Future at the New Frontier of Power.* New York: PublicAffairs, 2019.

Zylinska, Joanna. "Of Swans and Ugly Ducklings: Bioethics between Humans, Animals, and Machines." *Configurations* 15, no. 2 (2007): 125–50.

INDEX

Made in the USA
Las Vegas, NV
26 April 2024

89151429R00152